How to Make Love to a Despot

Also by Stephen D. Krasner

Defending the National Interest:
Raw Materials, Investments, and U.S. Foreign Policy

International Regimes

Structural Conflict:
The Third World Against
Global Liberalism

Exploration and Contestation in the Study of
World Politics (coedited with Peter J. Katzenstein
and Robert O. Keohane)

Sovereignty:
Organized Hypocrisy

Problematic Sovereignty:
Contested Rules and Political Possibilities

Power, the State, and Sovereignty:
Essays on International Relations

How to Make Love to a Despot

An Alternative Foreign Policy for the Twenty-First Century

Stephen D. Krasner

LIVERIGHT PUBLISHING CORPORATION

A DIVISION OF W. W. NORTON & COMPANY

Independent Publishers Since 1923

NEW YORK   LONDON

For information about permission to reproduce selections from this book, write to Permissions, Liveright Publishing Corporation, a division of W. W. Norton & Company, Inc., 500 Fifth Avenue, New York, NY 10110

For information about special discounts for bulk purchases, please contact W. W. Norton Special Sales at specialsales@wwnorton.com or 800-233-4830

Manufacturing by LSC Communications, Harrisonburg
Book design by Lovedog Studio
Production manager: Anna Oler

ISBN 978-1-63149-659-2

Liveright Publishing Corporation, 500 Fifth Avenue, New York, N.Y. 10110
www.wwnorton.com

W. W. Norton & Company Ltd., 15 Carlisle Street, London W1D 3BS

1 2 3 4 5 6 7 8 9 0

For Chase, Cole, Isla, and Liviya
with the hope that the world they
inherit will be more secure.

Contents

\

Preface

THROUGHOUT ITS HISTORY THE UNITED STATES HAS VACILLATED between two foreign policy models. One is an activist foreign policy designed to remake other countries in the United States' own image. The other foreign policy regards the rest of the world as essentially beyond repair, with the appropriate role for the United States being to demonstrate to other countries the benefits of consolidated democracy—including not only free and fair elections but also a free press, the rule of law, separation of powers, and an active civil society—but not to actively try to create these results. Because groups or individuals with few resources can now kill thousands or hundreds of thousands of people, the United States no longer has the luxury of ignoring the rest of the world. But it cannot create consolidated democracies, either. The United States must learn how to make love to despots. It should aim for good enough governance, not good government. Greater security, some economic growth, and the better provision of some services is the best the United States can hope for.

During the nineteenth century the United States was too weak to act far beyond its own borders. In the twentieth century the United States intervened in the First World War to make the world safe for democracy, in the words of President Wilson, but, because of domestic opposition, refused to join the League of Nations or to

sign the Versailles Treaty after the war. The United States then settled into splendid isolation while Germany and Japan rampaged
across Europe and Asia. The United States entered the Second
World War only after the Japanese attacked Pearl Harbor. Before
this attack the America First movement, led by Charles Lindbergh
and others, was politically stronger than those individuals, including the president, who wanted to join the nations fighting against
the Axis powers. President Roosevelt seized on the Pearl Harbor
attack to send American troops to North Africa, where they would
engage German—not Japanese—forces.

American leaders ended the Second World War convinced that
hypernationalism and competitive economic closures were a threat
to the security of the United States. They constructed an international order that was designed to prevent such threats in the
future, an order that included multinational organizations like the
United Nations, the International Monetary Fund, and the International Bank for Reconstruction and Development (the World
Bank). American leaders were very successful in state-building
in Germany and Japan. Both countries eventually became democratic and market oriented. An activist foreign policy could create consolidated democracy. When it became clear in 1947 that the
Soviet Union would oppose the United States, materially and ideologically, American leaders supported elites in the third world that
would at least not take their countries down a communist path.
Democracy was not a high priority.

When the Soviet Union collapsed, and along with it the appeal
of communism, American elites returned to what was a more natural instinct, remaking the world in the image of the United States.
This was especially true after 9/11, when it became clear that weak,
malign, and often badly governed states could threaten the security
of the United States itself.

The interventions in Afghanistan and Iraq have proved to be long
and costly and the administrations that followed that of George
W. Bush have looked for ways to retreat from the broader Mid-

dle East. Officials as well as public opinion in general have become convinced that nothing can be done. A dystopian vision, in which the United States can do nothing, has been embraced by those on the left and the right.

The greatest challenge for the United States now is to identify a set of policies that lie between the utopian vision that all countries can be like the United States, or at least some idealized version of America, and the dystopian view that nothing can be done. Americans would do well to begin with their own fraught history. The United States was the first major state to become a democracy. The Declaration of Independence was written at a time when all other major countries were monarchies. There was no guarantee that the United States would survive. It almost did not. The Civil War is still the costliest war in American history.

The language of the Declaration of Independence soars. At the time of its writing, however, the United States was a slaveholding country. Slaves were counted as three-fifths of a person in the Constitution of the United States, which was written in 1787 to increase the population of slaveholding states. Slaves were about 20 percent of the population of the thirteen states in 1776 even though slaves and slavery are not mentioned once in the Declaration of Independence. Racism still plagues the United States more than 240 years after independence was declared. The household income of African Americans is only about 50 percent of that of non-Hispanic whites.

Rather than trying to make other countries consolidated democracies or doing nothing, this book argues, the United States should aim for good enough governance. The best is often the enemy of the good. Pushing for free and fair elections may only get people killed. Trying to eliminate corruption entirely may preclude eliminating the worst form of corruption. The United States must learn how to deal with despots because despotism is much more likely than consolidated democracy.

Consolidated democracy is not the normal order of things. In most places in almost all of human history, elites in power have done everything that they could to stay in power. Power has meant material wealth and status, and power has usually come from the barrel of a gun or the point of an arrow, not from the voting box. Those who lose elections but have most of the guns will not go quietly into the night.

Good enough governance would aim for security, better health, some limited economic growth, and perhaps some limited protection of human rights. It would complement rather than undermine the interests of elites in despotic polities. Good enough governance will be anathema to many groups in the United States but it is feasible, and it would contribute to a world that is more secure and prosperous.

I have come to understand that the problem of weak, fragile, and badly governed states has dominated most of my career both within and outside of academia. In my early twenties I was a Peace Corps volunteer in northern Nigeria. Many decades later I worked at the State Department and the National Security Council, thanks to the generosity and confidence of my friend and colleague Condoleezza Rice. My time in government helped me to realize how many wise and competent people work for the federal government. Most governments are run entirely by professional civil servants; the American system allows for the presence of outsiders like myself. The many political appointments in the United States government do undoubtedly make for some degree of amateurism, but these appointments are also a conduit for new ideas. The United States has many failings, but no country has wielded such great power with so much wisdom.

How to
Make Love
to a Despot

CHAPTER 1

So You Want to Make the World a Better Place

Police are everywhere: therefore be careful! They are out to fleece us, and rob us of our last copeck.

—Innkeeper in *Boris Godunov*, act 1, scene 4 by Modest Petrovich Mussorgsky

THE UNITED STATES HAS LABORED UNDER A DELUSION. IT HAS been a costly delusion. And it has hurt American national interests for one hundred years. That delusion is that the world can be like us. We Americans have come to assume that democracy and material wealth are the natural order of things. We have assumed that the world, as President Wilson said in asking Congress for a declaration of war in April 1917, "could be made safe for democracy." These words were echoed by President Bush nearly a century later, in his transmittal letter for the 2002 *National Security Strategy*, which opened with the following sentence: "The great struggles of the twentieth century between liberty and totalitarianism ended with a decisive victory for the forces of freedom—and a single sustainable model for national success: freedom, democracy, and free enterprise."

When the rest of the world has failed to conform to American expectations, when America's utopian vision has not been realized, Americans have looked away, not comprehending why other countries have not adopted a model that seems to coincide so perfectly with human needs and desires. The concluding sentence of Donald

Trump's transmittal letter of his first *National Security Strategy*, published in 2017, reads as follows: "We will remain a beacon of liberty and opportunity around the world,"[1] but at the same time the Trump administration has embraced a dystopian view in which the United States can do nothing to improve conditions in other countries even when American security is at risk.

The United States has vacillated between active intervention to promote consolidated democracy and passive beckoning, the beacon on a hill. And it has been consistently disappointed. Weak and poorly governed states pose a threat to the United States. Modern technology has severed the relationship between underlying material resources and the ability to do harm. Millions of Americans could die as a result of actions taken by individuals in poorly governed and impoverished states because these individuals control nuclear or biological weapons. Pandemic diseases arising naturally in badly governed states could also kill millions of people in wealthier and more developed countries. The problem of governance cannot be solved through the creation of wealthy and democratic states but it cannot be ignored, either, without threatening the material security of the more powerful. The United States could make itself and the world safer if it learned how to support policies that would be acceptable to despotic rulers—if it learned how to make love to despots.

The best that can be hoped for is good enough governance, something that lies between the utopian vision of creating consolidated democracy and the dystopian view that nothing can be done about governance in other states. Governments capable of policing their own territory, generating some economic growth, and providing some basic services, especially those related to health: good enough governance can be supported by external actors. Corruption cannot be eliminated. Elections cannot be free and fair unless the distribution of votes matches the distribution of guns. In despotic states there may be rule *by* law but there will not be rule *of* law; the law will be used arbitrarily to punish those who threaten extant elites.

American naïveté about the possibilities for creating wealthy and democratic states has not been based on some simpleminded, atheoretical view of history. Rather, American policy makers have always been influenced by a widely held view of how development and democracy take place, namely, modernization theory. In this approach, wealth and democracy can be attained relatively easily. All that is necessary are population growth and technological change. If countries can find the first step of the up escalator they can ride all the way to the top.

American leaders have also been influenced, usually tacitly, by a second perspective on development, one that emphasizes institutional capacity. American leaders and those in other countries of the OECD (Organization for Economic Co-operation and Development) have assumed that rulers in poorly governed states want to do the right thing. Their failures are the result of a lack of capacity rather than their desire to stay in power.

This is a naïve view of history and human nature. Wealth and democracy are not the natural order of things. They are, in fact, deeply unnatural. Despotic leaders do not want to provide benefits for those whom they govern; they want to support with arms or money those that can keep them in office. Wealthy democratic states have existed for only a short period of history, perhaps 150 years, in a few places in the world—North America, Western Europe, and parts of Asia. Despotism is not an aberration.

The small number of states that have actually become wealthy democracies, states where political leaders can stay in power only by winning free and fair elections, have succeeded not because of structural conditions alone, but also because of luck. If the wind had blown in a different direction in June of 1588 the Spanish Armada might have been able to support the Duke of Parma's invasion force, which had been assembled in the Low Countries, then under Spanish rule. Queen Elizabeth I, a Protestant, would probably have been deposed. England would never have become the birthplace of the Industrial Revolution or the cradle of liberty. Catholicism would have become the official religion. If England had been invaded in 1588, rather than having the wealthy and democratic United Kingdom, we would all be speaking Spanish. If in 1940 the waters of the English Channel had prevented the small boats from rescuing the British Expeditionary Force from Dunkirk, the British government might have sought peace, and Nazi Germany would have been able to devote all of its resources to the defeat of the Soviet Union. The outcome of the Second World War might have been very different, as would the world in which most humans now live.

The Madisonian sweet spot, first described by Madison in Federalist 51, in which the government is strong enough to provide key services but does not repress its own population, has been achieved by a very few polities for a limited period of history. Since the Second World War, only one country has gone from being poor and autocratic to rich and democratic, South Korea. Most of the United States' interventions to create modern wealthy democracies have been failures, Afghanistan and Iraq being only the most recent examples.

Because we Americans have assumed that everyone could be just like us, we have failed to identify any salient markers between Somalia and Denmark: between poverty, violence, and chaos; and wealth, peace, and order. We do not know how to make love to despots, even though most of the world is ruled by despotic regimes. Political leaders in nondemocratic states will not accept changes that would threaten their ability to maintain power. Good enough governance is feasible, would protect American interests, and would not preclude changes that might ultimately lead to a more democratic system.

It is hardly a revelation to point out that democracy, effective government, and a free market economy cannot usually be achieved by outside actors. Japan and Germany after the Second World War were aberrations made possible by the power of the United States, the delegitimization of fascist governments, and the existence of local members of the elite who saw being allied with the United

States as the best alternative among difficult choices. The Marshall Plan worked in Western Europe, but the beneficiaries of the plan were already relatively wealthy and had some experience with democracy before the Second World War. Democracy was adopted by many of the former satellite states of Eastern and Central Europe after the collapse of the Soviet Union, not only because of the financial and ideological incentives that could be offered by the European Union, but also because extant regimes had been delegitimized. Communism had failed. Some of these countries, notably Hungary, are already backsliding.

External actors can only see through the glass darkly; they are often oblivious to local power dynamics. Saddam Hussein was able to maintain power in Iraq for more than twenty years despite having completely miscalculated how long the 1980s war against Iran would last (he thought a few months at most, not years) and how the United States would react to his invasion of Kuwait in 1990.[2] Only invasion by the United States in 2003 led to his ouster and execution. Stalin killed or imprisoned the wives and husbands of those close to him but died a natural death. Even though Muammar Gaddhafi died in a ditch, he stayed in power for more than forty years.

Good things do not always go together. Greater security may mean more violation of individual rights, including women's rights, and a limitation on the kinds of economic activities that would maximize individual well-being. No matter how much commitment the United States makes or how well coordinated its efforts are across the whole of government, the United States will fail if its goal is consolidated democracy, at least fail most of the time. Even if the best-intentioned international actors did not live in what Séverine Autesserre has called "peaceland," they would still not be successful, because their objectives would be inconsistent with the interests of local elites.[3] Despotic rulers will undermine or reject reforms that would weaken their hold on power.

Humility

Homo sapiens have been on earth for more than 150,000 years. For much of this period they lived only in Africa. As they spread across the land masses of earth they initially formed small hunter-gatherer societies, based on kinship groups. Only about 10,000 years ago did human beings begin to inhabit larger communities made possible by settled agriculture, which generated a surplus of food that could sustain groups of individuals, such as priests and rulers. The communities were governed by despotisms, usually hereditary, that maintained order through the arbitrary use of violence. Legitimacy was provided by tradition. These elites did not govern in the interests of the population as a whole. Their behavior and that of their minions was arbitrary and exploitative, as Mussorgsky so well captured in the innkeeper's lament from his opera *Boris Godunov*. Despots attended to the care and feeding of their own families (and sometimes not even that) and of those individuals or groups that controlled the instruments of violence. Throughout time, if individuals had the opportunity to run away from state control (because, for instance, there was inaccessible mountainous terrain nearby in which to hide), they did so.[4] Running away from the state meant less exploitation, more calories, and better health. Hobbes successfully captured our imagination: we fear the lack of effective government, but for most of human history in almost all places in almost all times, life has been nasty, brutish, and short, with or without effective governance.

Madison wrote in Federalist 51: "If men were angels, no government would be necessary. If angels were to govern men, neither external nor internal controls on government would be necessary. In framing a government which is to be administered by men over men, the great difficulty lies in this: you must first enable the government to control the governed; and in the next place oblige it to control itself." Only in the last century or two in a small number of countries have polities been created and sustained that solved the problem posed by James Madison: How is it possible to create institutions that are strong enough to govern and provide services and yet do not abuse individuals?

Most people cannot access the legal system, even if on paper a modern legal system exists. Despots need corruption to get the resources that they need to stay in power. They engage in rent-seeking; that is, they create economic rules that allow them to steal more easily. Most individuals cannot join together; they cannot form organizations because such organizations might threaten their despotic rulers economically or politically. Reaching the OECD world of rich and democratic states is extremely difficult and unusual.

The most important virtue that external actors seeking to promote better governance can possess is humility. External actors should seek to promote good enough governance, not good governance. Good governance is based on a Western ideal in which the government delivers a wide variety of services to the population based on the rule of law, and the laws are determined by representatives selected through free and fair elections.[5] Good governance will not be in the interests of national elites in most target states, which are closed access orders. Despots want to do what is good for them; only in special circumstances will what is good for them be good for the society as a whole.

External actors cannot be successful without the support of national elites, and national elites are usually despotic. They will at best support good enough governance—security, some service provision, some economic growth—because such policies will help them to stay in power. Most of the world's polities, perhaps 130 or so, are most easily understood as despotic. National elites in despotic polities will undermine efforts to create consolidated democracy or rule-of-law bureaucracies because the existence of such structures would mean their own political death.

There are a small number of countries, perhaps 30 or so, that can be classified as intermediate polities, in which the interests of national political elites will be mixed. In intermediate political orders, those between open and closed access, different members of the national elite, or even the same individual, might be torn between initiatives that protect their own position and initiatives that are beneficial to the society as a whole.

But even in intermediate polities there is no guarantee that external actors trying to promote democracy, rule of law, and higher incomes will be successful. Not only will external actors have to support the right individuals in target states, those whose interests would best be served by an open access order in which rent-seeking is limited or eliminated, but there is also an inescapable element of luck or unpredictability. Structural factors do not determine outcomes. Achieving the utopian vision is possible only in a small number of polities, and even in intermediate polities there is no guarantee of success.

False Expectations

In the late summer of 1963 I boarded a chartered plane that was carrying more than one hundred Peace Corps volunteers from New York City to Lagos, Nigeria. I was uncertain about going to graduate school, afraid to join the civil rights movement and face the racism and violence of the American South, happy to avoid the prospect of being drafted and sent off to Vietnam, but confident that my colleagues and I, mostly new college graduates, would make a positive contribution to Nigeria's future. John F. Kennedy's words in his inaugural address—"Ask not what your country can do for you; ask what you can do for your country"—rang true for me and for the other young Americans on that flight to Africa. We were American utopians.

Nigeria had become independent from Britain in 1960. It had held democratic elections. The military was playing no obvious part in politics when I arrived. Even though regional, ethnic, and religious divisions were evident, there was no organized violence among groups or tribes. I was, however, assigned to teach history and English at a secondary school in the North, Adamawa Provincial Secondary School, because the regional government of northern Nigeria did not want to hire southern Nigerians, who were often Christian and definitely from a different tribe than the Fulanis and Hausas, almost all Muslim, who dominated the North.

At one point, the several Peace Corps volunteers at the school were accused of proselytizing for Christianity. As a Jew, I felt more than comfortable rejecting the accusations being made against my colleagues and me, but I should have realized that something was amiss. I was, however, young and naïve—an American utopian. With the end of British colonialism, my American colleagues and I imagined that Nigeria would do well, would become a prosperous, peaceful, democratic state. The Nigerians that I met after I arrived expected the same. With the yoke of colonialism lifted, everyone saw a bright future for Africa in general, and in particular for Nigeria, sub-Saharan Africa's most populous state. Ethnic, religious, and tribal divisions were obviously salient—people looked and dressed differently and voted largely along regional and ethnic lines—but none of us Americans thought that these divisions would be a driver, perhaps the major driver, of Nigerian politics.

I taught at Adamawa Provincial Secondary School for two years. The school itself, established by the British, was located halfway between the provincial capital of Yola, a traditional walled city where the Fulani emir lived, and the commercial center, Jimeta, which was located on the Benue River near the Cameroon border. The teaching staff consisted of Brits, Nigerians, American Peace Corps volunteers, and Pakistanis, the latter because the government of northern Nigeria preferred Muslims from South Asia rather than Christians from southern Nigeria, and there were many educated people in Pakistan. (In the smallest of the small world moments that I have had, the son of one of the Pakistanis that I was teaching with, now a distinguished journalist in Karachi, participated in a summer program at Stanford in 2012.) The principal of the school was a Brit, as were the provincial commissioner (a simulacrum of Colonel Blimp) and several other provincial department heads when I first arrived. Over the course of my two years, most were replaced by Nigerians.

The school functioned well. Teachers always showed up for their classes. Classes were well taught, as far as I could see. Adamawa Provincial Secondary School was the only public high school in the whole province, and the selection of students, with a few exceptions, like the emir's son, appeared to me to be based on examination results. Some of our students went on to universities, at least one to graduate studies in the United States. One of our students, Atiku Abubakar, made a lot of money in the oil industry, was vice-president of Nigeria from 1999 to 2007, and founded the American University of Nigeria in Yola in 2003. On the whole, things appeared to be working pretty well.

Within months after I left the country in the summer of 1965, military officers staged a coup. Within a year after I left, most of the people from the South that were living in Jimeta and its environs, primarily shopkeepers or federal civil servants, had been killed. In 1967, the southeast part of the country, where Nigeria's newly discovered oil was located, declared its independence, precipitating the Biafran Civil War. There were tens of thousands of battle deaths over the three-year duration of the conflict. As an American utopian, I was surprised by all of this.

Since the late 1960s, Nigeria has lurched through a series of military coups, had anemic economic growth, squandered its oil revenues, suffered from massive corruption at every level of government, and, in the area where I served, experienced an Islamic fundamentalist insurgency organized by a group called Boko Haram, which means, in Hausa, "Western education is sinful." Nigeria's military—which, at least on paper, is very formidable—has had great difficulty containing and defeating Boko Haram.

Even if we hadn't been young and naïve, I do not believe that I, or any of my colleagues, Nigerian or foreign, could have come close to predicting Nigeria's experience over the last fifty years. I could not have imagined the several-decades-long closure of the railroad by which I traveled from the northern part of the country to the South on one of my school breaks. Nor do I think that in the early 1960s many scholars or government decision makers would have guessed at how wrong things would go.

For almost all analysts and policy makers during the Cold War, the problem of the twentieth century was not that modernity and progress could not be achieved but that modernity could be perverted, Nazi Germany being the obvious case in point. For Americans after 1945, the major threat to the liberal democratic capitalist model was Soviet communism. Both communism and capitalism were ideologies of modernity whose adherents expected that technology would be harnessed to progress, governments would effectively govern, and per capita incomes would rise. The Soviets, of course, denied human freedom and individual choice and presumed that progress could be effectively directed from the top through a more or less unconstrained bureaucratic apparatus; the Americans placed their faith in individual initiative, a limited state, and political and economic decisions that were made from the bottom.

The Soviets beat the Americans into space in the late 1950s. Nixon's famous kitchen encounter with Khrushchev in Moscow in 1959 was a real debate. The Soviet Union and the communist system under which it was organized appeared to be a serious alternative to American capitalism and democracy. The fatal flaws in the Soviet system were hardly visible when I left for Nigeria in 1963.

Fascism and communism were rationalized and legitimated by a high modernist ideology ostensibly grounded in rational thought. These modern autocracies killed tens of millions of their own citizens through domestic repression and the Holocaust, and tens of millions in other countries through war.[6]

The international institutions that were established at the end of the Second World War—the United Nations, the World Bank, the International Monetary Fund, the General Agreement on Tariffs and Trade—were initially motivated by a desire, especially in the United States, to prevent perversions of modernity, not to achieve it. Modernity, most Americans believed, would come with new technology and population growth. Rising incomes and democracy would naturally follow. The great challenge was to prevent the perversion of modernity, not to achieve it in the first place. Most Americans believed in a utopian vision in which consolidated democracy could be created relatively easily.

What was not anticipated in the decades immediately following the Second World War was that many polities would not progress. The issue would be not which of two paths to modernity would be followed, communist autocracy or capitalist democracy, but rather whether any path to prosperity could be found at all. The prospect that economies could stagnate, that states would not be able to govern, that despotisms would be inefficient and exploitative, that there might be no effective state at all, that services could crumble, that despots would regard the polity's resources as an entitlement that could be pillaged for their own personal satisfaction and that of their close supporters, that civil conflict could afflict large numbers of states, that millions of people could become refugees or internally displaced persons—these were not trajectories that were seriously considered.

It Is Very Hard to Get to Denmark

Denmark is a metaphor for a well-governed wealthy state; Denmark was ranked number one in the *World Happiness Report* for 2016.[7] Denmark's per capita income was almost $50,000 and its life expectancy reached eighty years. It is a full democracy.

For most of human history, however, life has not been so benign.

Homo sapiens have lived for about eight thousand generations. Increases in life expectancy for human beings began around 1850, only seven generations ago, and accelerated after 1900.[8] For almost all of human history, life expectancy was below thirty years (although infant mortality explained much of this very low figure), while today it is in the high seventies or above for wealthy countries and approaching seventy for many poorer ones. Women, rich and poor, died in childbirth. Pandemic diseases, such as the Black Death that spread through Europe in the fourteenth century, might have killed half the population. In the Western Hemisphere European conquerors used diseases to decimate the indigenous populations.[9] For most people, regardless of their social rank, violence was endemic. Random murders and other forms of violence were not unusual. About one-quarter of the English nobility died a violent death in the fourteenth century.[10] Murder rates in Western Europe declined from about 20 to 40 per 100,000 in the thirteenth century to about 1 per 100,000 today.[11] Western Europe became a world of wealthy democratic states only in the last part of the twentieth century. Most human beings who have ever lived have done so under despotic regimes.

The experience of people living in wealthy industrialized democracies since the end of the Second World War, with lives almost entirely free of violence, is the exception. The first half of the twentieth century in Europe and Asia was soaked in violent death: perhaps forty million casualties in the First World War and eighty million in the Second.

Only in the last century or two has per capita income grown significantly. Angus Maddison has estimated that world per capita income grew only very slowly from the year 1000 to 1820, at a rate of 0.05 percent a year from 1000 to 1500, and 0.07 percent a year from 1500 to 1820. Growth accelerated to 1.17 percent on average from 1820 to 1999 for all countries in the world. There was, however, significant variation in growth rates after 1820. The per capita compound growth rate in the now developed OECD West was 1.27 percent from 1820 to 1950, 3.64 from 1950 to 1973, and 1.80 from 1973 to 1995. In the rest of the world the figures were 0.50 percent from 1820 to 1950, 2.89 from 1950 to 1973, and 1.38 from 1973 to 1995.[12]

The nature of some domestic political systems has become more variegated. Most of the OECD world is populated by full, or consolidated, democracies. Of the thirty-six members of the OECD, only eleven receive a Polity score below the highest score of 10. Political authorities govern with the consent of the governed; they do not exploit or dominate. They cannot use violence in arbitrary ways. The rule of law is accessible, if not equally accessible, to all. These countries have reached the Madisonian sweet spot; government is effective and constrained.

In the past, only a few polities, such as the Greek city-states in the fifth and fourth centuries BC, the Italian city-states in the fourteenth and fifteenth centuries, and the Dutch Republic in the sixteenth century, approached anything like modern democracies where the arbitrary power of the state is constrained. Even in those societies, however, individual rights were much more limited than is the case in modern consolidated democracies, and these rights were enjoyed by only a fraction of the population. The Greeks, for instance, kept many slaves, and women did not vote.[13]

Consolidated democracy, or open access or inclusive societies, ones in which the arbitrary power of the state is constrained and in which almost all residents have access to the rule of law, is a recent and unique development in human history.[14] It is worth quoting Josiah Ober at length. In his 2015 book entitled *The Rise and Fall of Classical Greece*, he writes in the preface:

> I live in exceptional times. . . . Democracy and growth define the normal, although not yet the usual, conditions of modernity: Autocracy, while still prevalent, is regarded as aberrant, so that most autocrats pretend to be democratic. Economic stagnation is seen as a problem that demands a solution.

These conditions were *not* normal, or even imaginable, for most people through most of human history.[15]

Throughout human history there have been only three ways in which societies have been organized: small foraging groups of perhaps 150 individuals, closed access or natural orders, and open access orders.[16] In closed access orders, services are provided based on personal relationships with the elites; in open access orders, services are provided on the basis of impersonal entitlements accorded to citizens or residents. In closed access orders the use of violence is controlled by elites and can be arbitrary. In open access orders violence is constrained by the rule of law and is in the hands of an organized security apparatus that is controlled by legally authorized public authorities; these authorities, if they abuse their power, can be dismissed by a broad coalition of citizens. In closed access orders only some members of the society, elites, have the right to form organizations. In open access societies all members of the society have the right to form organizations.[17] In closed access societies only some individuals, members of the elite, can compete for office; in open access societies anyone can compete for office. In closed access societies elites can create rents by restricting the right to form organizations and to engage in exchange; in open access societies it is more difficult for elites to create rents because rents can be competed away by newly created organizations.

The political and economic spheres are intimately linked. In closed access orders, the political elite is constrained, if at all, not by the rule of law or accountability to a broader public but by a balance of power among elites. Despots can use violence, confiscation, and arbitrary changes in rules to seize economic assets. If there is political order in a closed access society, economic growth is possible, but it will be more erratic and cannot be sustained over the long term.[18] Economic growth can be sustained only if individuals have incentives to invest and if political elites have no choice but to accept the changes in the distribution of political power generated by creative destruction in the economic sphere. If any successful venture can be confiscated or shut down by political authorities, if individuals can be killed, sustained investment will not take place.[19]

That despots would want to pursue policies that keep them in power, that provide them with deference, status, and wealth, is hardly surprising. What is surprising is an incentive system that would reward political elites not for feeding their own families, or for paying off those in control of the means of violence, but for serving the best interests of the society as a whole.

There is no teleological trajectory, no natural and inevitable path from extractive or closed access orders to inclusive or open access orders. In the modern world some elements of technology, especially those related to health, have resulted in impressive improvements in the control of some diseases, infant mortality, and life expectancy. These improvements have been experienced across a very wide range of polities. But sustained economic growth and consolidated democracy have been more elusive. Elites operating in a closed order or extractive society will not necessarily have an incentive to expand rights, to make themselves accountable to the rule of law, to limit opportunities for rent-seeking, or to constrain their own use of violence. Just the opposite; in a closed access or extractive polity the loss of political power means the loss of status, wealth, and possibly life. Death in a ditch, the fate that befell Muammar Gaddhafi, is more likely than the golden parachute that landed Idi Amin in Saudi Arabia.

Although almost all of the countries that have achieved consolidated democracy are in Western Europe, East Asia, and North America, this end point was not foreordained by geography or culture. Rather, it was the result of a series of lucky accidents that encouraged elites to move toward a more inclusive, open access order. We cannot assume that consolidated democracy is a natural stopping point from which regression is impossible. Organizational structures can atrophy, and institutional arrangements locked in by constitutional rules that can be changed only by supermajorities can become dysfunctional because they were created to address different problems in a different era. The United States Senate, for instance, has become less and less representative over time as the ratio between the smallest and largest state populations has grown from about one to thirteen (Delaware to Virginia in 1787) to one to sixty-nine (Wyoming to California in 2018). Even in full democracies, public policy may fail to address pressing issues because political decision making is skewed by neo-patrimonialism, in which moneyed elites are more and more able to determine political outcomes, or by the fact that, at least in the United States, the members of Congress are hardwired by electoral incentives to be responsive to the interests of their districts or states and not to the interests of the United States as a whole.[20]

In 1963, my fellow Peace Corps volunteers and I, policy makers, and academics assumed (sometimes tacitly) a natural progression in human affairs. We were American utopians. We were wrong. Getting to Denmark is hard.

Understanding how rich and democratic states got to be rich and democratic is the greatest challenge for the social sciences. The most convincing argument, rational choice institutionalism, focuses on the incentives and strategic behavior of elites.[21] Transitions from despotic to more open polities, in which political leaders have an incentive to promote the well-being of the society as a whole, or at least a large part of it, are never instantaneous. Polities do not move from extractive, exploitative institutions to the Madisonian sweet spot overnight.

There are intermediate, or transitioning, polities. But this group is relatively small. Rational choice institutionalism provides a more convincing picture than do the other two major theoretical perspectives on development that have been explicitly identified by scholars and implicitly embraced by policy makers—modernization theory and theories of institutional capacity. All three of these approaches are discussed more thoroughly in chapters 3 and 4.

Development, Domestic Authority Structures, and External State-Building

The most important foreign policy objective has always been national security, the preservation of the territorial and political integrity of the state. The greatest threats to national security have historically come from the most powerful states, those that commanded the largest material resources and could deploy the most formidable military forces. The most common modalities have involved state-to-state relations, including diplomacy, sanctions, and war.

The international system is, however, anarchical. There is no authoritative actor that can prevent one state from pursuing its foreign policy objectives by trying to alter the domestic authority structures, leaders, or domestic political forces in another state. Efforts to alter domestic authority structures are challenging; they are relatively rare; but they have always been a policy option. There were about two hundred cases of forcible regime change, the most extreme form of external state-building, from 1555 to 2010,[22] fewer than one every two years but, in absolute terms, not a small number. The hot wars that the United States fought during the Cold War against Vietnam and Korea were primarily about the kind of domestic authority structures these two countries would have. Much of the foreign assistance that was disbursed during the Cold War was designed to support or bribe leaders that would ally their countries with the West or the East.

Covert or overt interventions by the United States between 1945 and 1990 were designed not to conquer territory but to influence domestic political arrangements, often just arrangements at the top. The Soviet Union imposed communist regimes on the countries that it occupied at the end of the Second World War, or incorporated these countries into the Soviet Union itself, as was the case for the three Baltic countries. Leaders in both the Soviet

Union and the United States understood that if, in the long term, the overwhelming balance of regime types in the world became either communist, or democratic and capitalist, it would pose a threat to the domestic integrity of the superpower that was losing this global struggle.

With the collapse of the Soviet Union, the menace of communism disappeared for the West, and the project of democracy promotion, broadly understood to include, for instance, human rights, became more consequential, especially for the United States and Western Europe. Democracy promotion was a more ambitious agenda than simply the support of regimes, autocratic or not, that supported the West. After 1990 a major goal, perhaps the major goal, of the European Union was to transform the former satellite states of the USSR through the appeal of membership, which involved both material and ideational attractors.[23] The United States could put more emphasis on supporting transitions to democratic regimes because it no longer had to be concerned about bolstering autocratic rulers who might align their countries with the Soviet Union. Most countries, however, remained despotisms with or without the Soviet Union.

Outside of Europe, though, there was not much urgency to these projects. Development assistance (only a small part of which was committed to political reform that included democratization) from all of the OECD countries fell from $91 billion in 1992 to $73 billion in 1997. Aid from the United States dropped from $17 billion to $9 billion for the same period, or from 0.2 percent to 0.1 percent of gross national income.[24] The benign period in which foreign policy was of limited concern for American leaders lasted, however, for only about a decade. It ended with the attacks of 9/11.

I began working at the State Department as a member of the policy planning staff at the beginning of September 2001. I had spent the previous thirty-five years in academia. I was anxious for exposure to the policy world, and the appointment of my Stanford colleague and friend Condoleezza Rice as national security advisor provided an opportunity. Despite the bombings of the US embassies in Kenya and Tanzania in 1998 and the attack on the USS *Cole* in Yemen in October of 2000, few in the policy world or academia expected that America's conception of the world was about to be transformed. 9/11 was a shattering event, especially for anyone living in New York or Washington. After I left the State Department building on the morning of 9/11, I biked over to the Potomac, a short ride from State, to look at the Pentagon burning across the river. I thought about trying to get closer but decided that it would be too painful.

George W. Bush had expected that his administration would be focused on domestic issues. 9/11 transformed that focus but did not dictate the nature of the response. The administration framed the problem of transnational terrorism in a very ambitious way, associating it with repressive regimes especially in the Arab world, and developed a coherent grand strategy consistent with this framing that was articulated in the *National Security Strategy* of 2002. This framing was completely consistent with America's utopian vision.

The 2002 *National Security Strategy of the United States of America* offered a coherent approach for addressing the threat of transnational terrorism. It identified "the crossroads of radicalism and technology" as the "gravest danger" to American security. It argued that the United States and its allies would have to redefine the conventional understanding of imminent threat and preemptive war because transnational terrorists would not engage in the "visible" mobilization of armed forces. President Bush wrote in his letter introducing the *Strategy* that "the events of September 11, 2001, taught us that weak states, like Afghanistan, can pose as great a danger to our national interests as strong states."

Islamic radicalism was understood as a product of political repression, especially in the Arab world. In the long run it was a challenge that could be addressed only by the spread of democracy and freedom. In an essay published in *Foreign Affairs* at the end of the administration, Condoleezza Rice, who had been Bush's national security advisor and secretary of state (and for whom I worked as director of policy planning), argued that "the United States does have permanent allies: the nations with whom we share common values."[25] While recognizing that there could be tensions between democracy and security in the short term, she argued that "in the long term, our security is best ensured by the success of our ideals: freedom, human rights, open markets, democracy, and the rule of law."[26]

The administration's ambitions were hardly aberrant. Like all of his predecessors, Bush argued that the United States had to support freedom and democracy. The idea of spreading democracy has always been part of American foreign policy, although sometimes only discernible in rhetoric.

The temptation to make values and regime change relatively more prominent is greater when a state has more power, and the United States occupied an unchallenged position at the beginning of the first decade of the twenty-first century.[27] Had the United States been more constrained, had its material resources been more limited, its leaders might have opted for less ambitious goals. They might have focused more on immediate security concerns and less on democratization, even if they believed that democratization was the key to American security in the long run.

I worked at the National Security Council in 2001 and 2002 and then as director of policy planning at the State Department from 2005 to 2007. While the ambitions of the Bush administration may look excessive in retrospect, in prospect they appeared, at least to me, to be entirely reasonable. At the beginning of the twenty-first century, the United States had overweening power. Democracy appeared to be on the rise around the world. Francis Fukuyama had written about the end of history in 1989, arguing that democracy and free markets were the only fully legitimated path to prosperity and human well-being. The Soviet Union had self-destructed. The Berlin Wall had fallen. After the collapse of the Soviet Union, the states of Eastern Europe, with significant incentives and assistance from the European Union, had become democracies, in some cases consolidated democracies. The idea that the United States could plant democracy or at least the seeds of democracy in the Middle East did not appear to be far-fetched.

A potent new threat, made manifest on 9/11, had arisen. Because of the nexus of alienated and radicalized groups, especially those motivated by Salafist Islam, and weapons of mass destruction (nuclear or biological), the security of even the most powerful nations might be at risk from groups protected by or finding safe harbor in malevolent, badly governed, or failed states. Of the fifteen states with the highest (worst) scores on *Foreign Policy* magazine's 2010 Failed State Index, nine were majority-Muslim countries. Zimbabwe might be ignored; Somalia, Pakistan, and Yemen cannot be.

Terrorists may come from many different backgrounds: a grandchild of a Jewish doctor, raised by hippie parents in Riverside County west of Los Angeles, became a spokesman for al-Qaeda; a college-educated American citizen of Pakistani origin tried to set off a car bomb in Times Square.[28] Terrorism, including terrorism motivated by Salafist Islam, may arise in the United States itself. Syed Rizwan Farook, an American-born son of Pakistani parents, who graduated from Cal State–San Bernardino and worked for the San Bernardino County Department of Health, killed fourteen people at the Inland Regional Center in San Bernardino in December 2015. His wife, who participated in the attack, was born in Pakistan, had lived in Saudi Arabia, and had studied in Pakistan.

Even if failing states are not the only source of terrorism they are one venue within which terrorists can be radicalized and seek refuge. Salman Abedi, who killed twenty-two people in a suicide bombing at a concert in Manchester, was born in England of Libyan parents but had recently returned from Libya. Failing states with many alienated young men can be hospitable environments for training camps, and trained terrorists are more likely to be successful.[29] Safe havens provide venues where extremists can seek refuge, indoctrinate, and train without fear of disruption.

Attacks with weapons of mass destruction, not just conventional explosives, could result in many deaths. Biological weapons will become easier to fabricate. Natural pathogens could occur in a state with limited governance capacity and increase among the local population for many years before spreading to the advanced industrialized world. Such pathogens would cause limited but hardly trivial damage if transmission was difficult, as has been the case of AIDS and Ebola, but could cause millions of deaths if they could be transmitted through the air rather than by human fluids.[30] Even AIDS, which is not transmitted that easily, has killed, according to the World Health Organization, about thirty-five million people.[31] Nuclear weapons are not beyond the reach of ISIS, al-Qaeda, Hezbollah, or some other group, given the nuclear programs in Pakistan, Iran, North Korea, and elsewhere.[32]

Advanced industrialized democratic societies are confronted with a world of uncertainty rather than risk, a world in which there might be black swans: very destructive events may take place but it is impossible to know with any confidence what their underlying probability distribution might be. States or non-state groups with relatively limited resources, but possessing nuclear or biological weapons, could kill thousands or hundreds of thousands of individuals residing within the boundaries of much more powerful states. Terrorist groups, national or transnational, could also inflict levels of death and destruction that have in the past been associated only with war and not with criminal activity. Global pandemics and transnational terrorism are two sources of mass death and destruction that could arise in poorly or malevolently governed areas. If Americans are concerned with their own security, they cannot ignore despotic regimes—but they cannot put such countries on the road to consolidated democracy either. We must learn how to make love to despots—how to get good enough governance rather than good governance.

Despite the Bush administration's understanding the sources of the national security challenge facing the United States, its grand strategy failed. Iraq and Afghanistan, the two countries invaded by the United States, are not on a path to democracy. Both are classified by Freedom House as "not free." Polity IV classifies Afghanistan as a failed or occupied state and Iraq as an "open anocracy." Disorder in both countries persists. Despite the campaign rhetoric of Bush's successors, Barack Obama and Donald Trump, American assets have not left either country.

The fundamental problem for the strategy of the Bush administration—"to seek and support the growth of democratic movements and institutions in every nation and culture, with the ultimate goal of ending tyranny in our world," as stated in George W. Bush's second inaugural address—proved to be impossible to realize in practice, because the objectives of American policy makers were inconsistent with the interests of political elites in targeted closed access or extractive orders. Bush's successors, Obama and Trump, have been very skeptical of American involvement in the broader Middle East. But they too have been unsuccessful. The United States has vacillated between a utopian vision, in which any country could be put on a path to consolidated democracy, and a dystopian view, in which the United States could do nothing.

The United States has been between a rock and a hard place. American leaders have tried to create a world of well-governed democratic states. This effort has failed outside of Western Europe and East Asia. At the same time, poorly governed states around the world cannot be ignored, because of the disconnect between underlying capabilities and the ability to do harm. Transnational terrorism in conjunction with pandemic disease, whether naturally occurring or artificially created, could kill thousands or even millions of people in wealthy, well-governed, democratic states. American leaders cannot create open access orders but they cannot ignore poorly governed states either. Wilsonian policies that try actively to remake the world will fail. The utopian vision will not be successful. But the dystopian vision in which the United States can do nothing is politically fraught and threatens American security.

The United States must content itself with creating good enough governance.[33] Good enough governance would have the following characteristics:

- Public authorities—a national, regional, or local government—would be able to provide order and security. Transnational threats, threats to other countries from non-state actors, could be contained, albeit not perfectly, by national authorities either alone or with support from external actors such as the United States.

- There might be rule by law but not necessarily rule of law; political, military, and economic elites would not be subject to the same legal constraints as the rest of the population. The law could be used to prosecute opponents of the regime.

- There could be some economic growth if not sustained growth, although the level of wealth that could be achieved would be limited by perverse incentives that are an inevitable consequence of arbitrary power: individuals will limit their investments in fixed assets if they know that those with guns or political power can simply grab their holdings, jail them, or kill them. Favorable global prices, migration from rural to urban areas, or the appropriation of new technologies might set off bursts of growth even in limited access orders, but positive growth rates cannot be sustained over long periods. What distinguishes the now wealthy countries from their more impoverished counterparts is the much larger proportion of years in which their growth rates have been positive. In closed access orders despotic rulers would always be attentive to maintaining rent-seeking opportunities that they would need in order to pay off their key supporters and stay in power.

- Clientelism and patronage, in which political leaders provide resources for those who keep them in power, would be accepted; corruption in which political leaders simply accumulate wealth for themselves, much of which they might hide in overseas tax havens, could be limited. Good enough governance would then involve not the elimination of corruption but rather the acceptance of corruption that kept funds in the country rather than gross theft.[34]

- The state itself or external actors would be able to provide some basic services, notably those services that do not threaten the position of despotic rulers in the short or medium term.[35] Such services could be most easily provided, especially with help from external actors, in the area of health, especially health services, such as immunizations, that can be provided without a complex logistical system.[36] Other basic services where corrupt practices are essential for the survival of national elites, such as education and infrastructure, which involve lots of people or lots of money, would be harder to provide.[37]

- Elections would be used to legitimate agreements that had been reached *ex ante* among political elites. Free and fair elections, where the outcomes from voting would be incompatible with the distribution of control over the means of violence, would be eschewed.

- Many rights, however, associated with political freedom and more extensive human rights would not be protected. Individuals would not necessarily have freedom of speech, the right to assembly, or the right to worship publicly. The best that could be achieved is what Rawls characterized as a benevolent absolutism, in which there was some toleration and respect for individual beliefs.

- Good enough governance might eventually facilitate the movement of a polity toward consolidated democracy, where freedom and the rights of individuals are protected from despotic state behavior, but there is no guarantee that such a felicitous outcome will be reached. In Brazil a major corruption investigation led to the imprisonment of a popular ex-president, the resignation of his successor, and the election of a politician with very weak democratic credentials. Structural improvements would have to be wedded to good luck for a polity to make the jump to consolidated democracy.

In most instances, good enough governance, or some of its elements, is the best outcome that an intervening power can achieve. Good enough governance is not utopian but it is not dystopian either. It is consistent with despotic rulers' staying in power. "In some cases even 'good-enough-governance' may be beyond reach, especially if it is impossible to establish some kind of effective authority, even arbitrary authority, over an entire country or significant parts of it."[38] If this is the case, the United States or other external actors would have to choose from among even worse options to achieve some internal order and security. Allying with local warlords might be the only way to engage local actors and contain transnational threats. In the worst case, external actors might need to function as external balancers, episodically supporting local groups that do not threaten the security interests of more powerful states.

Promoting good enough governance would not, at least, preclude movement toward a more open access order, even if such movement were not guaranteed. Order is a necessary condition for raising income over the long term. Order coupled with technological change can result in higher levels of per capita income over time, and higher levels of income make inclusive polities more likely, but they do not guarantee them.

This is a sobering policy conclusion. It is not one that would sit well with the electorates in the United States and Western Europe. Citizens of the OECD world, especially the OECD world in Western Europe and North America, believe that the stability, security, prosperity, and greater life expectancy that have been achieved in their own polities are the natural order of things. They are not.

Within the lifespan of many people now alive, one of the most advanced states in Europe was captured by a grotesque ideology that arbitrarily slaughtered six million human beings during the Holocaust and engaged in policies that resulted in the deaths of tens of millions of others through the direct and indirect consequences of war. Greater flows of people, goods, and ideas have benefited some more than others even in the OECD world. More information is not necessarily better. Technological change is disruptive. Populism is not an aberration. There are no safe havens. Reaching the OECD world does not guarantee that the OECD world will continue forever. Rich, well-governed polities are a rare achievement in the history of the human race. The United States must find a path between a utopian vision that is impossible in most polities and a dystopian rejection of the world in which nothing can be done. The United States and others must support policies that despotic rulers—most of the rulers in the world—believe will help them to stay in power. Good enough governance is a feasible middle path.

CHAPTER 2

The Nature of Threats in the Modern Era

CONSIDER A POSSIBLE SCENARIO. A NUCLEAR DEVICE EXPLODES near the intersection of Second Avenue and Sixty-Second Street on Manhattan island. Seven hundred thousand people are killed instantly; at least two million more die of radiation poisoning over the next two years. Several different Islamic jihadist groups claim responsibility for the initial explosion.

The origins of the device remain unclear to American authorities. The weapon might have come from Pakistan; not all of Pakistan's more than one hundred nuclear weapons have been accounted for, following its recent war with India. To prevent a decapitating first strike from India, Pakistan decentralized control of its nuclear arsenal. Weapons were placed around the country. The commanders of different bases were given control over specific weapons and were authorized to strike India without an explicit command from central authorities. At least some members of Pakistan's armed forces had embraced radical Islamist beliefs. They believed that the religion that informed many aspects of their lives was threatened by a godless America that had refused to accept Muhammad as the last prophet sent by God. Striking a blow against America would be a saintly act, one that would guarantee them a place in heaven.

The weapon might also have been sold to a transnational terrorist group by North Korea. Several American presidents, including

Clinton, Bush, Obama, and Trump, had tried to denuclearize the Korean peninsula. The North Korean regime was desperate for an independent source of money. Kim Jong-un could not resist several million dollars for a nuclear weapon that could not definitively be traced back to North Korea.

Or consider a second scenario. A respiratory disease strikes many individuals around the world. The disease has not been seen before. It is easily transmitted. There is no effective vaccine. The mortality rate is high, greater than 50 percent. The very old and the very young seem particularly vulnerable. The earliest cases, which are traced to tropical regions in Africa, are not monitored by any national or international authorities because administrations in the countries initially impacted are unable to effectively govern many parts of the territory nominally under their control. This global pandemic kills hundreds of millions of individuals.

Neither of these possibilities is far-fetched. All of the countries from which such threats (a loose nuclear weapon or a pandemic disease) might emerge have gross national products that are under 2 percent that of the United States. They are all despotic regimes. To an extent that has never been true before, poor governance in even the remotest areas of the world could threaten the security of major powers. This is a new challenge for the United States and other advanced industrialized countries. New technologies have severed the link between underlying resources and the ability to do harm. Even actors, state or non-state, with very limited material resources could inflict damage that in the past has been associated only with major-power conflict, with war. American national security could be directly threatened from areas that in the past could not have inflicted significant direct harm on the United States. North Korea, a despotic regime, could devastate its neighbors—China, Russia, Japan, and South Korea—and the United States as well. Non-state actors could secure weapons either nuclear or biological that could kill millions of people even in the wealthiest states in the world.

Global pandemics could emerge from areas where official

authorities do not have the capacity to monitor what is happening within territories ostensibly under their control. HIV/AIDS and Ebola have alarmed countries far from the tropical areas where the associated pathogens jumped from animal to human populations. These diseases are, however, difficult to transmit, because their spread depends on contact with bodily fluids. An easily transmissible disease vector, one that spread through the air, for instance, could be far more devastating. Governance, or at least the ability to effectively control and monitor national territory, in poorly governed and malign states matters now more than has ever been the case in the past.

By some measures the United States emerged as the most powerful country in the world in the first decade of the twentieth century. The lessons that American leaders learned from the interwar years were that the United States could not isolate itself from the rest of the world and that there would be a very high cost to pay for appeasing despots; competitive trade policies and hypernationalism have had bad results for the United States. The immediate aftermath of the Second World War, especially regarding what were understood as very successful democratization projects in Germany and Japan, convinced American leaders that the world could be remade in America's image. The outcome of the Second World War confirmed America's utopian vision: consolidated democracy could be promoted in any country. This conclusion was reinforced after the Soviet Union collapsed, really self-immolated, in 1991. The end of history was apparently at hand and with appropriate policies the United States could successfully promote a liberal world order composed of well-governed states that respected the rule of law and individual rights. These very optimistic assessments have been dashed by the events of the twenty-first century, leading to the dystopian view that there is nothing that the United States can do.

After the Second World War, Truman and his administration quickly came to recognize that the Soviet Union would be an implacable enemy, one opposed to American values. Of the fifty-one countries that founded the UN in 1945, six were members of the Soviet bloc or of the Soviet Union itself.

Most of the countries that subsequently became independent states were then under colonial rule. The United States opposed colonialism and undermined Britain and France, the major colonial powers, especially during the Suez crisis in 1956. At least some American leaders expected, hoped, that the end of colonialism would be a harbinger of a new global rise of democracy. Implicitly and sometimes explicitly, American leaders assumed that economic development would occur naturally, that the United States only had to get rid of colonialism, provide stability, and offer some foreign aid and all would be well. With the fetters of colonialism removed and a small amount of assistance, the countries of the developing world would come more and more to be like the United States.

It was not to be. Leaders in most other countries were despots, more concerned with staying in office than with helping their own populations. During the Cold War the United States focused on securing regimes, even authoritarian regimes, that opposed communism and the Soviet Union. Most of the successor states to the European empires started as democracies but then quickly succumbed to despotic rule. Many electoral gains were reversed as despots realized that their hold on power was threatened by reforms associated with democratization.

With the collapse of the Soviet Union, however, it appeared that the United States had defeated its enemies of the twentieth century, fascism and communism. Seeing the breakup of the Soviet Union as the end of history, as the end of any serious challengers at the global level to democracy and the free market, appropriately captured the euphoria that followed the fall of the Berlin Wall. American leaders and the attentive public assumed that they could help to create a world of effective sovereign states, states that were democratic and well governed. Utopianism was vindicated. The march toward a more just and effective liberal international order had only been temporarily derailed by the triumph of communism in Russia, in those territories that the Soviet army captured at the end of the Second World War, and in China.

WHAT IS UNIQUE about the contemporary moment is that even weak actors with limited material capabilities can threaten the security of the most powerful states in the world. The level of suffering that could be imposed by states with very limited resources, or by non-state actors with ideological or religious objectives, would be similar to the suffering that has in the past resulted only from war among major powers. Weak actors, state or non-state, could kill millions of people.

The impact of the poor governance of failed and failing states on the well-being of individuals in richer, better-governed, democratic countries is uncertain. What is clear is that the relationship between underlying material capabilities and the ability to do harm has been broken. In the past, individuals or small groups could not kill significant numbers of people (no more than a few hundred) or disrupt major infrastructures (only for short periods of time). The weapons that groups or individuals could acquire—knives, guns, even dynamite—could do harm but not the kind of harm that would result from warfare. This is no longer the case. Individuals or small groups could cause major damage through the use of biological pathogens, dirty nuclear or even conventional nuclear weapons, or possibly cyber attacks.

The fundamental problem for the United States is that all of its traditional ways of understanding the world have failed. The utopian vision, Wilsonianism, will not work for most of the world's polities, which are essentially despotic orders where political leaders are bent on staying in power. The dystopian view that the United States can do nothing is inadequate, given the security threats that could emanate from actors with limited resources.

Unconventional Threats

The defining characteristic of unconventional threats is that actors with relatively limited material resources can now deploy weapons that could kill hundreds of thousands or millions of people or permanently disrupt societies even in the most powerful countries in the world. Some of the risks are associated with internationally recognized states such as Iran, North Korea, and Pakistan, but others come from non-state actors, including covert organizations within the liberal industrialized West, extremist Islamic groups, other transnational actors, and even disgruntled individuals or lone wolves. Because of weapons of mass destruction, notably nuclear and biological, the absence of authority structures within some states, and the global linkages provided by the World Wide Web and air travel, the connection between underlying material resources and the ability to do harm has been ruptured.

Unconventional threats have created the possibility of "black swans." These are Rumsfeld's unknown unknowns: things that we have not even imagined, as opposed to known unknowns, such as flight cancellations, things that we know about but whose occurrence we cannot predict. Black swan events are by definition rare and treacherously difficult to address. Political leaders do not get credit for preventing bad things from happening. The US intelligence community, for instance, had dots that were never connected that might have prevented the 9/11 attacks, but if the intelligence community had connected the dots political leaders would not have been rewarded. A major security incident, however, that killed thousands or tens of thousands of citizens or more (with nuclear weapons or biological pathogens being the most likely source), or a cyber attack that disabled the power grid for a long period of time, or a massive flow of migrants that left wealthy advanced democracies with only very uncomfortable choices—this could change the boundary between individual freedom and public authority within liberal states, undermine democratic norms and values, and weaken presumptions of sovereign autonomy internationally. All we can know is that black swans might occur and that, if they do, political leaders in democratic states will lose support, even if they get no credit for preventing the appearance of a black swan in the first place.

Black swans must be distinguished from other kinds of events that are hard to anticipate but do not constitute existential security threats. For example, terrorist attacks that kill small numbers of people, such as the Boston Marathon bombing, the murder in Charleston by a white supremacist, and the attack on American military personnel in Chattanooga, are tragic but not existential. Likewise, transnational criminal organizations may steal millions of dollars from individuals or institutions in OECD countries. Such attacks, however, are best dealt with through domestic intelligence and law enforcement. Attempts by external actors to address transnational criminality may actually make things worse because of the close relationship between some despotic leaders and criminal gangs.[1]

The terrorist attacks in Paris, first on the *Charlie Hebdo* staff and then in November 2015 on the Bataclan theater and elsewhere, are on the cusp between ideologically motivated criminal attacks that kill small numbers of people randomly, on the one hand, and, on the other hand, nuclear or biological attacks that would result in large-scale death or cyber attacks that could disrupt the financial sector or power grid. Although the *Charlie Hebdo* attack killed just eleven people, it had a chilling effect on public discourse, and the carnage in Paris in November of 2015 probably affected people's behavior and sense of safety. Free speech and expression is a hard-won privilege that has become widespread in the world only since the end of the Second World War, as consolidated democracies have replaced despotisms in a few countries. Some novelists, analysts, or journalists will almost certainly be discouraged from engaging in activities that could be construed by extremists as anti-Muslim.

Clear security threats, by contrast, involve attacks that could kill thousands of people or more, or lead to fundamental changes in the principles and laws that govern liberal democratic states and the international sovereign state system. There are three possible kinds of black swan events that could kill large numbers of people or disrupt normal life in the OECD world: global pandemics, attacks using naturally occurring or artificially created biological agents; nuclear terrorism; and cyber acts of mass disruption. In addition, very large flows of migrants could upset the balance of political and ideational interests that has helped to sustain liberal democracy in Western Europe, North America, and East Asia. However, the level of refugee flows is sensitive to national policies. Germany, for instance, dramatically reduced the inflow of refugees in 2017 by imposing new rules on asylum seekers and by making deals with countries in North Africa and the Middle East to keep refugees in their home areas if not their home countries.

Some have suggested that the United States in particular has exaggerated the threats from poorly governed areas.[2] The threats, however, cannot be ignored. Poor governance, civil wars, state failure, and ungoverned spaces can have negative impacts on the wealthiest countries in the world. In some cases these impacts, as measured in terms of the number of people that could die or the potential disruptions to normal life, could reach very high levels. This is true for naturally occurring pandemic disease outbreaks, and it is true for transnational terrorism involving biological and dirty or conventional nuclear weapons and possibly coordinated cyber and physical attacks.

Pandemic Disease Outbreaks and Biological Pathogens

A global pandemic could arise naturally. About four hundred diseases have jumped from animals to human beings since 1940, mainly in the world's tropical belt where humans and animals are living closer together.[3] HIV and Ebola are two examples. Such diseases have spread among the population in poorly governed areas without being recognized. HIV, for instance, might have spread among humans in Africa for decades before it infected individuals in advanced industrialized countries, was recognized as a new illness, and was eventually treated. Greater trade and air travel have increased the chances that such zoonoses (infectious diseases that move from animals to humans) will spread internationally.

Civil wars and internal disorder make such contacts more likely.[4] Civil wars and poor governance increase the likelihood that the outbreak of some new communicable disease will not be detected at an early stage. The spread of Ebola in some West African countries offers vivid recent examples, both positive and negative. An Ebola epidemic broke out in Guinea, Sierra Leone, and Liberia in early 2014 and infected almost thirty thousand people. The disease overwhelmed the public health systems in these three countries, and some local practices, such as cleansing the dead, facilitated the spread of the disease. Although the World Health Organization (WHO) at first underestimated the magnitude of the outbreak, the disease was brought under control with the help of national and international organizations, including the US military. By early 2016, the WHO declared that the outbreak was over, but Ebola had killed more than eleven thousand people.

The most striking positive story from the Ebola outbreak was the effectiveness with which the disease was contained in Nigeria. An infected individual flew to Lagos, but because Nigeria had in place a Gates Foundation system for monitoring polio, all of his contacts were tracked down. There was no Ebola epidemic in Nigeria.[5]

The International Health Regulations (IHR), which have been endorsed by all members of the WHO, constitute the only international treaty that incorporates provisions for minimal detection and public health capacity. Though 196 countries have signed the IHR, only a small proportion have implemented them.[6] The IHR are voluntary. States do not have to report to or cooperate with the WHO. China's failure to cooperate with external actors contributed to the severity of the SARS outbreak in 2002; the infection spread to fifteen countries.[7]

What is needed in despotic states to address the threat of potentially global pandemics is not good governance but good enough governance. Communicable diseases must be monitored. Monitoring might be sustained by external funding. But the return on investment for wealthier countries would be substantial, which is not to say that all wealthier countries would be willing to make the necessary investment, as evidenced by the 2017 budget proposals of the Trump administration.[8] A relatively small but competent bureaucracy, perhaps supported by external funding, can make a major contribution to the detection and isolation of a communicable disease. Such an agency would not be a threat to despotic rulers.

Deadly pathogens might also be deliberately created and spread by transnational terrorist organizations or even by disgruntled individuals. Already-known pathogens might be used for malevolent purposes. One hundred kilograms of anthrax, for example, distributed over a populated area, could kill as many as three million people.[9] The technological skill and resources needed to produce a pathogen that could have devastating global consequences, either by tweaking an existing biological agent (for instance, by making such an agent transmissible through the air) or by creating a new pathogen, are becoming more easily obtainable. CRISPR technology for gene editing is cheap and readily available.[10]

There has been a robust debate in the scientific community, with no clear consensus, about how much work on deadly pathogens should be made public.[11] A safe haven in an ungoverned space in a poorly governed despotism would be an advantage, if the goal was to train relatively unskilled individuals in the use of such deadly biological agents.

Nuclear Terrorism

While the means that could produce a global pandemic are becoming more available, the financial and technological assets needed to produce a nuclear weapon exist in only a very few states. A nuclear explosion in a major urban area would be a game changer. There is almost zero probability that a nuclear weapon could be produced by a non-state entity, although such capacity might reside in quasi-autonomous substate actors in some countries. A transnational terrorist group could, however, procure a nuclear weapon from a country whose own internal controls were weak (possibly Pakistan, from which A. Q. Khan sold nuclear technology to North Korea, Iran, and Libya), or which harbored individuals sympathetic to a global jihadist movement (possibly Iran or Pakistan), or whose leaders needed cash (North Korea).

Obtaining a true nuclear weapon would be difficult but not impossible. Pakistan probably has more than one hundred nuclear warheads.[12] Some of the Pakistani officers in charge of the military intelligence service, the ISI, have been influenced by the radical Islamists. Pakistani nuclear scientists met with bin Laden shortly after 9/11, a meeting that could not have taken place unless it had been sanctioned by the ISI. By 2008 US officials were convinced that the senior ranks of the ISI were fully under control, but they were not so sure about the middle ranks of the organization or retired officers. Although the command and control structure for Pakistani nuclear weapons is a closely held secret, it seems likely that Pakistan has decentralized the ability to deploy such weapons to prevent a decapitating first strike from India. Pakistan is a nuclear-armed state, some of whose decision makers have been influenced by jihadist beliefs.[13]

Iran has the ability to produce nuclear weapons in a matter of months, although it may be constrained from doing so by treaty obligations or if its leaders calculate that it is better to be on the threshold of getting a bomb than to actually produce one. North

Korea has nuclear weapons. The possibility of North Korea selling a nuclear weapon to a transnational terrorist group cannot be ruled out.

Cyber Acts of Mass Disruption

Cyber threats are evolving far more quickly than policy or law, generating possible black swan acts of mass disruption emanating primarily from states, notably North Korea, Russia, China, and Iran, but also from non-state actors. Cyber threats are the embodiment of unknown unknowns. The full range of cyber threats is broad, including petty theft; espionage intended to give foreign states or organizations a bargaining advantage; theft of intellectual property, most notably from American corporations and universities; disablement of US military systems in times of conflict; corruption of elections in Western democracies; and attacks on critical infrastructure that could paralyze or fundamentally alter society. Many cyber attacks, notably financial crimes, are not black swans. They are known unknowns and the consequences of attacks on individuals are limited, if only because institutions absorb the costs of financial theft. Cyber black swans would involve attacks on critical infrastructure, such as financial institutions, power systems, or elections, that could fundamentally disrupt or alter the way society functions. In 2007 Estonia experienced a denial-of-service attack against many official and nonofficial websites. These attacks, which almost certainly originated in Russia, accompanied a dispute about the removal of a Soviet-era memorial from the center of Tallinn, the capital of Estonia.[14]

Cyber attacks pose a huge challenge for advanced industrialized democracies. The private sector and the government do not share the same interests. Private firms may want to conceal the fact that they have been hacked. Public agencies might not want to reveal that they have identified, followed, and traced foreign hackers. Apple wants to be able to encrypt its devices to assure its customers that the government cannot read their emails or other materials. The Justice Department took Apple to court to get access to the iPhone of the San Bernardino killers, withdrawing its request only after the government found a way to access the information on the phone without Apple's help.[15]

Wealthy societies are becoming increasingly networked. But every networked device in the universe of things could potentially be hacked. The internet was not designed for security. Autonomous cars have already been hacked. Hackers have claimed that they can control civilian aircraft in the air. Attribution is difficult. Deterrence might work against other states but some states that have engaged in hacking, such as North Korea, which launched an attack on Sony Pictures in the fall of 2014, are not networked to a very high degree. Even if the United States has the capability to strike back, there may be little to strike back against. Deterrence is completely useless against most non-state actors, where attribution might be even more challenging. Some cyber attacks might be as potentially disruptive as pandemics or terrorist incidents.

Refugee Flows

Refugee flows are a fourth issue area where rich consolidated democracies can be affected by developments in poorly or malevolently governed areas of the world. Unlike pandemics, nuclear attacks, or cyber combined with kinetic attacks, refugee flows do not pose an existential threat to Western democracies. The number of immigrants, if not the number of refugees, is responsive to national policies. The countries that were the source of the largest number of refugees in 2015—Syria, Afghanistan, Somalia, South Sudan, Sudan, Democratic Republic of the Congo, Central African Republic, Myanmar, Eritrea, and Colombia—were all, unsurprisingly, states where internal order had disintegrated at least in some parts of the country.[16] The number of displaced persons was between forty and fifty million per year from 2007 through 2013 but then rose above sixty million in 2016 and 2017.[17] Distance is still a challenge but modern transportation technologies have made moving over long distances much easier than was the case in the past. Large migration flows have been particularly challenging for Europe because of its closeness to parts of Asia and Africa.

A formal international regime for refugees emerged only after the First World War. The High Commissioner for Refugees was established under the auspices of the League of Nations to address the problems stemming from the flow of refugees from Soviet Russia. The assumption was that this would be a temporary problem. The League provided refugees with papers that made it easier for them to travel, but countries did not have to accept refugees. German Jews who tried to flee in the late 1930s were sometimes turned back and some of those were forced to return to Germany. (The most familiar example is the German ship *St. Louis*; carrying more than nine hundred Jewish refugees in 1939, it was turned away from Cuba and the United States.)[18]

During and after the Second World War, the UNRRA (United Nations Relief and Rehabilitation Agency) and the IRO (International Refugee Organization, replaced in 1950 by the UN High Commissioner for Refugees) were established. Initially their primary focus was on refugees in Europe. Palestinian refugees were addressed through a different UN agency, UNRWA, established after the 1947 war. The UN Convention Relating to the Status of Refugees was adopted in 1951. The convention defined refugees as those subject to persecution because of race, religion, nationality, membership in a specific organization, or political opinion. The convention also had a provision for non-refoulement, meaning that an individual could not be returned to a country if he or she had a well-founded fear of persecution.[19] Regional conventions in Latin America and Africa endorsed or extended this basic definition.

Claims of refugee status can, however, still be adjudicated by national governments which can, within the general principles of the Refugee Convention, set their own specific standards. The burden of proof is on the individual that is claiming refugee status. In countries that have not signed the 1951 convention, which includes many countries with a large number of refugees, such as Jordan and Pakistan, a representative of the UN High Commissioner for Refugees determines refugee status.[20]

Refugees can upset existing ethnic balances. The following countries had the largest number of refugees per 1,000 inhabitants at the end of 2015: Lebanon, 183; Jordan, 87; Nauru, 50; Turkey, 32. The European country with the largest number of refugees per 1,000 was Sweden, with 1.7.[21] Anti-immigrant sentiment played some role in the successful Brexit vote in the UK and in Donald Trump's victory in the American presidential election. In less wealthy, less well-governed states that are geographically close to countries that are generating large numbers of refugees, the political impact can be even more direct. Refugees can turn against their host country, as the Palestinians did against Jordan in 1971. Isolated refugee camps can become breeding grounds for terrorism.[22]

Migrants from poorly governed states do not, however, pose an existential security threat to wealthy industrialized countries. Migration would not directly be the cause of large numbers of deaths, as could be the case for transnational terrorism or pandemic disease. But migration can alter the level of support for existing parties and change the political discourse even in the most left-leaning countries, such as Sweden. The level of migration can, however, be dramatically affected by changes in national laws.

Some European countries have drastically reduced the refugee inflow. The number of asylum seekers in Germany, for instance, radically declined in 2017. Germany changed its rules for family reunification in late 2015. It began sending refugees from Afghanistan back to Kabul in late 2016. It signed an agreement with Tunisia in March 2017 that allowed Germany to more quickly deport rejected asylum seekers from Tunisia. These changes were spurred by the electorate's very negative response to Chancellor Merkel's openhanded policies, after widespread reports of sexual assaults on German women by refugees in Cologne and terrorist attacks by refugees in Berlin and other German cities. Sweden toughened its asylum regulations in June of 2016 to limit the number of new migrants. The legislation, which was introduced by the Social Democrats, passed overwhelmingly, 240 to 45.[23]

Hence, while international migration caused by strife in poorly governed states can confront the leaders of Western democracies with uncomfortable choices, given their normative commitments and international obligations, national governments in the OECD world can, if imperfectly, control the inflow of refugees through national legislation.

Transnational Crime

Unlike cyber attacks, biological agents, or dirty or conventional nuclear bombs, transnational criminal activity does not pose a black swan threat. Transnational criminal activities are often known knowns or known unknowns. Cyber crime is about money: thefts from banks, extortion of individuals, identity theft. The amounts are not trivial, reaching several billion dollars a year. A substantial amount of transnational criminal activity originates from states with at least moderately competent institutional structures, such as China, Russia, North Korea, and Ukraine.

Unlike pandemics or biological attacks, attacks with dirty or conventional nuclear weapons, or kinetic-cyber disruptions, transnational criminal activity cannot generate the kinds of threats that would approximate the casualties potentially incurred in a war or undermine or challenge the fundamental values of liberal societies. Transnational crime is still crime. It is best addressed through conventional means in advanced democracies. External interventions will be extraordinarily challenging, often impossible, fruitless, or even counterproductive.

TERRORISM, INCLUDING TRANSNATIONAL terrorism, is not a new phenomenon. Several heads of state were killed, mostly by anarchists, in the decades before the First World War, including President McKinley of the United States; President Carnot of France; and monarchs or members of the ruling family in Russia, Austria (Empress Elisabeth, Archduke Franz Ferdinand), and Portugal. The assassination of Archduke Franz Ferdinand, presumptive heir to the Hapsburg throne, by a Serbian nationalist was the spark that set off the First World War. Political groups also used explosives, primarily dynamite, to randomly target civilian populations. Irish nationalists were active in the United States in the late nineteenth and early twentieth centuries and supported their compatriots, who engaged in a variety of activities, including terrorism, designed to get the UK government to grant independence to Ireland.

Contemporary transnational terrorism is, however, potentially very different from its historical analogues. A terrorist attack could kill tens of thousands, even hundreds of thousands of people or more by deploying a nuclear or biological weapon. In the past the number of people that terrorists could kill was limited to the weapons available—knives or swords could kill a small number of people, bullets and TNT could kill scores—but a nuclear weapon or a pathogen could kill numbers that would approximate those killed in war. More than 2,500 people died in the attack on the World Trade Center when passenger jets were turned into missiles. A much smaller number died at the Pentagon. Many more would die if a terrorist organization was able to secure and use a weapon of mass destruction. It is not frivolous to argue that the United States should have simply absorbed the attacks of 9/11, that the Bush administration overreacted, but such a position would be impossible in the face of tens of thousands of casualties or more. Large numbers of casualties could result from a naturally occurring pandemic disease, most likely to originate in a tropical area from the use of biologicals as a weapon, and from dirty or conventional nuclear weapons.

Cyber attacks could fundamentally alter the way in which individuals in advanced industrialized societies conduct their daily lives, and a cyber attack combined with a kinetic attack could kill substantial numbers of people.

Biological weapons are easier to get than nuclear weapons. There are many known pathogens, such as salmonella and anthrax, that could be relatively easily obtained by individuals or non-state groups and could cause sickness or death. Lethal disease vectors such as for smallpox could be reconstructed from genetic pieces. Gene splicing machines are easily available. The skill needed to construct a lethal agent from natural or artificially created DNA is becoming increasingly widespread.[24] Individuals with malevolent intent could use the internet to wreak damage even in polities with very substantial resources. There are reasons to be attentive to weakly governed and failed states.

In the past, advanced industrialized countries focused on weaker polities for a variety of reasons. The United States, for instance, was concerned about developments in weak states during the Cold War because of its rivalry with the Soviet Union. Any state whose leaders appeared to be aligning themselves with the communist world was viewed as a threat even if that state had very limited resources. The United States intervened overtly and covertly in Korea, Vietnam, Guatemala, Cuba, Iran, the Dominican Republic, and elsewhere because American leaders saw communist or left-leaning regimes as a threat. They intervened even when their perceptions were warped by intelligence gathering that focused on left-leaning members of the elite.[25] Even before the Cold War the United States had intervened, especially in Central America and the Caribbean, when it feared that despotism, and, often, high indebtedness to a European power would lead to some great power challenging the United States in the Western Hemisphere. European states were engaged with weaker polities in Africa and Asia during the colonial period, especially in the nineteenth century, when colonies were viewed as a source of prestige and possible wealth. The great powers of Europe were also attentive to areas that could provide raw materials, especially oil in the Middle East after the beginning of the twentieth century, and even manpower; a large number of troops from India and other colonies fought for the UK in the First and Second World Wars.

The contemporary era is different. The relationship between underlying capacity and the ability to do harm, to kill large numbers of people, has been severed. In the contemporary world, state or non-state actors from impoverished areas could cause casualties at a level that was previously seen only in wars among great powers. The threats posed by poorly governed or malevolent areas are mostly black swans, low-probability but highly consequential events whose underlying probability distribution cannot be estimated. They are unknown unknowns. States with substantial resources have reason to be attentive to the possibility of black swans and their association with poor governance, but exactly what policies these wealthy states might plausibly implement has been contested.

The Bush administration explicitly tried to put Iraq and Afghanistan on the path to consolidated democracy. The Obama and Trump administrations viewed any sustained American engagement with deep suspicion. Both these visions, utopian and dystopian, are wrong. The United States must learn how to make love to despots: to find policies that are compatible with the interests of despotic leaders, that strengthen American national security, and that might, although we can never be sure, lead to consolidated democracy in the long run.

The kinds of policies that advanced industrialized countries might adopt depends, in the first instance, on how they understand the process of development, a problem about which there is no consensus in the academic or policy world. A better understanding of the process of development in all its aspects, political and economic, is the first step in providing policy guidance for external state-building. There is something between the very ambitious agenda of the Bush administration, which reflected an American utopian vision that any state could become a consolidated democracy, and the very reserved approaches of the Obama and Trump administrations, which reflected a more dystopian view that external actors could do little or nothing to affect governance in other polities.

Good enough governance is an objective that is neither utopian nor dystopian. Good enough governance could improve conditions in target states and protect the security of the most developed polities. External actors cannot securely put countries on a path to consolidated democracy, but they can do something. A better understanding of how development has taken place is the first step in empirically and theoretically grounding external state-building efforts.

CHAPTER 3

Accounting for History and Human Nature

THERE ARE THREE APPROACHES TO EXPLAINING HOW WEALTH and democracy have come to a small part of the human race. The first two are very familiar to academics, policy makers, and even the general public. The first is modernization theory, which basically asserts that technological change is the key driver of development. Technological change along with population growth leads to more wealth, more wealth leads to a larger middle class, and a larger middle class provides the social basis for democracy. The second approach focuses on institutional capacity and contends that without institutional capacity economic growth is impossible.

Policy makers, at least policy makers in the United States, have relied on these two approaches, especially modernization theory, believing that democracy and a market economy are the natural order of the world. If only repressive and autocratic leaders would get out of the way, or be forced to move out of the way, democracy would spring forth. Democracy is not a privileged possession of the West but rather a universal form of government that could triumph everywhere. Modernization theory is completely consistent with utopianism. Institutional capacity is at least not inconsistent with a utopian vision.

For many American leaders, not only could all countries become democracies but all countries would naturally become wealthy and democratic over time. The United States welcomed China into the World Trade Organization, which helped to sustain China's rapid economic growth. Part of the explanation for the very accommodating policy that the United States adopted toward China from the Nixon administration to the Obama administration was the assumption that China would become just like the United States. It was the same assumption about China that was made by George Marshall when he was the US special envoy to China immediately after the Second World War.[1] A wealthier China with a larger middle class would become democratic and would share American values.[2]

The second approach to development, institutional capacity, has also been relied on by American decision makers. The assumption, often tacit, is that elites want to do the right thing: They want to provide their societies with security and the rule of law. They want to provide their populations with health care and education. They are prevented from achieving these laudable goals because the institutions that they must rely on are weak. If only these institutions could be strengthened then development would naturally follow.

The third approach is less well known and has been largely confined to American academia. It is rational choice institutionalism. The basic contention of this approach is that both sustained economic growth and democracy require that self-interested political elites constrain their own freedom of action. They will do this only under certain special circumstances, when constraint is more attractive than arbitrary power. There is inevitably an element of luck and happenstance in achieving a government that is both effective and constrained. Small changes, not always under human control, could have outsize consequences. The triumph of wealth and democracy is not foreordained; we are lucky that it has happened at all.

Although none of these three approaches is completely compelling, rational choice institutionalism offers the best understanding of how a small part of the world became wealthy and democratic.

For external actors, rational choice institutionalism suggests that in despotic orders, which include most of the polities in the contemporary world, the best that external actors can hope for is good enough governance: security, some service provision, some economic growth. Good enough governance is neither utopian nor dystopian, but it does involve making love to despots and accepting some painful trade-offs. Most countries in the world have no clear path to consolidated democracy, but it is possible for external actors to do some things. In most of the world's polities—in other words, in closed access polities—an attempt by external actors to put them on the path to Denmark, on the path to democracy and sustained growth, is a fool's errand, because such a path would be antithetical to the interests of despots. On the other hand, there are possibilities for better security, better health, some economic growth, and perhaps even protection of some basic rights.

Modernization Theory

To repeat, modernization theory contends that wealth and democratization are the natural result of technology and population growth. Industrialization and urbanization lead to greater literacy and a larger middle class. A larger middle class is more tolerant, more accepting of diverse political perspectives, more willing to compromise, and more likely to reject extremism. The middle class is prepared to defend both rule of law (because middle-class individuals want to protect their property rights) and accountability (because they do not want public policy to be dictated exclusively by the rich and powerful, which can too easily act in its own interest).[3] Class conflict is mitigated. Democracy is not the result of some special set of cultural attributes possessed only by the West, but rather is a product of social and economic transformation.[4]

There is a kind of automaticity to modernization theory: wealth and democracy are produced by technological change and population growth; population growth occurs naturally and technological change will take place, especially if there is sufficient capital. In the 1950s and 1960s, ideas about growth saw rising income as a likely if not inevitable process. Academics, whose ideas were absorbed by the policy world,[5] were writing in the United States during an era when there was a market for developing alternatives to Marxist ideas. Although domestic savings in developing countries might not support the level of investment needed to sustain high growth rates, this gap could be closed by foreign assistance.

The goal of committing 0.7 percent of GDP to foreign assistance, an objective that is almost ritually endorsed at every UN meeting concerned with development, reflects the assumptions of modernization theory.[6] Poorer countries do not have the savings that would enable them to invest in their own national economies. If these investments can be provided through foreign assistance, then economic growth will take place. If there is economic growth there will be a larger middle class. If there is a larger middle class there will be democracy.

Even without foreign assistance, modernization theorists assumed, growth would take place, because technological change was unstoppable in a globalized world and capital would be available to commercialize innovation. There was one coherent process involving urbanization, industrialization, education, communication, and social mobilization that would lead to institutional development, a larger middle class, the triumph of democracy, and steady economic growth. Marxism provided a teleological view of human history in which there was inevitable progress; modernization theory, at least in the United States, provided an alternative to communism.

The relationship between per capita income and democracy has been thoroughly investigated.[7] The empirical findings are clear. Although there is a lot of movement between democratic and autocratic regimes, democratic regimes last longer in wealthier countries.[8] In 1985 the life expectancy for democratic regimes in countries with per capita incomes below $1,000 (in 1985 purchasing power parity [PPP] dollars) was eight years; for countries with incomes from $1,001 to $2,000, eighteen years. Once democracies achieve a per capita income of $4,000 (in 1985 PPP dollars) there has been virtually no chance that they would revert to dictatorship.[9] In recent years most wealthy countries (those with incomes above $10,000 in 1996 dollars) have held competitive elections; the vast majority of poorer countries with incomes below $2,000 have not.[10]

Modernization theory is, however, contradicted by several empirical findings. First, ever-higher levels of income do not make democracy more likely. Once income reaches a modestly high level, ever-higher levels of wealth are not associated with greater democracy.[11] There is no guarantee that China will become a democracy; despite rising income, President Xi Jinping is intent on maintaining the central role of the Communist Party in China. Second, there is also no relationship between per capita income and the longevity of autocratic regimes. Autocratic regimes remain in power regardless of income levels. Third, transitions from democracy, at least as measured by Polity scores, to autocracy and vice versa occur at all income levels; transitions to democracy, if not consolidated democracy, are not more likely at higher levels of income. Fourth, the relationship between wealth and democracy was very weak during the Cold War: the Soviet Union was never interested in supporting democracy; American leaders always gave lip service to democracy but during the Cold War they were in fact more interested in supporting regimes, even autocratic regimes, that opposed communism.[12] External actors can frustrate democratic changeovers. Finally, transitions to democracy have been clustered in specific periods of time, suggesting the importance of the external environment. There have been three waves of democracy since the first part of the nineteenth century. These waves have corresponded with major changes in the international system.[13] Economic growth and consolidated democracy both depend on institutions that are both effective and constrained. Without the right institutions, growth will never take place.[14]

Flaws in Modernization Theory

The fundamental challenge for modernization theory is to explain how sustained economic development occurred. Impressive technological, intellectual, and artistic achievements of the past, such as Platonic philosophy, Hellenistic bronze sculptures, and Roman aqueducts, were realized and then lost. The relatively small number of Hellenistic bronzes that have survived to the present era, several hundred, have mostly been found in shipwrecks in the Mediterranean. Many thousands of others were melted down over the centuries. These bronzes are stunning artistic achievements, such as one of a life-sized boxer sitting exhausted after a match. Only with the Renaissance, more than 1,500 years later, did European artists display similar aesthetic and technical levels.[15] The quality of construction of Hadrian's Wall, which was begun in AD 122 and completed within a decade, is more impressive than the English stone boundary walls that came centuries later. There were always differences in per capita income across the world, perhaps four to one in 1800, but nothing like the enormous variation that is now present because of the sustained economic development that has taken place in a small number of countries over the last two centuries.

Modernization theory has assumed that growth will take place more or less automatically. But this does not explain why growth took place only at a specific time and place, namely Western Europe and North America during the nineteenth century. Economic growth in Europe was modest until after 1800. Between 1500 and 1820 per capita income fell in Italy, Spain, and Poland. From 1820 to 1870 per capita income increased by 87 percent in the UK (more than in the previous three hundred years), and by 55 percent in the Netherlands (also more than in the previous three hundred years).[16]

Urbanization has not automatically led to growth. In the premodern world the largest cities were often centers of administrative control and economic exploitation. This was especially the case outside of Europe, where urban centers were the seats of imperial bureaucracies and despotic elites. "The European urban model had little to do with the political and economic nature of non-European towns. Asian, Middle Eastern and pre-Columbian American cities were the seat of despotic elites and their religious or royal bureaucracies. Absolutist monarchs built large empires through the force of arms. Despots extracted agricultural surpluses that they then could spend in lavish palaces and founded vast cities that could cater to their needs."[17] For instance, the city of Teotihuacan, which is northeast of the present Mexico City, may have reached a population of two hundred thousand by AD 400; as a religious and administrative center, however, it was not associated with sustained economic growth.[18]

Economists in the 1950s assumed that growth would naturally follow from increases in the factors of production: land, labor, and capital. The great impediment to development in poorer countries was understood to be the lack of capital, but additional capital could be provided through foreign assistance. By the beginning of the twenty-first century, however, despite hundreds of billions of dollars in assistance, many countries were still mired in poverty.

The dramatic disparities in economic growth and democratization that characterize the contemporary world present a huge challenge for modernization theory. Only a small number of polities have moved along the path described by modernization theory, around thirty. And this movement has taken place only over the last two centuries. For all but the past two hundred years of the ten thousand years of human history following the development of settled agriculture, the human condition was more or less stagnant. If growth is relatively easy, if it follows from technological change and increases in other factors of production, why did the Industrial Revolution not begin thousands of years ago? Why have some technological innovations been lost? Why is growth so uneven across the world, especially since the Industrial Revolution? Why did the Industrial Revolution, the engine of economic transformation, begin only at a specific point in time in a specific place? The evidence that, on average, higher levels of per capita income are associated with democracy is compelling, but the failure to explain how growth gets going in the first place is the great lacuna of modernization theory. If technological change and population growth were the only factors that mattered, economic growth would have occurred thousands of years ago in many different places.

Institutional Capacity Approaches

In the late 1950s and early 1960s modernization theory reigned supreme in American academic and policy circles. Modernization theory was completely consistent with American utopianism. It offered a direct challenge to Marxism. Both were teleological explanations of development. Both envisioned unidirectional movement toward a political, economic, and social order that would fulfill the highest aspirations of human beings. Human agency mattered, but only in the context of a given set of structural conditions. As Marx wrote, "Men make their own history, but they do not make it just as they please in circumstances they choose for themselves; rather they make it in present circumstances, given and inherited."[19] Once the wheels of history begin turning, whether as a result of Marx's dialectic or as the consequences of technological change and population growth, there could be only one end point: either the communist ideal society of free and associated producers or a polity in which individuals enjoyed the benefits of democracy and a market economy.

Although modernization theory was an attractive, perhaps an ideal, foil with which to counter Marxism at the high point of the Cold War, its preeminence in American academic discourse lasted for only about a decade.[20] Where modernization theorists saw the development of institutions, especially the institutions of liberal democracy, as the natural outgrowth of economic and social change, others argued that political order and economic growth were contingent on institutional capacity. Rather than being a product of economic and social change, effective institutions were a prerequisite for such change. For Samuel P. Huntington, one of the leading opponents of modernization theory, political mobilization without political institutionalization would lead to political decay. "Urbanization, increases in literacy, education, and media exposure all give rise to enhanced aspirations and expectations which, if unsatisfied, galvanize individuals and groups into politics. In the absence of strong and adaptable political institutions, such increases in participation mean instability and violence."[21] The key challenge for political life is order, and order can be achieved only through institutions that are adaptable, complex, autonomous, and capable of coercion.[22] Huntington wrote in 1968 that "the most important political distinction among countries concerns not their form of government but their degree of government."[23] Without an effective government there can be no development of any kind.

Huntington was not writing in a vacuum. In Western political thought the foundational statement of the importance of order is Hobbes's *Leviathan*, which was published in 1651. Hobbes argued in *Leviathan* that without order life would be nasty, brutish, and short. Order was best preserved by the Leviathan, the all-powerful state, whose legitimacy was based on an implicit social contract that had been entered into by all subjects. Subjects agreed to obey the Leviathan, the sovereign, in all things, and the Leviathan in turn provided order for the society.

When Hobbes published *Leviathan*, Britain was in the midst of a series of political upheavals. The king was executed. The monarchy would disappear for a decade. During the previous century religious wars had torn apart France. The Thirty Years' War in Central Europe, which killed more than two million people and whose ferocity was worsened by religious conflict, ended in 1648.

In what is now the industrialized world, social mobilization has followed or accompanied growing state capacity. Urbanization and education have depended on some level of state capacity. In the newly independent states of Africa and Asia that captured Huntington's attention in the mid-1960s, things were reversed. Urbanization and social mobilization took place without an increase in state capacity. The colonizing powers of Europe, especially Britain and France, were anxious to leave their former colonies. European powers wanted a quick exit even when this involved the loss of millions of lives, as was the case for Britain's departure from the Indian subcontinent.

In many countries capacity deteriorated even from the very modest levels that had been present during the colonial period. As I saw myself as a Peace Corps volunteer in the early 1960s, the Nigerians who replaced their British counterparts in the higher civil service were not obviously more committed or skilled. The number of trained individuals was limited. In some countries, the Congo being an extreme example, there were hardly any individuals with a college education at all.[24]

For new governments, the demands on them were unmanageable not only for reasons of limited capacity but also because the tasks that public authorities were expected to perform were now generated by a global template rather than by indigenous demands. In the advanced industrialized countries the scope of state activities increased gradually over time as a result of both the interests of elites and the demands from the broader society. Initially, public authorities were focused on external threats and the provision of courts with some reputation for fairness. Internal security came only later; the first police force was established in London only in 1829.

In the contemporary world, states are expected to be engaged in a much wider range of activities that include health; education; census taking; environmental protection; labor conditions; natural resource management; macroeconomic stability; fiscal stimulation; financial regulation; social security; protection of rights for designated groups such as children, ethnic minorities, indigenous peoples, and individuals with disabilities; infrastructure, including roads, railways, airports, and water supplies; recovery from acts of nature such as hurricanes, earthquakes, and fires; promotion of economic growth; regulation of specific industries; promotion of specific sectors; and subsidization of certain kinds of economic activities (farming being the most obvious).[25] The 1997 *World Development Report* from the World Bank included the following list of "functions of the state: minimal functions: defense, law and order, property rights, economic management, public health, antipoverty programs; intermediate functions: basic education, environmental protection, utility regulation, antitrust policy, insurance (health, life, pensions), financial regulation, consumer protection, redistributive pensions, family allowances, unemployment insurance; activist functions: fostering markets, cluster initiatives, asset redistribution."[26]

This is a daunting list and not all of the most advanced countries with the most exceptional competencies perform all of them, but it is a list that would have been incomprehensible to any political leader, say, two hundred years ago, when states had much less capacity.

These expectations regarding the responsibilities of the state have become part of a powerful logic of appropriateness that is both embraced by elites in the developing world and propagated by official and unofficial international and transnational organizations.[27] On a trip to Khartoum in 2005, the State Department motorcade that I was a part of drove through the center of the city. The signs in front of the government ministries were the same signs that would have been found in Washington or Berlin (although they were in Arabic as well as English)—the Ministry of Health, the Ministry of Education—but the functioning of these ministries, to the extent that they functioned at all, would have been very different. The Sudanese delegation that met with my State Department colleagues and me included a number of women, certainly more than would have played a significant role in the government of the Sudanese despot Omar al-Bashir. Equal, or at least some, representation of women was part of the logic of appropriateness that modern states were expected to follow.

In many developing countries there is a disconnect between the formal or legal scope of state authority and institutional capacity. The template for state responsibility is global. In the developing world this template has been embraced because newly independent states in the post–World War II period modeled their formal organizational structures on those already in place in Europe, and North America. The public officials of every state know that the state is supposed to have an organization that supports scientific research; they know this because officers from the United Nations Educational, Scientific and Cultural Organization (UNESCO) have made this part of the template of modernity. Every modern state must have an equivalent of Germany's Deutsche Forschungsgemeinschaft or America's National Science Foundation. This is true even for states that have no scientists and no research community to speak of.[28] These challenges—high social mobilization, limited capacity, and high expectations about the services that the government should provide—have provided a formidable challenge for many states in the developing world. There is a decoupling of logics of appropriateness (what the state is expected to do) from logics of consequences (what political leaders actually have an incentive to do based on their resources, interests, and the capacity of public institutions). There is a disconnect between the template provided by the international environment, the demands generated in a socially mobilized society, and what the state can actually provide or what political leaders have an interest in providing.[29]

For adherents of the view that state capacity is the key to development and modernity, the fundamental analytic questions are: How can state capacity be increased so that the state can effectively control activities within its own territory? How can the state meet at least the minimal expectations of its population by providing security, law and order, and the protection of property rights?

Attempts to understand how state capacity has developed have looked to the past, particularly, but not exclusively, to Europe's past. How did the powerful centralized states of the European continent, especially the states that became the major powers of the twentieth century, emerge from the fragmented and weak polities that characterized Europe in the Middle Ages? The focus for institutional capacity analyses is on the factors that might have enhanced the capacity of the state, in Huntington's terms the amount of government, and not on factors that might constrain the arbitrary exercise of state power.

The most prominent argument, and one that has been used to understand developments in China as well as Europe, is that state power emerges in response to external threat. Charles Tilly's famous aphorism, "War makes the state and the state makes war," captures this argument. States displaced other organizational forms in Europe, notably, leagues of city-states and empires.[30] In 1490 there were around five hundred political entities in Europe, including empires, states, city-states, principalities, and the papal states. By 1990 there were fewer than thirty states in Europe.[31]

After 1500 the fiscal-military state spread in Europe.[32] War, conquest, occupation, and defense demanded bureaucracies that could administer territory. The fiscal-military state was able to tax its population and use these revenues to pay for loans and a permanent bureaucracy, including an army and a navy. Over time, the fiscal-military states of Europe developed specialized military forces.

Mercenaries disappeared.[33] Feudal obligations became irrelevant even if the aristocracy continued to dominate the officer ranks.[34]

The most successful states in Europe developed first the ability to borrow at reasonable rates; this was especially the case for Britain after the Glorious Revolution of 1688. In the eighteenth and nineteenth centuries the major European powers came increasingly to rely on organized bureaucracies that could collect taxes effectively.[35] "War builds up an infrastructure of taxation, supply, and administration that itself requires maintenance and often grows faster than the armies and navies that it serves."[36] External wars may increase the identity of individuals with the state, facilitating resource extraction by political leaders and making it easier for them to enhance state capacity.[37] For Europe over the last several hundred years, there has been a positive relationship between tax revenue and war.[38] States that have experienced more years of war in the past have greater capacity to tax in the present.

Europe is not unique in how the pressures of war increased state capacity. A similar process took place in China almost two thousand years earlier. In 221 BC, the Warring States period in China ended after more than 250 years of fighting among seven major contending polities. Power was consolidated in the hands of one dynasty, the Qin. Technological change, the ability to cast individual weapons, provided an advantage to larger political entities that could arm more foot soldiers. At the end of the fighting around five hundred thousand men were mobilized, more than 10 percent of the population, a far higher percentage than what the Roman Empire had been able to muster at the height of its power.[39]

The most stunning escape from the trap of suboptimal domestic institutions occurred in Meiji Japan. Facing the threat of colonial conquest, a threat made manifest by the fates of China and India and the appearance of American naval vessels in Japanese waters in 1853, the Japanese political elite transformed the political, economic, and social systems of the country during the Meiji restoration. The Japanese elite essentially destroyed the political and social system of the Tokugawa shogunate. The samurai class was abolished; a conscript army replaced samurai bands; restrictions on travel were ended; international trade was opened; Western-style education was introduced in state schools; feudal holdings became prefectures of the central government; tax collection was centralized; an elected Diet was established; and, in 1890, a written constitution was promulgated, the first in Asia.[40] A country that had first tried to deal with Western encroachment under the Tokugawa shogunate by limiting Westerners to one port, Nagasaki, and abolishing firearms because they threatened the quintessential samurai weapon, the sword, systematically surveyed Western institutions during the last part of the nineteenth century and transformed Japan into a modern industrial power that was able to defeat Russia in the Russo-Japanese war of 1904–1905.

External threat provided a powerful incentive to increase state capacity, but these incentives were not always strong enough to counter the parochial interests of political and military elites. Poland, which experienced the same external threat as Prussia/Germany, was partitioned out of existence in the last decade of the eighteenth century by Prussia, Russia, and Austria not only because of its vulnerable geographic position but also, more importantly, because of the liberum veto, which allowed any aristocratic member of the parliament to block an agreement. China went through more than a century of turmoil before the reforms of Deng Xiaoping led to external autonomy and spectacular economic growth.

Thus, war did not always make the state. In many instances it unmade, destroying political entities. Some political entities were too small to defend themselves. Existing institutional structures in some larger political entities—Russia, Poland, Korea, the Ottoman Empire—created perverse incentives: the ruling elites could not reform without fundamentally undermining their own position. Their choice was death or death: death by conquest or death by domestic transformation.

Tilly's "War makes the state and the state makes war" may not be relevant in the contemporary era, where established boundaries have been protected by sovereignty norms and by the interests of elites in weak as well as powerful states. One of the most dramatic changes to take place after the Second World War is a decline in the number of violent state deaths.[41] This has happened despite the fact that many states have limited resources, military or otherwise, arbitrary boundaries, and a shallow sense of national identity. They are protected by international recognition. Political rulers in these states have to worry about many things, but external conquest is usually not one of them. Rulers are more likely to be overthrown by internal coups or revolts than by external invasions. There are a few exceptions, such as South Korea, which is threatened by North Korea, and Taiwan, which enjoys effective Westphalian/Vattelian and domestic but not international legal sovereignty and is threatened by China. But generally, foreign conquest is not an issue that domestic elites have worried about, even in states with very limited capacity.

For analysts who focus on the importance of state capacity, Tilly is, fortunately, not the only explanation for why central political authorities have been able to increase the competence and scope of their activities over time. A second explanation points to the importance of specific social or political coalitions, groups whose interests would be furthered by a more effective state. This is an argument entirely consistent with modernization theory. Such explanations have been offered for changes in state capacity in many different settings. In France, the centralization of state power began in the fifteenth century, before external threats were clearly manifest.[42] In a dramatically different setting, the development of greater state capacity in recent years in Somaliland, a piece of Somalia that has become de facto independent, was the result primarily of internal pressure: political leaders, merchants, and traditional elites all believed that their interests would be better served by creating an independent authority structure that was free of Somalia, where central authority had disintegrated.[43] Political coalitions also explain, at least in large part, the increase in state capacity in the United States in the latter part of the nineteenth century. The Pendleton Act of 1883 provided for the selection of federal civil servants based on meritocratic criteria, including examinations, and established the Civil Service Commission. In 1882 almost 90 percent of federal jobs were filled through political patronage; by 1945 the number had fallen to 15 percent.[44]

As in the case of external threat, greater per capita wealth and a larger middle class have not necessarily led to greater state capacity. In some countries, such as Italy and Greece, patronage has continued to dominate meritocratic standards in the selection of civil servants.[45]

Colonial legacies offer another explanation for state capacity. In general, colonialism was not a good thing. The occupying power usually provided only limited resources. Indigenous institutions, which might have provided effective building blocks for state capacity over the longer run, were undermined or destroyed.[46] The strongest case for the positive impact of colonial control can be found in Japan's colonies, Taiwan and Korea. In Taiwan, initial efforts to impose institutions from Tokyo and Japanify the population were resisted. The local Japanese governor, Goto Shimpei, a military officer, then was given considerable autonomy. Shimpei introduced a set of policies that greatly increased compliance, because of support that the Japanese received from community leaders, and ultimately led to a more effective state that persisted even after Japanese colonialism ended in 1945. "In Taiwan, state-society mediation was formalized. . . . Having dislodged the urban scholar-gentry and the rural strongmen from positions of political authority, the Japanese revived and reconstituted an alternative local governance structure centered around village- and neighborhood-level community leaders."[47] The Japanese encouraged industrial and agricultural development in Korea during their colonial occupation.[48] Colonialism is, however, a thing of the past. Colonialism has been delegitimized.

A final explanation for variations in state capacity is religion. Because of its independence and hierarchical structure, the Catholic Church was able to contribute to the rule of law in Europe by constraining warriors in a way that was not possible in parts of the world where religious and secular authority were joined (the Islamic world), where religious authority was not independent (China), or where religious authority was not hierarchical (India). The capacity of states in Europe was enhanced rather than undermined by the fact that religion offered some possibility, not always exercised, of constraining arbitrary state power.[49] Religion can make a critical contribution both by making the society more orderly and easier to govern and by motivating elites to commit themselves to the well-being of the polity, when order, discipline, and service are identified with religious salvation. Calvinism provided a particularly powerful set of organizational structures and beliefs because it was concerned with creating an ordered society that reflected the will of God. "In the 'confessional paradigm,' church-building and state-building go hand in hand."[50] The kings of Prussia populated their bureaucracies with Calvinists. In the Netherlands, Calvinism helped to create a well-ordered, self-disciplined society that made it possible for the Dutch to play an outsize role on the world stage.[51]

What unites all authors who understand institutional capacity as the key to state development is the assumption that it is possible to engage in state strengthening, that is, to construct a central state apparatus that can concentrate and effectively deploy power for collective objectives. State institutions must be able to set and enforce the rules of the game. They must be able to establish order, ensure rule of law or at least rule by law, and provide some collective goods. The state may be a stationary bandit but it is not a roving bandit. The provision of some order is a necessary condition for wealth.

The Flaw in Theories of Institutional Capacity

Theories that link development with institutional capacity suffer from one major flaw. While institutional capacity arguments have many different explanations for why institutional capacity develops, they do not explain why political leaders would adopt policies that would benefit the society as a whole, or even a large part of it, rather than their own narrow self-interest. Elites, if they have any choice, will not allow economic developments that would upend the existing political order.

Some autocratic regimes have dramatically increased their average per capita incomes from poverty levels to middle income, but they have not become rich. China is the most dramatic contemporary example. If China reaches OECD-level incomes and remains dominated by the Communist Party it will be a vindication of institutional capacity theory: an autocratic regime will have introduced policies that have benefited a large part of the population. Such an outcome is unlikely, because an autocratic state will not tolerate the kind of economic dynamism necessary to sustain substantial levels of growth. Sooner or later the bad emperor problem will rear its head. Mao killed tens of millions of Chinese through disastrous policies, including the Great Leap Forward and the Cultural Revolution.

In 1968 Huntington courageously (and he was nothing if not intellectually courageous) referenced the Communist Party of the Soviet Union as his example of an organization that had been autonomous, independent from societal pressures, and competent. The Soviet Union did have many impressive accomplishments. The Bolshevik government transformed an agrarian, backward polity into one of the two most powerful military powers on earth with a formidable industrial capacity of its own. The costs, however, for those living in the Soviet Union were very high. Tens of millions died in Stalin's purges, forced collectivization, and geographic displacement of ethnic minorities. Many millions more died because of Stalin's grotesque foreign policy errors: the Nazi-Soviet pact, which made it easier for Germany to invade the Soviet Union; and the purges of the military leadership in the 1930s, which made the Soviet Union's military weaker. The artistic avant-garde that emerged at the time of the Russian Revolution was forced underground or killed. The suprematist movement of the 1920s, which focused on radically abstract geometric shapes, was supplanted by socialist realism. Malevich, the leader of the suprematist movement, painted abstract and visionary canvases immediately after the revolution; his last paintings in the 1930s are painfully constrained by socialist realism. By the 1980s the Soviets had exhausted the technologies developed elsewhere (including those acquired through espionage, such as nuclear weapons) and exploited the available agricultural labor force by moving it into industry; Soviet economic growth stagnated. Life expectancy began to fall, an astonishing development for an industrialized society (and one that is now being repeated among poorly educated whites in the United States).

The goal of the Soviet leadership was not to further the well-being of Soviet citizens—materially or spiritually—but to stay in power. And that they succeeded in doing, until 1991, when Gorbachev's reforms, prompted in part by the realization that the Soviet Union was falling hopelessly behind the West, along with his clash with Yeltsin, precipitated the collapse of the Soviet system. Soviet per capita GDP was about 28 percent of that of the United States when the Bolsheviks came to power; it rose to a high of 37 percent in 1970 but then dropped back to 30 percent in 1990.[52]

The Soviet Union is hardly an exception. While the classic Chinese imperial state was impressive in its reach and administrative capacity, it did not promote economic growth or social change.[53] The imperial system (or rather, those officials, including the emperor, who were the beneficiaries of the system) had no interest in generating economic and social transformations that could alter the balance of political power. Trade with the outside world was heavily regulated and limited to only a few ports on the coast before the nineteenth century, especially after the emperor ordered the imperial treasure fleet destroyed early in the fifteenth century. For most of the centuries before the Industrial Revolution, China was wealthier and more technologically advanced than Europe, but this did not mean wealth for the average denizen of China.[54] A 2013–2014 exhibit at the Metropolitan Museum of Art in New York, *Interwoven Globe: The Worldwide Textile Trade, 1500–1800*,[55] had few examples of textile products that had been exported from Europe to China. Europe bought luxury goods from Asia, not the other way round. The British initiated the Opium Wars in the nineteenth century at least in part because there was nothing that the Chinese wanted to import from Europe. Thus, in China the state was strong but it was not constrained. It was a despotism. The state often abused its own population. To maintain their own base of power, emperors frustrated economic and commercial growth.

State power alone does not lead to sustained development. Nazi rule in Germany benefited some but crushed, exterminated, millions of others. Constraints on the state in Japan were not embedded enough in the social and political structure to prevent the exercise of arbitrary military and political power in the 1930s. Mugabe pillaged Zimbabwe, leaving most of his compatriots, black and white, worse off than they were under white rule. In countries as geographically different as Azerbaijan, Saudi Arabia, Myanmar, Equatorial Guinea, and Angola, oil wealth has allowed a small cadre, sometimes from the same family, to live in astonishing luxury, while most of the population is in misery. Despots may be efficient, or they may not, but one characteristic they all share is the desire to prevent economic and social change that would weaken their hold on power.

So long as the despots can command enough control over the instruments of violence to stay in power, they will engage in rent-seeking that damages most members of the society. In most situations, the state is a protection racket. In all of the pre-industrial states—Athens, Rome, the rice-growing states of Asia—power depended on population; population depended on slaves; slaves were secured through warfare.[56] The apotheosis of state power and oppression arrived in the twentieth century with the combination of growing bureaucratic control, autocratic authority structures, and high modernist ideology—a belief in progress and rationality.[57]

Thus, while analysts focusing on the institutional capacity of the state have suggested a number of different ways in which state power can be established, they have failed to explain why this power might lead to sustained economic growth and democratization. Political elites are self-interested. In nondemocratic polities their interests, logically and historically, have resulted in oppression and exploitation. Some level of security may be a necessary condition for economic growth, but security alone is no guarantee of sustained economic growth, well-being for all or almost all, and responsive rather than repressive government.

BOTH MODERNIZATION THEORY and institutional capacity approaches are fatally flawed, albeit for different reasons. Modernization theory cannot explain how economic growth begins, and institutional capacity approaches cannot explain why a powerful state would not be self-serving. Economic development and democracy cannot be achieved unless the institutions in a country reach the Madisonian sweet spot, unless institutions are both effective and constrained. Without effective institutions, there will be chaos and sustained economic growth will be impossible. Without constraints, institutions will be used for the narrow self-interests of elites. Neither modernization theory nor institutional capacity approaches provide any guidance as to how the Madisonian sweet spot can be reached, how institutions can be effective and constrained. If the flaws of modernization and institutional capacity theories are ignored, both are consistent with a utopian vision of what external state-builders can achieve.

CHAPTER 4

The Difficulty in Replicating Success

RATIONAL CHOICE INSTITUTIONALISM OFFERS A THIRD PERspective on the trajectory of political and economic development. Whereas modernization theory emphasizes social and economic change leading to political transformation, and institutional capacity theory focuses on the factors that might promote the development of state institutions, rational choice institutionalism sees development principally as the result of self-interested decisions made by elites, especially the elites that control the instruments of violence. Full development, economic wealth and democracy, can occur only if institutions are both effective and constrained, rather than primarily extractive.[1] Institutions must reach the Madisonian sweet spot. Institutions must open up opportunities for all (or almost all) members of society, encourage rather than frustrate individual initiative, and reduce rent-seeking by elites. Reaching the Madisonian sweet spot is no easy feat, and only a few polities have made it.

The great mystery is why elites would ever create such institutions, why those who control the means of violence within a polity would ever agree to constrain their own freedom of action. Why would rulers ever tolerate or accept social and political change that would undermine their own ability to stay in power? As Madison recognized in Federalist 51, people are not angels; if they were, no government would be necessary. In human history, present-day Somalia is much closer to the average state than Denmark or Norway.[2]

Reaching the Madisonian sweet spot is a matter of luck, not basic conditions. Certain structural circumstances, especially a larger middle class, make the development of effective but constrained institutions more likely but do not guarantee them.

The country that first developed both effective and constrained institutions was Great Britain. Had Britain not developed effective but constrained government in the eighteenth and nineteenth centuries there would have been no Industrial Revolution and no modern democracy. Britain was the shining light, but that light could have been extinguished by fortuitous events.

Elizabeth I's speech to her troops at Tilbury on August 19, 1588, and Winston Churchill's address in Parliament on June 4, 1940, are two of the most famous perorations ever given in the English language. Both came at perilous moments in English history: the first, shortly after the Spanish Armada was forced north from the Straits of Dover, and the second, only a few days after the last evacuations from Dunkirk took place at the beginning of the Second World War. Elizabeth said in 1588: "I know I have the body of a weak, feeble woman; but I have the heart and stomach of a king, and of a king of England too, and think foul scorn that Parma or Spain, or any prince of Europe, should dare to invade the borders of my realm."

Churchill's words are more familiar:

Even though large tracts of Europe and many old and famous States have fallen or may fall into the grip of the Gestapo and all the odious apparatus of Nazi rule, we shall not flag or fail. We shall go on to the end, we shall fight in France, we shall fight on the seas and oceans, we shall fight with growing confidence and growing strength in the air, we shall defend our Island, whatever the cost may be, we shall fight on the beaches, we shall fight on the landing grounds, we shall fight in the fields and in the streets, we shall fight in the hills; we shall never surrender.

When Elizabeth spoke, the English did not know that the Spanish Armada was already sailing for home. Elizabeth and her advisors saw invasion as a very real possibility.[3] The Armada consisted of about 130 ships, only 6 of which were lost through military action by the British. If the Armada had been successful in its main task of protecting an invasion force from the Netherlands (then controlled by Spain), and the Duke of Parma had landed his forces, Protestant and Tudor England would probably have been finished.[4] Elizabeth's hold on power was hardly secure, with many in the country still Catholics. If the weather in the Channel had been more favorable, the Duke of Medina Sidonia, who commanded the Armada, might have succeeded in protecting Parma's troops as they crossed the Channel and this Spanish force might have encountered little resistance both because of the poor state of the English army and because of religious divisions in England.[5]

Whatever else one might imagine, the history of England—the leader in constraining the arbitrary power of rulers—would have been very different if Philip II had become the king of a Catholic England in 1588. England was hardly a democracy in the sixteenth century, but Philip II, the Hapsburg ruler of Spain, embraced a far more autocratic set of principles than did the Protestant Elizabeth. Had the Spanish Armada succeeded in facilitating an invasion of England, a very different historical trajectory would have followed.

Britain found itself in an equally perilous situation in June of 1940. Hitler's armies had rampaged across Western Europe. By June 1940 Britain was left to fight Germany alone in the west. The British cabinet was divided. Appeasers, especially Chamberlain, still held key positions in the Conservative government.

Had Britain failed to evacuate more than three hundred thousand troops from Dunkirk, more than two hundred thousand of them British, history would have been different, perhaps decisively different. The British would almost certainly have sued for some kind of peace with Germany; Germany could have turned all of its might against the Soviet Union; there would have been no North African campaign that allowed Roosevelt to engage Germany after the Japanese attack on Pearl Harbor. Perhaps the Second World War would have had the same outcome—America did, after all, develop nuclear weapons—but the world would have been very different than it is today had Britain surrendered or reached a peace with Germany in 1940.

The favorable weather in the Channel was, though, one of the factors that made the evacuation a success. Many "small ships" participated in the extraction of the British Expeditionary Force and some French forces from Dunkirk. Had the weather in the Channel been as bad as it could have been, the evacuation would have failed and history would not have been the same.

Luck, including the weather, has played a decisive role in creating the OECD world. For most of human history, political authority has been despotic, malevolent, and rapacious. Democracy is a rare occurrence. There is no set of structural conditions that foreordains democratic outcomes. Luck, even good and bad weather, has played a decisive role.

For analyses that focus on institutional capacity the most important goal is to create state institutions that are effective and autonomous, because such institutions are viewed as a necessary condition for order: no order, no economic development. In contrast, for rational choice approaches, such autonomous institutions are fatal. Institutions must constrain elites, not just empower them.

Consolidated democracy requires political leaders to be responsive to the collective benefits of at least a large part of the society, if they hope to stay in office. A market economy involves both the protection of property rights from the arbitrary power of the state and, in addition, creative destruction, technological change that upends the economic order and is inescapably disruptive for the political order as well. Schumpeter wrote in 1942: "The opening up of new markets, foreign or domestic, and the organizational development from the craft shop and factory to such concerns as U.S. Steel illustrate the same process of industrial mutation—if I may use that biological term—that incessantly revolutionizes the economic structure from within, incessantly destroying the old one, incessantly creating a new one. This process of Creative Destruction is the essential fact about capitalism."[6]

In the United States in the late twentieth century, technological innovations turned Silicon Valley from an area of fruit orchards to the center of high technology in the world, in the process creating many multimillionaires, even billionaires, individuals with substantial resources, some of whom also had political interests. The United States, because of its rule of law and protection of property rights, also attracted many investors, engineers, and programmers from other countries, some of whom became citizens and played a role in American politics. An autocratic regime would have stifled such development not only because autocracies cannot guarantee property rights or rule of law but also because new players with time and money would be a threat to the existing political order.

Unconstrained elites will never allow creative destruction because it would undermine the social and economic basis of their own power. History is filled with examples of situations in which despots have crushed technological, social, or economic changes that might have threatened their own power. At the beginning of the fifteenth century, the Chinese had the most formidable seagoing fleet in the world, with ships that not only were much larger than anything in Europe but outnumbered Europe's as well. But the emperor ordered that the Chinese treasure fleet, which had sailed as far as the east coast of Africa, be destroyed. Had the Chinese treasure fleet been allowed to continue unimpeded, the Chinese might have reached Europe; instead, the much smaller caravels of the Portuguese sailed into the Indian Ocean and on to China a century after the Chinese vessels ended their voyages. The Chinese might have discovered Europe rather than the other way around. But such voyages would have been a threat to the Chinese imperial system.

Investment and technological innovation, the drivers of economic growth, can flourish only in a polity where the holders of state power can act effectively but not arbitrarily. Despotisms, where there is centralized state capacity, may experience growth, but such growth spurts are not consistently sustained.[7] Since 1950, the richest countries (those with per capita incomes above $20,000) had positive growth rates in 84 percent of their country years, while poorer countries (those with incomes below $2,000) had positive growth in only 56 percent of their country years.[8]

For rational choice institutionalism the contemporary world is divided between open and closed access polities. In closed access polities, violence is endemic. In open access orders it is exceptional. The level of violence in the richest developing countries is closer to that in the poorest developing countries than it is to that in the OECD world.[9]

For rational choice institutionalism, moving from a closed access to an open access order requires simultaneous change in many different issue areas, including economic activity, military structures, the application and determination of laws, and the choice of political leaders. Such change across many different activities is difficult. Since 1840 only 10 percent of all regimes have lasted for more than fifty years. Most people have experienced violent regime change in their lifetime.[10] Effective states, capable of delivering services but at the same time refraining from exploiting their own populations, states that have reached the Madisonian sweet spot, have existed for only the last century or so.[11]

Rational choice institutionalists do, however, point to some distinctions among closed access or extractive polities. One discussion based on rational choice institutionalism distinguishes among fragile, basic, and mature natural or closed access orders.[12] In fragile natural orders the only organization that exists is the state itself;

in basic natural orders there are organizations other than the state but they are all directly tied to the state; in mature natural orders there are organizations outside the state. Closed access orders are all despotisms, but they may rule with varying degrees of effectiveness. Making the transition from despotisms to open access orders is challenging and never guaranteed. The jump to open access orders can occur, North, Wallis, and Weingast argue, only if a set of "doorstep" conditions, which are present only in mature natural orders, are reached. Reaching the doorstep conditions, which include rule of law at least for the elite, perpetual organizations, and centralized control of the military, does not, however, guarantee a transition to an open access order.[13] Not every state that meets the doorstep conditions makes the jump.[14]

Path dependence matters. Path-dependent explanations have two essential components: first, some random conditions, possibly combined with structural features of a polity, precipitate change; second, this change is then locked in. In classic path-dependent arguments, the random events that led to lock-in did not result in optimal outcomes, such as the adoption of the QWERTY keyboard (named for the first six letters on the top line of a typewriter keyboard) as opposed to the DVORAK keyboard, which places all vowels on the middle row. (It should be mentioned that the suboptimality of the QWERTY keyboard has been challenged.)[15]

The jump to open access does lead to a virtuous cycle. Openness in the political system supports openness in the economic system, which in turn reinforces political openness, leaving the society as a whole, and potentially everyone in it, absolutely better off. But even this virtuous cycle is not guaranteed, as present-day developments in the United States suggest.

Many different specific answers have been offered for the random events and possibly underlying structural prerequisites that can transform social orders. One way of thinking about when this transformation might take place is the doorstep conditions in which the control of violence is centralized, some organizations are perpetual and independent of the state, and at least some members of the elite have access to the rule of law. If these doorstep conditions exist, then elites may find it to be in their interests to extend impersonal rights, including the rule of law, to a broader segment of the society. The extension of rights might be attractive because it could increase economic payoffs to the elite by, for instance, making ownership in joint stock companies available to a wider public;[16] or a more constrained state might be more militarily effective because it can more easily raise money from a commercial elite that might otherwise live in perpetual fear of a sovereign default.[17]

There is, however, no teleology at work here. Even if the doorstep conditions are reached, polities might revert back into more primitive forms of a despotism.

> No teleology pushes states through the progression from fragile to basic to mature natural states. The dynamics of natural states are the dynamics of the dominant coalition, frequently renegotiating and shifting in response to changing conditions. If adjustments lead to more power and rents based on personal identity, institutions become simpler and organizations less sophisticated, and the society moves toward the fragile end of the progression of natural states. If adjustments lead to more power based on durable agreements, institutions become more complex and organizations become more sophisticated, and societies move towards the mature end of the progression. No compelling logic moves states in either direction.[18]

There are a variety of conditions that might lead elites to give up power. Elites may relinquish control when they face a credible threat of being overthrown. In this situation elites may accept more democratic institutions because this is the only way that they can make a credible commitment that allows them to avoid the even worse outcome of a successful rebellion. Elites may accept fundamental reforms that give more power to citizens because only constitutional concessions will be credible.[19]

Concessions will be more acceptable if elites are vested in more-movable industrial and human capital rather than land. Elites with human or industrial capital can exit a country with their assets; landed elites cannot. Movements toward democracy are more likely when there is a middling level of inequality: if inequality is very high, elites will be very resistant to change; if it is relatively low, citizens will be less likely to revolt. A more robust civil society facilitates democratic change by making it easier for citizens to overcome collective-action problems.[20]

Individual leaders might hold values that transcend their own narrow self-interest. Some individuals are indeed angels. Seretse Khama, who led Botswana's independence movement, is one prominent example. Botswana has not experienced any armed conflict, an unusual although not unique circumstance for a sub-Saharan African country.[21] Over the last twenty-five years it has been one of the fastest-growing countries in the world; it reached middle income status, with a per capita income of $17,700 at purchasing power parity, in 2015.[22] The literacy rate is 85 percent. Despite being highly dependent on diamond exports, it has escaped the resource curse. All of these successes took place despite unpromising beginnings: Botswana had almost no paved roads and very few university graduates when it became an independent state. The one area in which the country has not performed well is life expectancy, which is relatively low at fifty-four years, primarily because of a very high HIV/AIDS rate of 23 percent, the third highest in the world.[23]

It is difficult to explain Botswana's largely very attractive performance without taking account of the country's leaders, especially at the time of independence. A number of important and farsighted decisions were made by the post-independence political elites, in particular Seretse Khama and Quett Masire. Khama, who was heir to one of Bechuanaland's major kingships, was studying in

England in the 1940s when he fell in love with an English woman. In 1951, under pressure from the white racist governments of South Africa and Southern Rhodesia, Britain banned Khama from what was then the British protectorate of Bechuanaland. He was, however, allowed to return in 1956, after he renounced his kingship. The time he spent in London gave him a deeper appreciation of democracy. He led the independence movement in the 1960s, and he played a leading role in introducing modern institutions into his country. Most strikingly, he did not engage in personal aggrandizement.[24] The path to greater inclusivity, openness, and economic prosperity is not structurally determined. The quality of individual leaders is one factor among other kinds of fortune that can propel polities along one path rather than another.

There is, however, no guarantee that a polity will move to consolidated democracy. As Madison recognized, angels do not always appear. Democracy has emerged in some polities, for instance Britain in the nineteenth century; has been resisted for a long period, such as South Africa under apartheid; has failed to arise even though underlying conditions appeared supportive, such as in Argentina; or never existed at all despite considerable economic prosperity, as in Singapore.[25] Economic crises can lead to democratization, but can also precipitate coups that end democratic regimes. High levels of development, Singapore being the exemplary case, do not necessarily lead to democracy.

For most people for most of human history, life has been nasty, brutish, and short whether or not there was an effective state. Violence has been endemic. Political power has been used in arbitrary ways. Warriors killed the defenseless and one another. Political elites pillaged, taxed, and conscripted. For almost all of human history in almost all parts of the world, human beings have lived in despotic states.

Only in the last two centuries has some part of humanity escaped from these conditions. How and why this escape took place has occupied the attention of many observers. Analyses have relied on the three perspectives discussed here: modernization theory, institutional capacity, and rational choice institutionalism. Although these approaches are not mutually exclusive, rational choice institutionalism provides, in general, the most compelling explanation for why in a small number of countries in limited parts of the world, these conditions have been transcended. Transcendence is possible only if political elites accept constraints on their own power and if they are able to create and sustain effective institutions. Reaching the Madisonian sweet spot is, however, a rare occurrence, requiring both the right structural conditions (a larger middle class is helpful but not a guarantee) and luck.

Modernization theory and approaches that emphasize institutional capacity are compatible with a utopian vision in which any country may become a consolidated democracy. Rational choice institutionalism is not. There is no certainty that a country will reach consolidated democracy. Rational choice institutionalism suggests that consolidated democracy is usually a bridge too far. Most countries have despotic regimes. Rulers want to stay in power. They will undermine changes that threaten their rule.

Flaws in Rational Choice Institutionalism: The Empty Middle

Rational choice institutionalism makes no claim to being able to predict *ex ante* what the conditions might be that would allow a polity to be transformed into an open access or inclusive order. Only after the fact can institutions that are both effective and constrained be explained. Given the incentives confronting national elites, external actors cannot in most polities adopt policies that would put countries on a path to consolidated democracy. Even in those few countries that are in an intermediate position, in which the interests of elites might be mixed, it is difficult for external actors to understand the incentives facing national elites.

The more damaging lacuna for rational choice institutionalism is that it has no way to understand, or even to describe, polities that might be intermediate, in the middle, polities that have elements of both closed and open access orders. Even if most countries can be characterized as either closed or open, or either extractive or inclusive, there are some polities in the middle, or at least aspects of some polities are open access while others are closed access. Polities do not move instantaneously from extractive to inclusive institutions. The middle could mean a number of different things: polities in which some aspects of state policy are effectively constrained and others are not; polities in which the percentage of the population with access to the rule of law and with the right to form organizations is substantial, but not universal; polities in which the members of the political and social elite are divided with regard to their preferences for open access or closed access institutions. Paraphrasing Tolstoy, all happy countries (open access or inclusive) are alike, but unhappy countries (despotisms) are unhappy in different ways.

Even, however, in the country that was the trailblazer in extending the rule of law and the right to form organizations, the United Kingdom, the transition to constrained but effective authority was gradual. Britain was not suddenly changed by the Glorious Revolution of 1688 from a country that was subject to the arbitrary power of the Crown to one in which the sovereign and landed elites were constrained.

The constraints that were imposed on the Crown after the Glorious Revolution applied primarily to the military part of the state's budget. In 1700–1701 the total British budget was 3.76 million pounds, with the army and navy accounting for a little more than half; between 1792 and 1800 the average annual expenditure of the British Treasury was 25.36 million pounds, with 61 percent accounted for by spending on the army and navy.[26] In the 1740s British spending jumped by two-thirds over previous years; almost the entire increase was accounted for by the military.[27] During the second half of the eighteenth century, spending on the army and the navy accounted for about 9 percent of Britain's GDP, reaching 11 percent of GDP in 1800.[28]

The British military budget was controlled by the Parliament in the eighteenth century. The Crown had given up despotic control because Parliament had demonstrated that the king could be killed or removed. Parliament had the power to specify the spending plan for the army and navy, to collect revenues that would be needed to fund the plan, and to control any departures from the plan.[29] The military budget had to be passed every year. If a budget was not passed, the king's right to collect taxes for the military, or to make allocations for the military, would lapse.[30] After the Glorious Revolution, Britain had what Gary Cox has labeled a rule-of-law budget for the military but not for other public activities. The rule-of-law budget for the army and the navy allowed Britain to create a formidable military apparatus, one that ultimately triumphed over France in the Napoleonic Wars despite the fact that Britain was a smaller and poorer country than its main continental rival at the beginning of the eighteenth century.[31]

In the eighteenth century, however, other parts of the British budget remained in the hands of the Crown or local aristocratic authorities. Britain was in many ways a highly corrupt country in the eighteenth century. Britain had a relatively efficient fiscal military state, but a highly corrupt civil administration. Each new monarch at the beginning of his reign was provided with a sum of money with which he could do as he pleased. Moreover, there were many autonomous local authorities that were seen by Parliament in the eighteenth century as a bulwark against royal absolutism. Only slowly over time were royal appointments and local sinecures brought under the control of the Parliament. Officeholders were converted from independent actors who enjoyed the benefits of fees that they were authorized to collect for their lifetime (some positions could be inherited) into salaried civil servants whose budgets were controlled by the Parliament.[32]

In Britain, rule-of-law budgets for the military were an island of excellence that had positive impacts on the civil budget over time. The Crown was willing to accept rule-of-law budgets in the eighteenth century for the military because major continental powers presented a mortal threat. Spain, Austria, and, most obviously, France had the potential to conquer Britain and extinguish its independence. "War makes the state and the state makes war," Tilly's famous aphorism, can be applied to Britain in the eighteenth century. The Crown accepted constraints not only because the events of the English Civil War made it clear that the sovereign could be executed, that kingship could even disappear, but also because of external threats from continental powers with larger populations and a larger potential tax base.

The external pressures on Britain were unrelenting. Britain provisioned its army and navy, including not only food supplies (through the Victualling Board), but also (through civilian contractors) boots and uniforms, ships, fortifications, and gunpowder. Of the tonnage of new warships provided to the British navy for the period 1793 to 1815, 71 percent came from commercial shipyards.[33] The bakers, grain suppliers, and makers of cannons and cannonballs were commercial contractors. Britain relied on its private sector to provide the instruments of war. Spain and France, which attempted to provision their militaries through the activities of the state itself, were less efficient and less effective. When Britain lost the American Revolutionary War to the Americans and to France, one of its few defeats in the eighteenth century, it prompted a parliamentary investigation and the introduction of reforms to make the military more effective.[34]

The rule-of-law budget that had first been applied to the military demonstrated especially to members of Parliament that there were mechanisms that could be applied to the civilian sector as well as to the military. The members of Parliament came to understand that the mechanisms that they had used to frame and fund the military budget, such as committees of inspection, transfers of revenues from one activity to another, and the setting of standards, could be applied to all aspects of the budget, civilian as well as military. The members of Parliament learned how to create centralized boards, to conduct investigations, and to set standards of performance.[35] The organizational instrumentalities that had first been developed to make sure that commercial contractors were honoring their obligations to the army and the navy could be applied to non-military activities as well. These factors—external pressure, a parliament that had shown it could kill kings regarded as despots, the experience of the commercial class with a rule-of-law budget for the military in Britain, and the organizational innovations made by Parliament for this budget—explain why what had at first been an island of excellence (the military budget) spread to the civilian aspects of the state during the nineteenth century. (It might be more appropriate to call it a continent of excellence, given the relative importance of the military budget in Britain in the eighteenth century and through the Napoleonic Wars.)

It was not only the budget in Britain that did not change instantaneously from extractive activity controlled by the Crown, which could act arbitrarily or despotically, to a more inclusive activity controlled by the Parliament, but also the franchise. In the eighteenth century only a tiny part of the population had the right to vote for members of Parliament. The franchise was extended gradually throughout the nineteenth century. The reform acts of 1832 (separate acts for England and Wales, for Scotland, and for Ireland) extended the franchise, eliminated some constituencies (rotten boroughs that had de minimis populations), and gave more seats in Parliament to cities, which had growing populations. Even after the reform acts, only about 7 percent of the population could vote. The Second Reform Act of 1867 expanded the suffrage to 16 percent of the population.[36] The right to vote was not extended to all the citizens of the UK, including women, until 1928.

In the United States, African Americans, some white males, and women did not initially have the right to vote. By 1820 all white males in the United States, regardless of property holding, were given the franchise. The Fifteenth Amendment formally extended the vote to all citizens regardless of race, although this right was suppressed for African Americans in many states, especially in the South. The right to vote was not given to all women in the United States until the Nineteenth Amendment to the Constitution was ratified in 1920. Germany adopted universal manhood suffrage after unification in 1871, although only the second chamber of the legislature, the Reichstag, was selected through direct voting. Germany, however, did not introduce the secret ballot until 1903, a reform that resulted in a large increase in votes for the Social Democratic Party.[37] Change was not instantaneous in the United Kingdom, the United States, Germany, or any other country that has become a consolidated democracy. It is challenging, especially empirically as opposed to theoretically, to identify the boundaries among open access or inclusive polities; countries in the middle, or intermediate polities; and limited access or extractive orders.

External threats, internal pressures, learning, and luck have all played different roles for the few polities that have reached the OECD world of wealthy full democracies. There has been no single path. The British merchant class adopted the rules of the eighteenth-century military budget for the nineteenth-century civilian budget. Germany became a fully democratic polity only after Nazism and a devastating defeat in the Second World War. Japan became a consolidated democracy only after a wartime defeat and pressure from the United States. External threat, one of the central arguments of institutional capacity approaches, and a larger middle class, one of the basic arguments of modernization theory, help to explain why some polities have reached the Madisonian sweet spot, but they do not guarantee that it will be reached.

In the contemporary world, the threat of external invasion has virtually disappeared. International legal sovereignty has become an effective shield, defended by political leaders in weak states that are anxious to keep their prerogatives and by political leaders in strong states that do not want the obligation of intervening in weak states. One of the major motivations for state strengthening in the past, external invasion and the disappearance of the state, has vanished.

There is no structural data that can predict whether or not a country moves from closed to open access. Per capita income provides only a starting point.[38] If the income break is set at $12,750 per capita then the contrast between countries scoring 10 (the highest democracy score given by Polity IV) and all others is stark. For the countries with incomes greater than $12,750 in 2015, 72 percent received a score of 10. For countries in the income range of $5,000–$12,749, only 6 percent received a score of 10; for countries with incomes below $2,500, none received a score of 10.[39] This data is completely consistent with modernization theory; democracy is correlated with income level. It does not, however, solve the causality problem: Are richer countries democratic or are both high income levels and democracy a function of inclusive or open access institutions?

If per capita income and institutional development (as indicated by Polity IV scores) are used as a guide, there are a small number of countries in the middle, countries that might make the jump to open access orders. Of countries with per capita incomes of $20,000 or above, 81 percent received the highest score of 10 from Polity IV. These countries have reached the Madisonian sweet spot. No countries with per capita incomes below $2,500 received a score of 10. There are some transitioning countries, some countries between open and closed access orders, that are likely to fall within a per capita income level around $12,000 plus or minus $5,000. There were thirty-eight countries with per capita incomes between $7,000 and $17,000 in 2015, according to the World Bank.[40] Of these thirty-eight, twenty-eight had a large enough population to receive a score from Polity IV in 2015. Of the twenty-eight countries in the per capita income range between $7,000 and $17,000 with Polity scores, five were heavily dependent on oil exports

(Gabon, Russia, Kazakhstan, Equatorial Guinea, and Oman). None of these five countries had a Polity IV score higher than 4. Of the twenty-three other countries, eight had Polity IV scores of 10, suggesting that there are fifteen countries that could obviously be placed in the intermediate category. This group of fifteen includes the Dominican Republic, the Czech Republic, Brazil, Romania, Mexico, Malaysia, Croatia, Argentina, and Lithuania. These are countries that might make the jump to consolidated democracy, although rational choice institutionalism suggests that there is no guarantee that this will happen.[41]

These fifteen countries might, or might not, transition to open access, fully democratic orders. And there might be some countries with lower per capita incomes in which the elite, for a variety of reasons, including personal beliefs, might make the jump to an open access order. Nevertheless, the number of countries that are intermediate between open and closed access, countries where the preferences of elites are divided, is relatively small, about seventeen countries, based on per capita incomes and polity scores.[42]

Regardless of which set of quantitative indicators is used, there is a clear set of countries that are rich, stable, and democratic and an even larger set that are poor, afflicted by violence, and autocratic. Simple measures of per capita income or per capita income combined with some measure of regime stability also suggest that there is a relatively small set of countries someplace in the middle. Polities that fall between inclusive and extractive orders are those in which some members of the elite, political or economic, might have an interest in preserving rent-seeking limited-access opportunities, while others would benefit from a more inclusive polity or economy.

This was the case in Britain in the eighteenth and nineteenth centuries. The elite, including the Crown, had an interest in defending the country from powerful states in continental Europe, but this could be done most effectively if the Crown accepted some limitations on its own freedom of action. All of the key actors were following their own self-interest. Britain was, then, a mixed polity in the eighteenth century, not because anyone was committed in principle to an open access inclusive order but because key actors—the Crown, some members of Parliament, and merchants—benefited from an open access order in some spheres. In the nineteenth century, commercial actors saw the advantages of extending a more constrained but effective state to civilian activities. In the British case, the movement toward a more open access order was the result of a concatenation of events that could not have been predicted a priori.

In basically extractive or despotic orders there might be insulated bureaucracies staffed by technocratic individuals with strong ties to open access transnational or international organizations. These individuals might have advanced degrees from Western universities, work experience in international financial institutions, or memberships in transnational organizations. Autocratic rulers might need them as interlocutors with donor agencies or to manage essential state functions, like the central bank.[43] These individuals might be more willing to use their voice in favor of reforms because the consequences of failure would be limited (they could always move back to Potomac, Maryland, home to some of the officials based in Washington's international financial institutions) and they would be less bound by traditional loyalties. Their bargaining power would be greater because exiting would be an option for them.[44]

One example: Ngozi Okonjo-Iweala was appointed the finance minister of Nigeria in 2011 by President Goodluck Jonathan, a politician who has been accused of stealing billions. The Nigerian government has been afflicted by rent-seeking, military coups, and high levels of corruption. Most of those holding office can secure much more wealth and power inside the government than outside. But there are exceptions, like Okonjo-Iweala. She had served as finance minister and foreign minister in a previous Nigerian administration. Prior to her 2011 appointment she had been a managing

director at the World Bank. She served as the Nigerian finance minister until 2015. After leaving the Nigerian government she became
the chair of the board of the global Vaccine Alliance, and she has
been listed by *Forbes* and *Time* magazines as among the most
influential or powerful people in the world. Okonjo-Iweala earned
an AB degree from Harvard and then a PhD from MIT. Her four
children also have undergraduate degrees from Harvard. One of
her daughters, who has a degree from Harvard Medical School,
became an internist in Durham, North Carolina.[45]

No social science theory does a very good job of explaining
exceptional political leaders, individuals who, even in an environment where rent-seeking offers the most obvious path to personal
wealth and power, support policies that increase the provision of
collective goods for the population as a whole. These are angels.
Social science, at least American social science, is good at explaining behaviors and outcomes that are motivated by power and economic self-interest and not very good at explaining outcomes that
are driven by ideas, norms, religious beliefs, or identities. Individuals, including individuals in positions of power and authority,
might defy expectations for reasons that are not obvious.

A final factor that may explain how polities might become rich
consolidated democracies is consistent with rational choice institutionalism but is not a part of the core theory. It is the role that
external actors might play in fostering the creation of specific institutional arrangements that are potentially consistent with open
access orders.[46] External actors can realize their utopian vision
only in intermediate polities, but identifying local allies, those with
an interest in an open access order, is a daunting task. In despotic
orders the best that external actors can hope for is good enough
governance that falls short of their utopian vision but is not dystopian either. Something can be done but it is not ideal.

Even if, however, there are some open access elements of a polity, or some individuals in the political or economic elite that for
either idiosyncratic or self-interested reasons are more interested

in an open access, inclusive order, this does not necessarily mean that there is any teleological movement toward such an order. Full democracy and a genuinely open economy might or might not evolve. Islands of excellence might wither away, might be flooded over by widespread corruption, might be sustained in isolation, or might diffuse and be models that influence the evolution of the polity more generally.

In polities where the position of elites would clearly be threatened by more open access institutions, the leverage that could be exercised by external actors will be limited. In despotisms, good enough governance is the best that can be hoped for. The utopian vision of consolidated democracy cannot be achieved, but good enough governance is better than the dystopian view of doing nothing. Elites in despotic polities will frustrate efforts by external actors to put in place more open access institutions, because wider access would threaten the tenure of extant leaders.

Political elites act primarily to serve their own interests. For most of human society in most places in the world, elites could better protect themselves and stay in power by supporting despotic institutions. These institutions could provide benefits directly or indirectly to key actors, especially violence-wielding agents, whom political elites had to cultivate to stay in power. Under some circumstances, political elites in limited access or extractive orders may implement policies that improve the circumstances of others in the society as well. Only, however, under exceptional circumstances will they tolerate or be forced to accept changes that would undermine the social and economic basis of their own power. They may accept islands of excellence if they believe that such islands can be isolated. The fundamental conclusion of rational choice institutionalism is that in most of the world's polities, attempts to create an open access order, in which there is full democracy and an open market, are fruitless.

CHAPTER 5

Good Enough Governance

ASSUME THAT LEADERS IN TARGET STATES ARE SELF-interested, not too heroic an assumption. Assuming that external actors are not going to take complete control of some target state, that they are not going to incorporate conquered territory into their homeland or engage in genocide or the wholesale slaughter of the local elite, a necessary implication of the assumption of self-interest and limited legibility for external actors is that foreign actors can be successful only if their incentives are aligned with those of key national actors.[1] At a minimum, state-building efforts by external actors cannot make it more likely that political leaders in target states will lose power in the short or medium term.

If leaders are self-interested, then utopian aspirations held by external actors will fail, except in those few polities where national elites will see it as being in their interest to support consolidated democracy. It does not, however, follow that the dystopian view that nothing can be done will apply in most polities. Rather, external actors can support measures that are compatible with their interests and those of national elites; they can support good enough governance.

Peace builders, those who occupy, in Séverine Autesserre's term, "peaceland," are not likely to be able to understand local environments. Their ability to secure an accurate picture of the local environment is impeded by the inevitable biases in how they gather information, by their inevitable need to maintain a distance between themselves and local actors, and by their valuation of technical expertise over local knowledge.[2]

National elites can also manipulate the behavior of NGOs, who are often the implementers of policies that are designed, for instance, to promote political as well as economic and social change. To survive, NGOs need access. To secure access, NGOs have an incentive to avoid programs that directly threaten autocratic rulers. Sarah Bush writes: "In order to survive and thrive, NGOs seek out tamer types of aid."[3] She goes on to note that "incumbents want to stay in power and can and do block access to democracy-assistance organizations that threaten them."[4] Rather than confront autocratic regimes, democracy-assistance NGOs focus on issues like women's participation, local governments, and some types of election monitoring, which can show measurable results but may not threaten despotic regimes.[5]

Interest alignment obviously depends first on the objectives of the intervening state. A basic distinction is between actions designed to enhance the security of the intervening state by, for instance, keeping a friendly ruler in power, and policies whose goal is to alter institutional structures in the target state.[6] Interest alignment also depends on the mechanisms available to rulers in target states for staying in power. The more rulers depend on rent-seeking, the less receptive they will be to institutional changes that open the political and economic systems. If a leader can stay in power only by robbing the public till to secure money to pay key supporters, he or she will not be interested in anticorruption campaigns, at least not anticorruption campaigns that actually work.

If interest alignment is the necessary condition for success, then, in any polity where political leaders stay in power through rent-seeking, promoting consolidated democracy is a fool's errand. National leaders in such polities will not accept political changes that could undermine their own base of support. The alternative to staying in power in such polities is exile, death, or oblivion. In the one hundred plus countries that can confidently be classified as despotic regimes, the opportunities for external state-builders will be limited to good enough governance.

The 2002 *National Security Strategy of the United States of America* offered a coherent grand strategy for addressing the problem of global terror—specifically that terror was a product of political repression in some parts of the Islamic world (especially the Middle East), which had to be addressed by promoting democracy. This approach was doomed to fail. In 2002, not a single country in the Arab world was classified as being in the Polity IV democracy range of 6–10. The highest-scoring Arab country in that year was Jordan, with a score of –2.[7] By mid-2015, despite the Arab Spring, there was still only one Arab country in Polity IV's democracy range, Tunisia, with a score of 7,[8] but Tunisia became a major source of foreign fighters for ISIS.

Attempts at building institutional capacity, understood as creating Weberian rational-legal bureaucracies through the provision of technical assistance or material resources, will fail. Rulers will be intent on protecting their rent-seeking opportunities, exactly the kind of opportunities that rational-legal bureaucracies are designed to eliminate. In despotic polities the opportunities for external actors are limited.

A great challenge for leaders in advanced democratic countries is to constrain their ambitions, to recognize that their utopian vision cannot be realized. Democracy and openness are goals that are easily understood by publics in the West. It is tempting to regard every state as a potential Denmark or at least to put every state on the path to Denmark.

Only a relatively small number of states, intermediate polities in which elites are torn between open and closed access orders, should be targets for the full array of democracy-promoting activities. In despotic polities, most of the states in the world, the best that can be achieved is good enough governance, not Denmark or even a path to Denmark. Elites in advanced industrialized democracies should aim for good enough governance.

There are three policy arenas in which the interests of external and national political leaders might be aligned, even in polities governed by despotic elites with a narrow base of support: better security; better provision of some services, most notably health; and some economic growth. There is in addition a fourth policy area, respect for some human rights, where the interests of external and internal actors might be aligned. What external actors cannot achieve is what Rawls called societies of reasonable liberal peoples, societies in which citizens believe in reciprocity, tolerance, and fairness, in which commitments are honored, and in which human rights are respected, even if full democracy is not present.

The fundamental challenge for external state-builders is that their success is hostage to the preferences of national elites. Successful solutions will be nonangelic; the best is the enemy of the possible. Arrangements must have the support of violence-wielding elites who might act as veto groups. Governance structures must be inclusive enough, but not necessarily fully inclusive.[9] It may be necessary, as was the case in Iraq in the 1990s, to accept confederal or federal solutions, because the level of distrust of the central government is so high that certain groups or geographic areas will accept only arrangements that allow them to protect members of their own community. In Iraq, for example, Saddam Hussein imposed collective punishment on the Kurds because the regime did not have enough resources by the late 1980s to make the Kurdish population intelligible. Collective punishment, however, increased sectarian identities.[10]

In a closed access order the ability of rulers to seize wealth, take lives or freedom, or arbitrarily alter property rights precludes sustained economic growth, although there may be growth spurts.[11] Security might be improved, but political elites will insist on the ability to use the military and police to keep themselves in power.

Services might be enhanced, but only if such service provision does not constrain the ability of political elites to pay off their supporters (such payoffs often take the form of government jobs, sometimes ghost jobs). Health, which is often heavily dependent on external actors, offers the most compelling example of a service that might be improved, because health services usually enhance rather than weaken the position of rent-seeking elites.

In despotic polities, political leaders will limit their ability to arbitrarily punish individuals only if these individuals could threaten them. The development of religious toleration in Europe provides one important example of a situation in which autocratic rulers accepted limitations on their arbitrary power. The English Civil War, the French Wars of Religion, and the Thirty Years' War all threatened the aristocratic/autocratic closed access orders of Europe in the sixteenth and seventeenth centuries. Autocratic rulers, however, could not manage conflicts between Protestants and Catholics. In Britain and Ireland hundreds of thousands of people died from war-related causes; Charles I was beheaded; and Oliver and then Richard Cromwell became the Lord Protectors of England, Scotland, and Ireland in the 1650s, only to be replaced by the Stuart Kings, Charles II and then James II. James II was deposed in 1688 and replaced by the Protestants William and Mary. In France, the religious wars of the sixteenth century, which directly or indirectly killed millions, led Henry IV to issue the Edict of Nantes in 1598, which provided for religious toleration of French Protestants, the Huguenots, but not for religious equality or full religious freedom. The Edict of Nantes was revoked by Louis XIV in 1685, and almost all Protestants fled from France. While Henry IV had in some sense provided an island of excellence, at least an island of tolerance for French Protestants, Louis XIV saw it as being in his interest to end religious toleration in France, an act that allowed him to further consolidate his power. The center of Europe, the Holy Roman Empire, was torn by conflict in the Thirty Years' War. Both power politics and religious differences exacerbated the carnage. Millions died. The Peace of Westphalia, signed in 1648, enshrined religious toleration, not religious freedom, in parts of the Holy Roman Empire.

No European ruler in the sixteenth and seventeenth centuries believed in religious freedom or even religious toleration. The conflicts engendered, however, by religious beliefs were so volatile that they threatened the political order itself. While religious toleration was suppressed in some countries, notably France after 1685, it was accepted in others. However, one of the products of the French Revolution, a century later, was *laïcité*, a militant rejection of religion in politics. Nevertheless, when Louis XIV reversed the Edict of Nantes, he did so because it was in his short- and medium-term interests. Forcing the Huguenots, with their capital and technical skill, to leave France was not in that country's long-term interests, but the long term is always opaque.

Europe, at least parts of Europe, became somewhat more tolerant only because autocratic rulers could not manage conflicts between Protestants and Catholics. Repression failed; toleration could prevent civil strife. Toleration did not mean religious freedom or religious equality but it did mean in most cases that individuals could practice their religion in private, in homes, or outside of city walls.[12]

Good enough governance is a more realistic objective in closed access polities. Good enough governance, especially improving the ability of governments to control their own territory, enhances the security of the OECD world. With more security, extractive polities can limit transnational terrorism and better monitor disease outbreaks that could become global pandemics.

Autocratic rulers might also accept improved services, especially in the area of health, because this makes their own tenure in office more secure. They might be willing to see the size of the economic pie increase, provided that economic activity does not threaten their own rule. And they might accept some basic human rights if they fear that trampling on these rights would create a more threatening public, which is why religious toleration was accepted in parts of Europe.

Key Components of Good Enough Governance

In despotisms, efforts by external actors to introduce reforms that would confidently put a country on the path to consolidated democracy will be rejected. Attempts to create Weberian rational-legal bureaucracies will fail. Corruption cannot be eliminated. External state-builders must be satisfied with, at best, good enough governance.

Merilee Grindle, a faculty member at the Kennedy School at Harvard, coined the term *good enough governance* in 2004.[13] She argued that the good-governance agenda adopted by many of the major aid agencies, such as the World Bank, Department for Internal Development (DFID), United States Agency for International Development (USAID), United Nations Development Program (UNDP), and International Monetary Fund (IMF), was overly ambitious and failed to take into consideration the institutional context and needs of specific states. The number of items included in the good-governance agenda, she pointed out, had grown willy-nilly.

This problem is clearly manifest in the Sustainable Development Goals (SDGs) adopted by the UN in 2016, which were the successors to the Millennium Development Goals (MDGs), adopted by the UN in 2001. There were eight MDGs. There are seventeen SDGs. Fully 169 specific targets are associated with these seventeen overall goals. The SDGs are extraordinarily expansive and include the elimination of poverty and hunger, decent work conditions, affordable and clean energy, and responsible consumption.[14]

The utopian aspirations that have motivated some of the state-building efforts engaged in by the United States, and more recently by the European Union and some of its individual member states, are profoundly misguided in despotic polities where the political elite's ability to remain in power depends on resisting rather than facilitating such external initiatives. Truly free and fair elections can remove elites from power; rent-seeking political elites will subvert such projects. Security forces constrained by the rule of law cannot act arbitrarily; despotic political elites will resist the creation of such forces.[15] Weberian bureaucracies limit corruption; political elites, who must pay off their followers to stay in power, will prevent the establishment of such agencies.

Recognizing the limited opportunities for external state-building in extractive or closed access polities need not lead to inaction; there is an alternative to the dystopian view that nothing can be done. External actors must identify realistically achievable goals; more specifically, they must identify projects that will enhance, or at least not threaten, what members of the national elite believe to be their core interest, that is, their ability to stay in power. While despotic elites may sometimes misperceive the consequences of institutional reform, thinking that reforms will not be consequential, despotic elites in general are much more likely to understand the consequences of changes in their domestic environment than are external actors. External actors should assume that national elites know what they are doing. There are at least three areas, possibly four, where the interests of external actors interested in promoting development and state-building, broadly understood, could be complementary with those of rent-seeking elites in target countries: security, the provision of some public services, economic change that does not threaten the rent-seeking opportunities of indigenous elites, and respect for some human rights.

Security

The first goal of good enough governance must be to provide some level of security. Without a minimum level of security, economic growth and the provision of many services will be impossible.

Effective security is also necessary for policing transnational terrorist groups.

Security is an aspect of governance in which the interests of internal and external elites may be aligned, albeit for different reasons, provided that external elites recognize that security forces will be directed by local or national elites and will not necessarily be constrained by the rule of law. External actors can train local police, armed forces, and militias to fight more effectively; they can provide them with better weapons; they cannot, however, in a despotic polity, train them to operate as Weberian entities dedicated to the well-being of the society as a whole. National elites will support programs that strengthen the capacity of local forces, provided that they are confident that these forces will serve their interests. In closed access polities, lectures to police about the rule of law, or to military officers about the importance of control by civilian officials accountable to the population as a whole, will be rejected or be regarded as quaint.

In despotic polities, external actors will have to make painful choices about how to improve security. Simply dumping large amounts of money into the security sector in a rent-seeking state and engaging in technical training designed to inform the military and police about logistics, tactics, and the law of armed conflict may be less than useless. In a posting on Lawfare,[16] Richard Sokolsky and Gordon Adams point out that American military assistance in many countries, but not in all, has been ineffectual at best and useless at worst. Between 2011 and 2015, Afghanistan, Israel, Pakistan, Egypt, and Iraq were the five-highest recipients of military and police aid from the United States.[17] Although American forces, allied with Afghan groups, were able to displace the Taliban government within three months of 9/11, with losses of only twelve American and allied troops and one CIA employee,[18] Afghanistan, the largest recipient of American assistance, has been floundering for years. ISIS captured large amounts of military equipment when the Iraqi army disintegrated and the Iraqi army only slowly recovered to reconquer major cities such as Mosul. Pakistan has continued to play a two-faced game, supporting terrorists and the United States at the same time.[19] President al-Sisi in Egypt is governing in ways that are much closer to American interests than were the policies of his predecessor, Mohammed Morsi. Al-Sisi, however, is not ruling as a democrat and it is not clear that he will find the right formula for "good enough" inclusion.

The basic problem in despotic states, failed or not, is that such governance is inconsistent with the core interests of political elites and yet without the support of these elites no assistance program can be successful.[20] Among the countries that received the highest security assistance from the United States, only Israel approaches being an open access order. Somalia is a failed state. Pakistan, Egypt, and Iraq are rent-seeking polities in which accountable, efficient, and uncorrupt governance contradicts the fundamental political interests of elites. Under President Karzai, Afghanistan suffered from gross corruption; even Ashraf Ghani, who was elected president in 2014 and whose background is far more cosmopolitan than Karzai's, was not able to free himself from a society dominated by warlords.

Without national elites committed to a more open access, inclusive political order, external actors must accept that they confront trade-offs. They cannot secure better and more just governance and, at the same time, more security. A more effective security force will be used in arbitrary ways. External actors have to craft their security assistance to objectives that are attainable. In despotic orders the best possible outcome is an authority structure that can maintain security over all of the territory within a state's boundaries even if the security forces are not constrained by the rule of law. Pure utopianism is a pipe dream; but a completely dystopian view that nothing at all can be done should be avoided.

This first-best realistic outcome of effective but unconstrained security forces may not, however, be possible. Decentralization and warlordism are second-best alternatives. If central authority structures have disintegrated and cannot be reconstructed, leaders that can exercise control over some parts of a country's territory but not others may be the best available option. Subnational leaders will have varying levels of commitment to better governance within the territories that they control. The leadership in the Kurdish area of Iraq has been more committed to the collective-goods provision than most of the warlords of Afghanistan, but the Barzani and Talibani families control political power and most economic activities.[21] Even if subnational leaders are committed to good governance within their own area of control, they will be indifferent to the provision of public goods in other parts of the country. When central authority structures have broken down, individuals and groups are more likely to fall back on ascriptive identity.[22]

Warlords, however, will find it difficult to agree on a balance of power that limits conflict among themselves. They have no mechanism that allows them to make credible commitments to one another. They may be unsure of the strength of their opponent or even of themselves. Civil war may be the only way to reveal relative power.

External actors might be able to limit conflict among warlords, but this is a daunting task. Success is most likely if external actors are in agreement with one another and if warlords depend on these outsiders for economic and military resources. Maintaining peace among warlords also requires an intimate understanding of local conditions, a level of understanding that has eluded most external state-builders.

If central authorities are too weak and the balance of power among warlords too uncertain, the only remaining option to provide a modicum of security would be external balancing. External actors might be able to engage in selective raiding that could provide some order. This is the least-good option, but it might be the only one available.

Despite limited resources and information, security is a good that external actors can help provide even in badly governed polities, or at least in some parts of badly governed polities.[23]

Developments in Egypt demonstrate the difficult trade-offs for external actors. Hosni Mubarak, who had been president of Egypt for three decades, resigned in the face of popular pressure generated by the Arab Spring in February 2011. External actors, American officials not least among them, were enthusiastic about the prospects for democracy. Democracy advocates in Tahrir Square, such as an Egyptian employee of Google, got lots of coverage in the American press. (That individual, Wael Ghonim, now lives in the United States.) In June of 2012 Mubarak was sentenced to life in prison, but he was later freed. In June of 2012 Mohammed Morsi, who represented the Muslim Brotherhood and was an American-educated engineer, was elected in Egypt's first free and fair presidential election. A year later Morsi was overthrown by the military. In June of 2014 Abdel Fattah al-Sisi, the commander of the Egyptian military, was elected president. Less than half of Egypt's eligible voters cast their ballots, but of those that did, more than 95 percent supported al-Sisi. In 2015 Mohammed Morsi was sentenced to death, but this sentence was overturned the following year and Egypt's Court of Cassation ordered a new trial.[24] Morsi died in court in 2019.

The United States froze foreign aid after the Egyptian military coup but refused to call the coup a coup because US law would have required that all aid be terminated. Saudi Arabia became Egypt's main foreign backer. In 2015 the United States resumed military shipments and committed to continuing foreign aid, a decision justified by American national security.[25] In September of 2018 the State Department authorized the release of more than $1 billion in military assistance to Egypt.[26] Even with foreign assistance, al-Sisi had not provided security for the entire country. In late 2017 insurgents killed more than three hundred Egyptians at a mosque in the Sinai, an area where ISIS had launched many attacks. There have been several attacks on Copts in different parts of the country.

The United States and other external actors have resources—economic, military, and diplomatic—that can enhance the ability of a ruler to provide security. It is a much more daunting task to move a country along the path to full democracy, including free and fair elections (as opposed to the limited elections that were held in Egypt), legal-rational bureaucracies, a robust civil society, civilian control of the military, and a free press; the success rate for the United States and other countries has been much lower than when they aimed for security alone.

Better security is not a guarantee of stability in the long run but there may be no better short- or medium-term options. Better security is the necessary condition for the better provision of other services and for economic growth. Security is a necessary but not a sufficient condition for an open access order. A more effective security force may simply cement in place a despotic regime.

Better Service Provision

Even in despotic polities, external actors can contribute to the improvement of some service provision. The key constraint is that such activities, if they are to be successful, cannot compromise the ability of political elites to secure rents, especially rents that they need to pay off those that keep them in power.

Health is the most obvious example of a service whose provision has dramatically improved the condition of billions of people around the world, even those living in closed access, impoverished polities. Although many countries have remained poor, life expectancy has risen in almost all countries over the last thirty or more years, in some cases dramatically. The increase in life expectancy for poorer countries over the last several decades mirrors a dramatic increase in life expectancy in richer countries that began around 1850 largely as a result of improvements in sanitation and greater knowledge, especially about the germ theory of disease, which led to immunization programs that greatly reduced childhood mortality from communicable diseases.[27] In Afghanistan, life expectancy for females increased from thirty-three years in 1960 to sixty-five in 2015; in Angola, from thirty-five to sixty-four; in Bolivia, from forty-three to seventy-one; and in Uganda, from forty-six to sixty-two.[28]

International actors have contributed to these gains, although many are the result of national initiatives. Smallpox has been eliminated as a result of a campaign organized by the World Health Organization. The last case of smallpox occurred in Somalia in 1977. In the fall of 2018 more than fourteen million people worldwide were receiving antiretroviral treatment from PEPFAR, a US government program initiated by the Bush administration.[29] Reported polio cases decreased from 350,000 in 1988 to 27 in 2017.[30] Many health interventions improve the lives of people and do not threaten the rent-seeking opportunities of political elites. Political elites may even gain some support from such health programs, whose success may be attributed to government policy.

However, even immunization programs can encounter resistance from local elites whose authority might be threatened by the acceptance of modern medical practices. Religious activists and others have opposed polio immunization programs in Pakistan and northern Nigeria. Salafists have accused workers of sterilizing Muslim women. Workers carrying out such programs have been killed.

Health-related programs have, however, generally been successful and this success has led to a significant increase in funding. Since 1990, annual disbursements for health-related activities have increased substantially. In 1990 developed countries contributed $9.6 billion for health; in 2014 the figure was $35.9 billion. Annual disbursements for health increased at 5.4 percent annually from 1990 to 2000, at 11.3 percent from 2000 to 2010, and at 1.4 percent from 2010 to 2014.[31] The overall level of official aid commitments in constant dollars increased by 75 percent from 2005 to 2016.[32]

Health aid has come from a wide variety of sources, including bilateral official aid, where the United States has been the biggest donor; multilateral aid, primarily from UN agencies; private entities, especially the Gates Foundation; and public-private partnerships such as GAVI. US agencies accounted for 22 percent of total giving from 1990 to 2014, UN agencies for 17 percent, private foundations for 16 percent, and public-private partnerships for 12 percent.[33] Health aid has been disbursed for a wide variety of purposes, including HIV/AIDS, communicable diseases, maternal health, and child health.

Not surprisingly, noncommunicable diseases have received relatively little attention. Noncommunicable diseases, unlike communicable diseases, are contained geographically. More important, however, may be the fact that improving outcomes in noncommunicable diseases requires a more developed indigenous health-care system. Support for strengthening health-care systems in general has also been relatively small, amounting to only 6.1 percent of total health assistance in 2014.[34] This may reflect the fact that it is easier, especially in the United States, to secure congressional authorizations for treating specific health issues such as HIV/AIDS and child health, but it also reflects the fact that interventions to accomplish specific objectives may be easier than improving the health infrastructure in general, especially in rent-seeking states.

Analysts that have addressed the question of health-system governance have, in general, implicitly relied on institutional capacity approaches in stipulating the characteristics that such governance structures must possess. In its annual report in 2000, *Health Systems: Improving Performance*, the World Health Organization suggested that good health governance must incorporate the concept of stewardship. State institutions ought to be concerned with the welfare of the population as a whole. Health-care systems should set and enforce basic rules and provide strategic direction. "The careful and responsible management of the well-being of the population—stewardship—is the very essence of good government," the organization's director general Gro Harlem Brundtland argued in her introduction to the 2000 report.[35]

In 2002 the Pan American Health Organization enumerated

eleven essential public health functions (EPHF), including monitoring, evaluation, research, health promotion, and public health
planning.[36] Like the World Health Organization's notion of stewardship, fulfilling the essential public health functions stipulated
by the Pan American Health Organization would be a demanding
task, one that would assume that a state had developed a rational-
legal bureaucratic structure that was responsive to the overall needs
of the population.

A decade later a group of professionals associated with the
World Health Organization and the Bloomberg School of Public
Health at Johns Hopkins University suggested ten principles for
assessing the governance of public health systems. These ten principles are "strategic vision, participation and consensus orientation,
rule of law, transparency, responsiveness, equity and inclusiveness,
effectiveness and efficiency, accountability, intelligence and information, and ethics."[37] Building on the earlier work of the World
Health Organization and the Pan American Health Organization,
these principles reflect a view of development that focuses on the
importance of institutional capacity.

From a rational choice institutional perspective, however, such
an approach is misleading. It assumes that the interests of political
elites will be served by delivering adequate or excellent health care
to all members of their society. In extractive or closed access orders,
however, political elites have no such interests. Like all political
elites they are focused on staying in power, and remaining in power
principally depends on keeping the support of a small selectorate,
not of the population as a whole. Better health care might serve
the interests of rent-seeking political elites. They may be indifferent to or even supportive of services provided by other actors,
including international aid agencies and nongovernmental organizations. They have no interest, however, in implementing the kinds
of improvements in health-care governance that might optimize the
delivery of health care to their own publics—in fact are unable to
implement them. Rent-seeking political elites will resist such efforts

because they are inconsistent with maintaining the elites' ability to arbitrarily provide payoffs and services to their own key supporters. External actors focusing on improving health-care governance in general will be discouraged. External actors focusing instead on providing targeted health interventions in specific areas may be supported, or at least not frustrated. Health care has improved in many places around the world not because national health-care systems have become centers of excellence but because external or private actors have effectively intervened in specific sectors, and because such interventions were supported by despotic elites.[38]

Even in rent-seeking environments, external actors might be able to improve health-care performance in specific issue areas. The International Centre for Diarrhoeal Disease Research, located in Dhaka, Bangladesh, is internationally recognized for the quality of its research. The center is supported by more than fifty donors, both public and private, including the government of Bangladesh. It is staffed by professionals from Bangladesh and from many other countries. The center is an island of excellence, but corruption is rife in Bangladesh. Transparency International's corruption rankings placed Bangladesh at the 146th position out of 183 countries in 2017.[39] The International Diarrhoeal Centre has been able to insulate itself from the larger environment in part by providing medical services to the general population. These services have created a base of popular support for the center, and this popular support has in turn made it possible for the center to operate according to professional standards that would be difficult to find in other issue areas in Bangladesh.[40] But the center has remained an island of excellence. Its practices have not spread to other arenas.

In sum, even in despotic polities in which rent-seeking is rife, service improvement may be possible in some issue areas. The national elite must perceive itself to be no worse off, and possibly better off, if service provision improves. Health is one issue area where such improvements have taken place. In many countries, health outcomes, including longer life expectancies, have improved dramatically. Non-state actors, internal and external, can significantly reduce deaths by disease, often with relatively simple interventions. Immunization against communicable diseases offers the most straightforward example. In health at least, a dystopian view in which nothing can be done is not warranted.

Economic Growth

Even where political elites use rent-seeking to pay off key supporters and repress independent organizations, external actors might be able to support some economic growth policies. The empirical support for the proposition that foreign assistance can increase economic growth is weak to nonexistent. Some studies have found no relationship between foreign assistance and growth, others a negative relationship, others a small positive one. In 2009 one meta-analysis of the aid literature, based on ninety-seven studies published through 2004, concluded that "after 40 years of development aid, the preponderance of the evidence indicates that aid has not been effective."[41]

There are a number of reasons to suspect that aid would not lead to higher economic growth. By providing foreign assistance, external donors disrupt the relationship between political elites and their citizens; if rulers get resources from foreign actors, they will have less incentive to be responsive to their own populations.[42] Foreign assistance may increase the level of spoils in a country and thereby promote rather than repress violence. Empirically, for instance, American food aid has been associated with higher levels of civil conflict.[43] Foreign assistance may push up exchange rates and undermine the competitiveness of traded goods from poorer countries.[44] Often, external donors will be most interested in the external policy compliance of recipient countries' leaders and not their domestic policies.[45] Even when donors are interested in promoting economic growth, they may support initiatives that are suboptimal or even counterproductive because they lack intimate knowledge of the local environment.[46]

Despite skepticism about aid, some forms of assistance could contribute to economic growth. Multilateral aid may work better than bilateral aid. Aid from countries that have no foreign policy agenda may be better than aid from countries that want recipients to follow specific policies. Aid may also be more effective in target states where there is a better policy environment. Political rulers that are highly dependent on foreign assistance might conclude that they are better off accepting some institutional and policy reforms that promote growth rather than risk losing foreign assistance.[47]

However, even the more or less intuitive proposition that aid is more effective in countries with better policy environments has been challenged. There is no statistically significant relationship between the effectiveness of aid flows and better institutions and policies.[48] In the words of two economists: "In other words, our regressions suggest that aid has no systematic effect even after controlling for any effect of strategic aid on policies and institutions."[49]

In general, then, aid might promote economic growth under specific conditions, such as foreign donors' being more focused on growth than on strategic objectives. Where foreign assistance was a large part of the national budget, where rents from natural resources were limited, and where external actors did not have strategic or security interests (allowing donors to make credible threats to withdraw aid), rulers in recipient countries have accepted policies and institutional changes that increased economic growth. Reforms in post-conflict environments may create islands of excellence. Once, however, there is an uptick in economic growth and recipient states become somewhat more self-sufficient, the most likely outcome is that rent-seeking rulers will limit, even if they do not stifle, the impact of these islands of excellence. The fundamental problem is that in despotic polities, economic growth might weaken the position of extant elites. The Ming emperor ordered that the Chinese treasure fleet cease its operations because overseas trade was a threat to his rule.

External actors could change the incentives of political and economic elites in target states by, for instance, adopting policies that would allow actors, even in despotic polities, to more fully participate in the global market by reducing tariffs or guaranteeing foreign investments. Such opportunities might be acceptable to target elites because they could increase rent-seeking opportunities as well as economic payoffs, at least for some. Global market–opening policies could be beneficial even to despotic elites.[50]

Rent-seeking elites might be willing to accept economic growth resulting from outsourcing of governance to transnational or international actors if it provides them with some economic payoffs. Bilateral investment treaties (BITs) offer an example. These treaties provide for dispute settlement by international arbitration panels, whose decisions can be enforced in third-party courts. Participation in a BIT between a wealthy state and a poor one increases international investment.[51] Higher levels of investment could increase economic growth. Higher levels of investment might also provide opportunities for rent-seeking elites. More than 2,500 BITs have been signed, even between states with no capital to invest; such a large number suggests that for elites, at least, this particular form of outsourcing is not threatening.[52]

In closed access, extractive orders, the best that external actors can confidently aim for is benevolent absolutism. Decision making will be monopolized by the national elite, but there might be some security, some economic growth, and some protection of basic human rights, if only because national elites fear that violating these rights will weaken rather than strengthen their hold on office.[53] Ruling elites in such polities will not, however, accept democracy, defend all human rights, be accountable to a broad cross section of the public, or promote rational-legal bureaucracies. Such measures would directly threaten their ability to stay in power.

Security, some service provision, and job growth are achievable expectations—good enough governance—for external actors seeking to implement changes in poorly governed or malevolent states. Under some circumstances some human rights might also be respected. More ambitious efforts, such as putting countries securely on a path to consolidated democracy, are not only doomed to fail but will inevitably result in disappointments and wasted resources, which can undermine longer-term public support in wealthy democratic polities for engagement with poorly governed polities. More ambitious goals may even worsen conditions in target countries by misdirecting resources or attempting to put in place policies that raise the population's expectations but that will inevitably be undermined by national elites who understand that such policies would weaken their ability to stay in power, protect themselves and their supporters, and accumulate wealth.

Policies that resonate with domestic publics in wealthy democracies, such as equal rights for women or the equal treatment of the LGBT community, may contradict indigenous norms in poorly governed countries and provide rent-seeking leaders with opportunities to deflect pressures for reform. One of my friends, who worked for a major NGO in Afghanistan, told me that his organization had turned down a USAID request to bid on a project to construct a large number of schools for girls over a relatively short period of time, because he knew that a girls' school, if placed in an area unacceptable to the relevant population, could exacerbate local conflicts. Some other organization, of course, took the contract.

Programs designed to secure equal rights for women in Afghanistan have been appealing to publics in the United States and Europe. But in a society where decades of conflict have strengthened patriarchal practices, such efforts are doomed to failure. A *New York Times* story in April 2016 reported on the sad fate of women's athletic teams in Afghanistan. The story began with the following sentence—"Women's sports programs in Afghanistan, long a favorite of Western donors, have all but collapsed"—and went on to describe a pattern of gross corruption and even sexual abuse of athletes. In January of 2017 the *Times* reported on an invasive virginity test that continued to be ordered by officials and practiced by hospitals despite being legally banned by the government. In November of 2017 the *Washington Post* reported that the US Department of Defense had suppressed reports that Afghan security forces had sexually abused children.[54]

In sum, ambitious efforts to put extractive closed access polities on a path to consolidated democracy are doomed to failure. The utopian vision cannot be realized. The institutions that characterize consolidated democracy, including the rule of law, protection of property rights, the full panoply of human rights, and rational-legal bureaucracies, are antithetical to the interests of rent-seeking elites.

THE HOPELESSNESS of trying to put countries on the path to consolidated democracy need not lead to despair, or to the conclusion that nothing can be done. The dystopian view that external actors can do nothing is not warranted, either theoretically or practically. Marginal improvements in governance that make the lives of people somewhat more secure and prosperous might better position polities to make the jump to inclusive or at least mixed orders over time. Good enough governance might alter the incentives of elites in ways that would make them more amenable to supporting changes that would embed their polities in a new equilibrium, an intermediate polity and ultimately an inclusive or open access order. No matter what external actors do, there is no guarantee that the incentives of national elites will change enough to make them prefer inclusive rather than extractive orders, or that initial reforms will create societal pressures to apply such reforms to more and more arenas of government activity. In the future, as in the past, historical contingency, random events, unpredictable accidents, and either malevolent leaders like Stalin or Mugabe or benevolent ones like George Washington or Paul Kagame will be critical determinants of the trajectories along which different polities might move. History can be understood *ex post* but not *ex ante*.

In general, the most promising initiative that could be taken by external actors trying to encourage movement toward a world of consolidated democratic states would be to encourage economic growth. Greater prosperity does not guarantee consolidated democracy but it does make it more likely. Growth requires some reasonable level of public order. This level of order would initially have to be provided by rule *by* law, not rule *of* law, and by security forces beholden to despotic political elites. In trying to improve conditions in autocratic regimes, whether failed or not, aspirations for democracy, for rule of law, for efficient and rational bureaucracies, have to be put aside. External actors must focus on more modest objectives where there is some complementarity between their preferences and those of national elites.

CHAPTER 6

Corruption Is Unavoidable

A S A TEENAGER, I TOOK THE A TRAIN FOR MORE THAN AN HOUR each way from my home in upper Manhattan to my public high school in Brooklyn. The station was cold, very cold in the winter. If there was a subway schedule, I had no idea what it was and I don't believe my fellow passengers did, either. Sometimes, if I was late, I was excused because the official at my high school was able to call someone in the subway system. Who that someone might be, I had no idea.

Many decades later, the *New York Times* had a front-page story on why the New York City subway was such a torture for its riders. The *Times* found that the costs for construction on New York City's subways were about four times higher than for equivalent projects. These higher construction costs reduced the amount of funding available for maintenance, which increased delays and stoppages. At least part of the cost was the result of the close relationship between New York politicians and labor unions. The unions have successfully insisted on staffing levels four times higher than in other parts of the world.[1] Workers could be paid as much as $400 per hour. Construction companies, which had paid millions in campaign contributions, could increase their costs with limited oversight. Work rules and salaries were set in negotiations between companies and unions; the government, which paid for the project, did not participate. Consulting firms hired many people who had been employed by the Metropolitan Transportation Authority. The "soft costs" in New York City, preliminary design and engineering, are much higher, as a percentage of the total, than for comparable projects.[2]

The higher construction costs and accompanying maintenance failures and system delays are not the result of any explicit violation of the law. But they do reflect the fact that even in long-standing democracies, corruption, broadly understood to include both legal and illegal actions, is unavoidable. The delays that I experienced on my way to high school many decades ago were not a fluke. They were the result of public decisions that had been influenced by private actors, both unions and corporations.

Corruption in more or less open access orders is not always limited to practices that are formally legal. Many American states have suffered from illegal corruption. Illinois has one of the worst reputations for corruption of all the American states. Four of the last nine governors of Illinois were sent to jail, including Rod Blagojevich, who tried to sell Barack Obama's Senate seat after the 2008 presidential election. Thirty-three Chicago aldermen have been sent to jail since 1973.[3] Illinois, despite its reputation, is hardly unique. In per capita terms, the District of Columbia is far worse.[4] There is plenty of corruption in the United States, a country with free and fair elections, a vigorous civil society, and a free press. In unambiguously closed access orders, corruption is an even greater problem, and the chances of being prosecuted are small.

Oil was discovered in the southeast region of Nigeria in 1956 and the first commercial sales took place in 1958. Oil is not always a curse, but in Nigeria's case it has been.[5] For Nigeria, annual oil revenues have amounted to $200–$300 for each person, a lot of money but not enough to provide the government with the resources that it needs to guarantee security and stability. In contrast, Saudi Arabia gets revenues of about $4,000 per person.[6] Even after a successful democratic election in 2011, northeast Nigeria has been riven by an Islamist insurgency.

Billions of dollars' worth of oil has been extracted on- and off-shore in Nigeria. The failure of oil revenues to provide benefits for Nigeria's citizens has been partially the result of the misallocation of revenues (billions of dollars have been spent, for instance, on the Ajaokuta steel plant, which was nonoperational at the end of 2017). The population of Nigeria as a whole, and almost all of the residents of what is now known as the Rivers state, have seen few benefits from the oil that is extracted from their territory. Some is stolen by small-time operators or gangs tapping into pipelines on land. But there are also major thefts. Some oil is stolen and sold on the world market. It is hard to imagine that this could happen without the complicity of public officials. Tankers are not very hard to find.

In 2004 the Nigerian navy intercepted and took possession of a tanker. The tanker's cargo had been stolen. The ship was escorted to the Lagos harbor. There it sat for several months. Then it disappeared. NATO traced the ship to Venezuela. No one was ever prosecuted. Some Nigerians almost certainly got very rich.[7] There was no lack of capacity or information in this case. NATO ships had been dispatched to the Gulf of Biafra with the approval of the Nigerian government. NATO officials and their Nigerian counterparts knew where the ship was, at least most of the time. No one with appropriate authority, however, in the Nigerian government had any interest in making sure that the stolen oil on the tanker was used for the benefit of the Nigerian people. A 2013 Chatham House report stated that one hundred thousand barrels of oil per day was being stolen in Nigeria, about 5 percent of the country's official production.[8]

Corruption has undermined the ability of the Nigerian government to provide even the most basic level of security, at least in some parts of the country. Since 2009, the northeast of the country has suffered from the depredations of an Islamic radical group, Boko Haram. Boko Haram has destroyed villages, set off suicide bombs in Maiduguri, Zaria, Yola, and other major cities, and captured hundreds of children, among them girls who have been sold off to Boko Haram fighters or worse. In 2014 Boko Haram was identified as the deadliest terror group in the world, killing 6,644 people in that year, although it was supplanted in the following year by ISIS.[9]

Under President Goodluck Jonathan the Nigerian government was completely unable to deal with this threat. The Nigerian army, despite being the biggest in West Africa and having participated in a number of peace-keeping missions, was completely helpless. In 2015 Boko Haram's fortunes began to decline after troops from neighboring states, notably Chad, intervened, a humiliation for Nigeria and the Nigerian military. Under President Muhammadu Buhari, the situation began to improve in 2016. Buhari is from the North; as a northerner he was more concerned with the threat from Boko Haram, which has been limited to Nigeria's mostly Muslim North. But even under Buhari, the Nigerian government has not been able to defeat Boko Haram.

Corruption is an important part of why Nigeria's military has been so ineffectual, although poor training and the South's disdain for the North (President Goodluck Jonathan is a Christian from the South) may have played some role.[10] Officers and officials stole supplies, weapons, and bullets, or the money that was supposed to be used to buy them. Nigeria has become something of a poster child for corruption in Africa. But it is hardly a unique case.

Corruption has dramatically impacted security in Afghanistan and Iraq. Transparency International's 2018 corruption index ranked Iraq 168 out of 180 countries, and Afghanistan 172.[11] In 2010 about $800 million was stolen from the Kabul Bank, equal to about 5 percent of the country's gross output, mostly by President Karzai and Vice-President Muhammed Qasim Fahim and their entourages.

Iraqi security forces collapsed in 2015 in Anbar Province in the face of the Islamic State's assault, in part because the military was so weakened by corruption. Soldiers were told to stay home and to kick back half of their salaries to their officers. One Iraqi analyst estimated that there were twenty-three thousand ghost soldiers, that is, troops that were absent, before the confrontation with ISIS in Ramadi. Iraqi police had to beg for donations from private individuals to secure weapons. Weapons that were shipped by the Baghdad government to Anbar Province in 2012 ended up in the hands of insurgents.[12]

As the New York subways and the state of Illinois illustrate, it is wrong to associate corruption only with poorer countries, or with countries whose political systems have been disordered by foreign occupiers. Understood in the broadest terms as either the use of public office for private benefit, or the use of money (whether deployed legally or illegally) to secure particular legislation or policies for private benefit, corruption is pervasive. It affects every country in the world.[13] Corruption cannot be completely eliminated.[14]

In most cases corruption reduces economic activity and the utility of the society as a whole. The arbitrary power of a state that is for sale discourages initiatives or investments by individuals without ties to the state. In Tunisia under President Ben Ali's reign, individuals and companies that were closely associated with the ruling family were able to avoid more than $1 billion in import duties between 2002 and 2009. This not only deprived the public treasury of revenue but also gave these well-connected firms an advantage over their competitors.[15]

The resource curse is a familiar syndrome. In general, if a state has not already reached the Madisonian sweet spot, oil has increased the likelihood of civil war, worsened prospects for women, and impeded democracy.[16] Oil resources encourage corruption by freeing the political elite from dependence on local taxation and by multiplying the rewards of staying in office.

Equatorial Guinea offers a particularly egregious example of the oil and corruption syndrome. Equatorial Guinea had a per capita income of more than $10,000 in 2014 (although per capita income dropped to $7,050 in 2017), making it, according to the World Bank's classification scheme, a high-income non-OECD country. The poverty rate, however, was 77 percent in 2006, the latest figure available from the World Bank. Immunization rates for measles in 2012 were 35 percent, down from 55 percent in earlier years, and the primary school completion rate was 55 percent. These outcomes are far worse than those for all of sub-Saharan Africa, where the immunization rate was 72 percent and the primary school completion rate 69 percent, and where the per capita income was only 16 percent that of Equatorial Guinea.[17] The UN's Human Development Index ranked Equatorial Guinea at 141 out of 189 countries in 2017, while the country's per capita income would place it in the top quartile of all countries.[18]

Where has all the money gone? In this case, into the hands of President Teodoro Obiang Nguema Mbasogo, his family, and his close associates. Obiang has been president since 1979, when he overthrew and later executed his uncle. He has ruthlessly suppressed any opposition. In a speech at the Open Government Partnership in 2013, the prime minister of the UK, David Cameron, stated that "for decades in Equatorial Guinea, that country has seen its mineral wealth siphoned off by a corrupt elite, all under a veil of secrecy. A few people have got rich, but the majority have stayed gut-wrenchingly poor. A tragic result of broken institutions and a closed, secretive government."[19] The president's son Teodorin, who has owned property in Paris and Malibu as well as expensive sports cars, has been investigated in France and the United States. An American judge in 2014 announced a settlement with Teodorin in which he was forced to forfeit $30 million, including property, a Ferrari, and a life-sized statue of Michael Jackson that had been bought with money looted from the people of Equatorial Guinea. In the fall of 2017 a French court found Teodorin guilty in absentia of money laundering, corruption, and embezzlement and ordered that his home near the Champs-Élysées in Paris, worth more than £100 million, be confiscated, along with eleven luxury cars.[20]

Corruption is an endemic challenge for growth and accountability in closed access and transitioning polities, and it is not related just to natural resource wealth. The law has been used against those who have accused the powerful of malfeasance. In India in the summer of 2015 the Central Bureau of Investigation spent the better part of a day combing through the belongings of Teesta Setalvad. Setalvad was one of the most persistent critics of Narendra Modi, who had become prime minister of India in 2014, accusing him of encouraging ethnic rioting in 2002 when he was the first minister of the state of Gujarat, rioting that led to many deaths, mainly of Muslims. A judge ordered her jailed on the grounds that she was a threat to India's national security. The state of Gujarat accused her of committing fraud by appropriating money that was meant for riot victims. Setalvad's bank accounts were frozen and her passport seized. The Supreme Court of India has come to Setalvad's aid several times but the charges brought by public agencies have blunted her ability to investigate links between the prime minister and the 2002 disturbances.

The most obvious explanation for the interest of central and state officials in Setalvad is that the investigations are an effort to discredit her because of her accusations against the prime minister.[21] In India there is clearly rule by law; rule of law is more problematic. Public officials can use legal rules to serve their own narrow political purposes.

This case in India is hardly the only example of the use of the legal system by political leaders who want to punish their opponents. Mikhail Khodorkovsky spent nearly ten years in jail after being prosecuted for fraud and tax evasion by the Russian government in 2003. Khodorkovsky was a leading critic of Vladimir Putin and one of the richest men in Russia at the time of his arrest and conviction. Anwar Ibrahim, a former deputy prime minister of Malaysia and an important critic of the dominant party, spent six years in jail after a sodomy conviction in 1998 and was sent back to jail again on the same charge in 2015, but was pardoned in May

2018.[22] The American embassy in Kuala Lumpur issued a statement in 2015 reading, "The decision to prosecute Mr. Anwar, and his trial, have raised serious concerns regarding the rule of law and the independence of the courts."[23] The government of Singapore and its leaders have brought defamation suits against a number of international news media outlets, including the *International Herald Tribune* and the *Wall Street Journal*, as well as political opponents.[24]

Brazil has been one of the most successful countries in Latin America. Brazil's military dictatorship ended in 1985, after more than twenty years in power. There have been elections ever since. Freedom House has rated Brazil as "free," its highest category, since 2000; in 2015 Brazil received a score of 8 from Polity IV, placing it in the category of democracies but not full democracies. Brazil's per capita gross national income increased from $3,850 in 2000 to $11,530 in 2014. The poverty rate in 2014 was 7.4 percent; life expectancy, 74 years.[25] These are impressive accomplishments. Brazil could, according to Polity IV and per capita income numbers, be classified as an intermediate country, somewhere in between closed and open access.

In 2015, however, a corruption scandal involving Petrobras, Brazil's largest oil company, which is 51 percent government owned, pushed the country toward recession, tarnished those at the highest political levels, was associated with the impeachment of the president, Dilma Rouseff, and resulted in thousands of workers losing their jobs. A conservative, Jair Bolsonaro, was elected president in 2018.

The scheme basically involved fake contracts and kickbacks for work performed by corporations favored by Petrobras. Most but not all of these companies were Brazilian. Rolls-Royce, a British company, was also named in the investigation. The proceeds of the kickbacks were shared among Petrobras officials and political parties, primarily the ruling Workers' Party. Dilma Rouseff was the chair of the Petrobras board during part of the time when these thefts were ongoing, although she denied any involvement. One investigator stated that $3 billion had been stolen. A lawyer involved in the investigation said, "It was kind of like, in Brazil, we know that corruption is a monster. But we never really see the monster. This was like seeing the monster."[26]

Brazil is no Equatorial Guinea. It is not an exclusively closed access order. The fact that the scheme has come to light is impressive in and of itself. Brazil has some dedicated and honest prosecutors, investigators, and judges. The temptations of corruption, however, are omnipresent. In a country in which there are elements of both closed and open access orders, corruption is more likely to come to light and to be contained but not eliminated. Reaching consolidated democracy is hard, very hard.

Once corruption becomes deeply entrenched, which is most likely in despotic orders, it can become an equilibrium outcome. If many others are corrupt the chances of being caught are less, even if there is someone to do the catching. In a world of pervasive corruption the reputational consequences for any individual's corruption are low. It is difficult to challenge corruption once the practice becomes widespread.[27] The relationship between formal legal frameworks that criminalize corruption and the level of corruption is weak.[28]

Even if some kind of corruption exists in almost all polities, its consequences, resulting from both the kinds and extent of corruption, are dramatically different. The provision of public services in countries that score best in Transparency International's surveys, such as Norway, Finland, New Zealand, and Denmark, is not materially affected by corruption. In countries that score near the bottom of the surveys, including Somalia, South Sudan, Sudan, Afghanistan, and Iraq, corruption is crippling.

Quantified corruption indicators (quantified even if they are based on subjective opinions) do provide a readily available way to assess the level of corruption in a country, but they are misleading in suggesting that the most useful way to understand corruption is to assume that all countries can be arrayed along a continuum. Such a perspective, with its suggestion of the possibilities for linear progress, is much more consistent with theories of development derived from modernization theory, which suggests that it is possible to make incremental progress that will take countries from the bottom, Somalia, to the top, New Zealand.[29]

The empirical support for rule-of-law programs consistent with modernization and institutional capacity approaches is weak. Rule of law became a shibboleth for the international community after 1990. Billions of dollars were spent on rule-of-law programs such as anticorruption commissions, new laws defining corruption, prison reform, police training, new courthouses, and education for judges. Despite these investments corruption has, if anything, increased. Laws are manipulated by elites who have privileged access to courts and superior local knowledge. Anticorruption agencies are often just a box that must be checked to get international assistance. Changes in formal institutions will have little impact if there is no commitment to these new institutions from those that must actually put new practices in place. In closed access orders, where corruption is an essential resource for leaders to stay in power, there will be no such commitment.[30]

While modernization theory sees development as taking place more along a continuum, rational choice institutionalism sees basic differences between closed and open access orders. The number of intermediate polities is small. There will be some opportunities to contain corruption in intermediate polities, where some members of the political and economic elite will see it as being in their interest to support the rule of law, but not in extractive or closed access orders. In despotic orders, corruption, the ability of political leaders to secure resources, is an essential, inescapable part of the political system. At best, political leaders need resources that they can use to pay off their key supporters; absent these resources, they would lose office, and losing office would mean a dramatic decline in status, a precipitous loss of income, and possibly exile or death. At worst, political leaders simply grab as much in the way of state-controlled resources as they can, and share these gains with a small number of followers; the rest of the country gets nothing at all. Accountability mechanisms and an independent police and judiciary are inconsistent with the logic of the political order. Political leaders will subvert institutional reforms that would prevent corruption.

In intermediate polities there may be some political actors that see the benefits of an open access order for material or even non-material reasons. They may be willing to support an array of public policy measures that can limit some types of corruption. There are more opportunities for external actors in intermediate polities, but the task is challenging. External actors must have enough knowledge of the local political environment to be able to identify politically consequential actors within an intermediate polity that would support more accountability and a more effective legal system. External actors might be able to create islands of excellence that function according to the rule of law and meet international standards if they have local allies. In an intermediate polity these islands of excellence might diffuse to other institutions.

In open access orders, corruption persists because the temptations presented by the gap between official prices and market prices is too large for everyone to resist. At the same time, however, accountability mechanisms, including elections, civil society organizations, and the press, are robust. Police can investigate, courts function, and prisons punish. Corruption cannot be eliminated but, in open access orders, it can be contained. Some practitioners of corruption will end up in jail.

Classifying Corruption

A first step in understanding how external actors might combat corruption in closed access or intermediate polities is to develop a classification scheme that can identify different kinds of corruption. With better identification of different varieties of corruption and of the role that they might play in different political systems (inclusive, intermediate, or extractive), it is easier to identify reforms that might be acceptable to political elites and therefore might actually be implemented. Not all forms of corruption are equally bad with regard to security, some economic development, and better public services. The move from one kind of corruption to another is not necessarily an inconsequential change. The dystopian trap of doing nothing can be avoided but not by eliminating corruption entirely, at least not in despotic polities.

There are many different dimensions along which corruption can be categorized. These dimensions are not mutually exclusive. Corruption may be petty, many small thefts or bribes involving low-level officials, or it may be gross, involving large sums paid to a small number of individuals at the top of the political order. Money may flow down from the people at the top to a small or large number of their supporters, or the money may flow up from the population to a small number of people at the top. There may be a small number of rules of thumb that everyone in the system understands (more likely with centralized corruption), or there may be no clear mutual understanding among private and public actors about appropriate payments (more likely when corruption is decentralized).

Michael Johnston's 2005 book *Syndromes of Corruption*[31] offers a very useful classification assessing different forms of corruption and their impacts on economic growth and democratization. Johnston argues that there are four kinds of corruption, which he labels influence markets, elite cartel corruption, oligarchs and clans, and official moguls.[32] In influence markets, private actors pay off public officials, often legally, to secure policies that are favorable to them. For influence markets to function, government institutions must be competent and consequential. With strong institutions and accountability, however, officials are constrained in the extent to which they can favor particular private groups. There are many different groups whose interests are not necessarily complementary. Too much favoritism for particular private groups might undermine the support that a leader might get from the general electorate. Influence markets may weaken economic performance to some extent, but this kind of corruption does not preclude economic growth, security, and effective service provision even though growth and service provision might not be beneficial for all.

The United States, especially after the *Citizens United* Supreme Court decision, is an example of a polity in which influence markets are pervasive and consequential. An August 2015 *New York Times* article reported that almost half of the contributions to presidential candidates came from fewer than four hundred families. The total amount contributed was $388 billion, most to super PACs.[33]

In the advanced industrialized economies of North America and Europe, influence market corruption is not easy to escape. In Germany, public officials as well as representatives of management and labor sit on the supervisory boards of German companies. The former German chancellor, Gerhard Schröder, became chairman of the boards of two Russian-controlled energy companies, Nord Stream and Rosneft. In France, graduates of the grand écoles circulate between the private and public sectors. Emmanuel Macron, elected president of France in 2016, graduated from the elite École Nationale d'Administration and worked at the Inspectorate General for Finances in the public sector and as an investment banker with Rothschilds Bank in the private sector before being elected president. In Japan the practice of *amakudari*, "descent from heaven," includes the placement of government officials in lucrative private-sector positions when they leave public employment.

Elite cartel corruption involves mutually dependent relations between political and private elites. Elite cartel corruption develops when public officials depend on wealthy private actors for support and private actors depend on the state for favorable policies. Elite cartels are most likely to develop when a country is transitioning to democracy; South Korea under Presidents Park and Chun was an example of elite cartel corruption. Favored *chaebols* got privileged access to credit. But success was not guaranteed by the state. And some officials did go to jail. Corruption rules were mutually understood. The environment was predictable. In the 1970s, with General Park as president, South Korea's annual GDP growth rate exceeded 10 percent in six out of ten years; and in the years 1980–1988 under General Chun the growth rate exceeded 10 percent in four years and 7.5 percent in the rest.[34] Korea's dramatic economic rise provided a foundation, as suggested by modernization theory, for the country's transition to democracy in the late 1980s.

Even after the transition to a democratic regime occurred under President Roh in the late 1980s, elite cartel corruption continued. In 2017 President Park (the daughter of the 1970s military dictator) was forced out of office in a corruption scandal involving an unofficial advisor and the Samsung corporation, and was sentenced to more than twenty years in jail.[35] In August 2017 the de facto head of Samsung was sentenced to five years in jail for bribery, among other crimes.[36] The mutually supportive relationship between major *chaebols* and the state had continued long after the democratic transition, although, under an open access order, the president could actually go to jail.

All of the Asian tigers, the fastest-growing economies in the post–World War II period, experienced elite cartel corruption, not just South Korea. In Taiwan, Japan, and Singapore there was also a symbiotic relationship among political elites and the major private-sector corporations that was driving growth. The members of *keiretsu* in Japan and the *chaebols* in South Korea benefited from favorable public policies. The governments in South Korea and Japan would, however, support only companies that were internationally competitive. Payoffs to public officials did not guarantee economic success. And there were companies, at least in Japan, such as Honda, that succeeded without government support.

Historically, early industrializers, including the United States and the United Kingdom, also experienced elite cartel corruption. The Gilded Age in the United States in the last part of the nineteenth century was characterized by rapid economic growth, income inequality, and corruption. The so-called robber barons, individuals who dominated major industrial sectors, were emblematic figures of this period of American history. They did make payments to public officials, but they also contributed to economic growth. In sum, influence market corruption and elite cartel corruption have occurred in countries that have experienced sustained growth.

Johnston's other two kinds of corruption, oligarchs and clans and official moguls, are far more problematic for basic security, economic growth, and public services, in other words, for good enough governance. Money flows from the society as a whole to political elites. The state is closer to a roving bandit than a stationary one, because political leaders highly discount the future. Violence is always possible. Courts do not protect property rights.

Russia in the 2000s is an example of oligarchs and clans. Privileged individuals were able to seize privatized state assets. Many people were killed. Russia under Vladimir Putin has deteriorated. Access to the state is the key to wealth. Opponents of the regime such as Khodorkovsky can be put in jail or exiled. There are no competing elites that are independent of the state.

Kenya from 1978 to 2002 under President Daniel arap Moi is another example of mogul corruption. The courts were completely controlled by political elites. There was no free press. Growth rates were relatively low.[37]

Classifying corruption into these four categories—influence markets, elite cartels, oligarchs and clans, and official moguls—can incorporate many of the factors associated with corruption that have been noted by other analysts. These include whether money is moving up or down, whether it is centralized or diffuse, whether payoffs are petty or grand, and whether there are clear rules. Influence market corruption is concentrated at the top; money may move from the privately wealthy to the political elite but the political elite generally will deploy these resources for political purposes, to secure and keep public office. Outright theft is difficult because institutions, including legal institutions, are robust. Elite cartel corruption is also concentrated at the top of the political order. The rules are clear. There is a symbiotic relationship between political and economic elites. They mutually support each other. Personal theft is somewhat constrained by institutions, including legal institutions, by potential competition among competing elites, and by the competence of public institutions that can control decentralized petty theft. Both influence market corruption and elite cartel corruption are consistent with security, economic growth, and some provision of government services—with good enough governance.

Corruption associated with oligarchs and clans and, especially, with official moguls has been much more problematic. In these situations, resources flow from the society to the political elite. Money often leaves the country. There is no sustained economic growth.

Corruption in official mogul states may be widespread and decentralized, crippling economic activity. After the moguls get what they want, petty and debilitating corruption becomes pervasive. A December 2015 *PBS Newshour* report on corruption in Nigeria described an incident in which a policeman stopped a taxi driver and demanded the equivalent of ten dollars. When the driver refused to pay, the policeman shot the driver and also shot and killed his wife; the children were also present.[38] In Georgia, before the Saakashvili government introduced changes, the traffic police were so pervasively corrupt that their behavior had delegitimized the previous regime. The Saakashvili government fired the entire force.

Afghanistan after the American invasion offers an example of official mogul corruption. Sarah Chayes has written a stunning indictment of the extent to which the Afghan government under President Hamid Karzai was riddled with corruption. Chayes first went to Afghanistan shortly after the American invasion as a reporter for National Public Radio. She stayed on for a decade, mostly in Kandahar. The Karzai government was essentially a gang of thieves organized to steal money. Much of this money came from the United States and other foreign donors. Aid funds that were designed to build public infrastructure, such as roads, ended up in the pockets of Karzai's cronies or his family members. This theft was visible to the population. It completely undermined the legitimacy of the Karzai government.[39] Chayes writes: "The fraud perpetrated in the 2009 Afghan elections was so egregious and widespread as to stun even seasoned election monitors, several of whom declared it the most pervasive they had ever seen. Later, US officers who spoke to Taliban detainees found that the election had generated a spurt in support for the insurgency, as Afghans lost faith in a 'political process that only seemed to strengthen power brokers and maintain the status quo,' as one put it."[40]

In 2010 the Kabul Bank nearly collapsed. Hundreds of millions of dollars had been stolen. The former president of the bank described it as a Ponzi scheme in which the owners took in deposits that were then distributed to Karzai, members of his entourage, and those of his vice-president, Muhammed Qasim Fahim.[41]

Rather than being able to combat corruption, the Americans and other foreign players were trapped by it. Americans and others did not know Afghan languages; they were almost always dependent on local translators. Officials and soldiers were in-country for too short a time to build relationships or fully grasp the local cultures. They could not fulfill their concrete tasks, whether military or civilian, such as building schools or killing Taliban forces, without the help of local elites. These elites had their own interests, including payoffs, which were not necessarily complementary to those of external actors seeking to promote better governance.

In Afghanistan, mogul corruption has posed a lethal threat to even the minimal goals of the international community. Afghanistan has consistently been ranked as one of the ten-worst countries in the world by Transparency International. To stay in power, politicians need money. In an environment where administrative and judicial checks are weak, despite the anticorruption programs of the international community, the temptation to steal is difficult to resist. Billions of dollars in aid money have flooded into the country, providing many opportunities for rent-seeking elites to line their own pockets.

Many external agencies have tried to reduce corruption, but it persists. On my last trip to Afghanistan, in 2011, it was very difficult to get through airport security without paying someone. Even in the airport, a limited physical space with high symbolic importance, corruption could not be eliminated.

In sum, some corruption is inescapable. But not all corruption cripples economic growth and security. Influence market and elite cartel corruption have both occurred in countries that have experienced sustained economic growth and democratization. Influence market corruption is more likely in open access or inclusive orders; the rule of law matters and those who violate legality may be prosecuted, but the benefits of influencing public policy may be too tempting to ignore, and the legal system itself can be torqued in ways that protect the rich. Elite cartel corruption is most likely in intermediate polities. Influence market corruption and elite cartel corruption can persist even in open access orders. In contrast, corruption associated with oligarchs and clans and official moguls is part of a self-replicating system that precludes positive economic and political change.

Proposals to eliminate corruption entirely in closed access and intermediate polities are fruitless because they are incompatible with the incentives confronting elites in these polities. Corruption is essential for holding on to political power.

The standard set of proposals that is offered to limit or end corruption tacitly assumes a modernization theory or institutional capacity approach to development. Corruption can be tamed or dramatically curtailed. The list of possible changes is long: anticorruption commissions can be created, competition might be introduced by having different bureaus perform the same tasks so that customers/citizens have the opportunity to shop around, bureaucrats might be paid higher salaries so the corruption will be less tempting, public officials can be asked to sign an integrity pledge, training for the police and the judiciary can be improved, civil society should be strengthened, government programs that are particularly susceptible to corruption should be eliminated, an independent judiciary should be created, and a professional civil service that is not beholden to particular parties or politicians should be established.[42]

The problem with conventional anticorruption proposals is that they are incompatible with the incentives that exist in polities characterized by corruption associated with oligarchs and clans or with official moguls. Accepting an independent or just better-trained judiciary, a more active civil society, a professionalized and independent bureaucracy, the elimination of government programs that facilitate rent-seeking, and multiple bureaucracies that open opportunities for citizens to avoid corruption—all these are fundamentally mismatched with the incentives that confront elites in closed access, extractive political orders. In such polities elites rely on corruption either to pay off their supporters (in a world of oligarchs and clans) or simply to steal (in a world of official moguls). Utopian policies in which corruption is eliminated are bound to fail.

Contracting Out

Even in a despotic world in which rent-seeking provides the resources that keep elites in power, there are some opportunities for reform, but they are limited. External actors can aim for good enough governance. Outsourcing governance to external actors, or contracting out, as is provided for in bilateral investment treaties (BITs), might provide some benefits for national elites. Most BITs provide for third-party adjudication of disputes between foreign investors and host-country governments. The economic pie might grow and national elites might secure more resources. Even political elites in closed access orders have accepted these treaties because they are better off with some foreign investment (even if this investment is walled off from corruption) than with very little or no foreign investment, which would be the case if the domestic judicial system were the only available avenue for resolving disputes.

Ambitious shared sovereignty arrangements, such as the Governance and Economic Management Assistance Program (GEMAP) in Liberia, can have a positive, but limited, impact on corruption. Under GEMAP, which was formally in effect from late 2005 until the middle of 2010, external donors had cosigning authority for contracts from many government agencies and parastatals. The program was initially resisted by Liberian elites, who were running the transitional government and enriching themselves through corruption. They ultimately accepted GEMAP because external donors, especially the United States, could credibly threaten to withdraw foreign assistance, because Liberia was strategically unimportant.[43]

Despite reservations about GEMAP, Ellen Johnson Sirleaf, who was elected president of Liberia in 2006, endorsed the program. Johnson Sirleaf had deep personal ties in the West. She had received an MA from the Kennedy School at Harvard, had worked at the World Bank and at Citibank in Nairobi, and had served as the director of the UN Development Program's Africa bureau. Without her support, GEMAP would have failed completely. However, even with the endorsement of the head of state, and high dependence on external donors, corruption persisted in Liberia. In 2017 Liberia ranked 122 out of 180 countries, according to Transparency International's Corruption Perceptions Index.[44] Per capita income in Liberia remained below $400, although the country's Polity score in 2014 was 6. Capacity building under GEMAP was weak. GEMAP made a positive contribution to development in Liberia but the country remained far, far away from the OECD world.[45]

Countries recovering from civil strife may accept external actors' proposals for institutional reforms that constrain corruption, if the external actors can credibly threaten to withdraw foreign assistance. Such threats are more likely to be credible if external actors have no strategic interests in a country's development, as was the case in Liberia.[46] Both Afghanistan and Iraq, after the American invasions, were highly dependent on external funding, especially from the United States, and both were profoundly corrupt. American leaders could not make a credible threat to withdraw aid because these countries, unlike Liberia, really mattered to American decision makers.

In Guatemala, government officials accepted CICIG (the International Commission against Impunity in Guatemala), another example of shared sovereignty. CICIG had the right to conduct investigations and to suggest legal changes, but not to conduct prosecutions. It was staffed by non-Guatemalans and created by an agreement between the Guatemalan government and the office of the UN secretary general. CICIG was a watered-down version of an earlier proposal (CICIACs), which would have had more legal authority but was rejected by the Guatemalan Constitutional Court. CICIG's budget, provided by external actors, was substantial. In 2015 a CICIG investigation of President Pérez Molina led to his resignation and ultimately to his conviction, and that of his vice-president, for corruption. Had the chief of state understood that CICIG would lead to his being indicted he would have rejected the proposal. But the government of Guatemala did rely to some extent on external funding from the United States, which conditioned its aid on the acceptance of CICIG. The vice-president, Joseph Biden, was a strong supporter of CICIG. Civil society clamored for CICIG's mandate to be renewed in 2015, only a few months before Pérez Molina resigned. A national panel, which included representatives from the attorney general's office and the Supreme Court, had also recommended that CICIG be renewed. Civil society in Guatemala did matter. CICIG became the most trusted institution in the country. Despite all of this support CICIG was suspended by the new president, Jimmy Morales, who had run on an anticorruption platform but was being investigated by CICIG.[47]

Guatemala can be understood as a mixed polity rather than an extractive order. Its Polity score was 8 in 2014 although its per capita income in 2015 was $3,900. There were members of the Guatemalan government that believed that pervasive corruption and violence weakened their own position and threatened their personal safety.[48] Even members of the government were uncertain which of their colleagues might be associated with criminal gangs. But only a special set of circumstances, including misperceptions by the political elite, allowed CICIG to be created in the first place.

An effort to replicate CICIG in Honduras led to the creation of the Mission to Support the Fight Against Corruption and Impunity in Honduras (MACCIH) in 2016 under the auspices of the Organization of American States (OAS), but the head of MACCIH resigned in 2018, complaining of a lack of support from the national government and the OAS.[49] MACCIH got little support from the Honduran government. The leaders of Honduras had learned from Guatemala and what they had learned led to MACCIH being stillborn.[50]

Mo Ibrahim, the very successful founder of cell phone companies in Africa and the source of funding for the eponymous prize for African leadership, reports that by creating a high-profile board of directors and implementing stringent rules about corruption, his companies were able to operate successfully and honestly. The board of Celtel (founded by Ibrahim in 1998) initially included prominent business leaders from Europe and political leaders from Africa, including the first CEO of Vodafone and a former Tanzanian prime minister. Ibrahim, a Sudanese by birth, spent his early career as an academic and working for British Telecom, a company that refused to set up operations in Angola and Guinea because of corruption. Ibrahim's board had to approve all contracts over $30,000. Ibrahim was successful because most African countries had few landlines, licenses were cheap, cellular communications had immediate benefits for many individuals, the industry itself did not exist so there were no extant corrupt practices, and the technology allowed the company to operate without relying on public infrastructure. At least in the short term, cell phones did not threaten national elites, who could take credit for better service provision. Moreover, the company offered service that many Africans wanted, creating an interest group that would support the company if it were threatened. Cell phone technology allowed the company to largely circumvent the state, unlike landlines, which required infrastructure (the lines themselves, rights of way) that had to be provided by the government. The company did have to withdraw from Sierra Leone in the midst of the civil war but was able to return with British forces. Celtel was sold in 2005 for nearly $3 billion, by which time it was operating in thirteen African countries and had millions of customers.[51]

In 2014 the successor to Celtel was operating in fourteen sub-Saharan African countries. In terms of the World Bank's percentile corruption indicator rankings, these countries had not particularly improved in the period from 2008 to 2014.[52] A visionary leader could bring an important service with peculiar attributes (direct benefit to many individuals and autonomy from public sector infrastructure) to many countries with high levels of corruption, but this activity did not have an impact on the broader environment for corruption. Cellular telephones remain an island of excellence in at least some African countries.

National legislation in the OECD world, such as the American Foreign Corrupt Practices Act, is another mechanism through which external actors might create islands of excellence, but in closed access orders these islands are likely to remain isolated. National legislation in OECD countries can change the incentives of foreign investors. The threat of prosecution in their home countries makes corporate officials less likely to offer bribes to political leaders in their host countries. Even in despotic polities, external actors may create islands of excellence that will not diffuse to other parts of the polity. They will not turn closed access orders into open access orders.

RATHER THAN ATTEMPT to eliminate corruption, or to put in place in closed access orders an institutional simulacrum of what already exists in the OECD world, external actors would be more successful if they sought to introduce reforms that would be incentive compatible with the interests of political elites in closed access orders. The minimum condition for reforms would have to be that they do not threaten the ability of the national elite to stay in power. In some cases of official mogul corruption, this might be a null set, or at least the best that external actors could hope for would be isolated islands of excellence that would wither and die when external actors departed.

If, however, political leaders believe that they might have some future, then the most promising reforms would be ones that might move them away from an official mogul behavior, in which they are simply extracting as much as they can from the society and possibly shipping it overseas, to clientelism, in which leaders use corruption to pay off the minimum winning coalition that they need to stay in power.[53] The larger the minimum winning coalition, the better for the society as a whole. Patronage and clientelism are preferable to gross mogul corruption and might be compatible with incentives of leaders in closed access orders.

Focusing on the possibilities of altering the incentives of leaders in closed access polities in ways that lead them to focus on payoffs that can help them to stay in power, rather than on outright theft, which extracts and removes resources from the polity, is more promising than the current set of prescriptions for ending corruption. A second-best policy that leaves more resources in a country is better than a first-best set of policies that will never be implemented.

In intermediate polities there will be more opportunities for external actors. Some members of the national elite in intermediate polities would prefer a more inclusive order with less corruption. Economically, a more open access order might be more attractive because it would allow some companies to become more competitive internationally rather than being dependent on national markets. Some members of the national elite might feel threatened, even physically threatened, by a closed access polity in which violence is tolerated and even sometimes encouraged. Normative values might change, because some members of the elite will have been educated in or have access to the open order OECD world. Islands of excellence might diffuse across the polity.

The challenge is to find fine-grained information about the national elites with which external actors are engaged. National elites that are committed to closed access orders have every incentive to convince external actors that they are interested in better governance. If they are fluent in English, all the better for them. If they have been educated in the West or are familiar with what the Americans, French, British, Germans, or Australians would like to hear, better still. Even if, in reality, a polity is mixed, external actors will not necessarily be able to identify internal actors with whom they share a commitment to better governance.

In sum, conventional prescriptions for eliminating corruption are useless or worse than useless in closed access polities. The best that external actors can aim for is to move national elites from gross mogul theft to clientelism and patronage, activities that at least benefit a larger part of the polity. In intermediate polities there are many more opportunities for introducing reforms, but external actors will always be challenged by their own lack of knowledge.

CHAPTER 7

Elections Sometimes Lead to Bad Outcomes

I N THE SUMMER OF 1989 FRANCIS FUKUYAMA PUBLISHED AN essay entitled "The End of History" in which he argued, "What we may be witnessing is not just the end of the Cold War, or the passing of a particular period of post-war history, but the end of history as such: that is, the end point of mankind's ideological evolution and the universalization of Western liberal democracy as the final form of human government." Fukuyama's 1992 book *The End of History and the Last Man*, which, according to Google Scholar, has been cited more than thirteen thousand times, has been both praised and criticized.[1]

The divided reactions to the idea of an end of history, more precisely, to the end of ideological contention and the triumph of Western liberal ideas about politics and economics over other contenders, reflected the developments of the last thirty years— at least until Donald Trump became the president of the United States. Democracy is everywhere praised. Virtually every regime describes itself, sometimes incredibly, as democratic. Democracy, a government and political leaders that reflect the will of the people, is the only universally accepted basis for political legitimacy. Elections are held almost everywhere. In this sense Fukuyama was not wrong. There are no ideological rivals to liberal democracy, but this does not mean that liberal democracy is everywhere triumphant.

The one essential ingredient for a democracy, the one attribute without which a regime cannot call itself democratic, is elections.[2] Elections provide at least a minimal definition of democracy, a necessary if not sufficient condition for democracy.[3] Many elections, however, are not free and fair. Incumbents win almost 70 percent of all elections. In the last decade there has been more backsliding than progress. Autocratic leaders have learned how to manipulate elections. They have engaged in gerrymandering, voter suppression, preventing opposition candidates from running, vote buying, and violence.[4]

Ink-marked fingers became an iconic image from the 2005 Iraqi elections. The purple finger became a source of pride. All the better for demonstrating the universal appeal of democracy that the women were often shown dressed in traditional garb.[5]

Elections have not only become a universally known form, they are also a potent symbol, one that can be invoked by both internal and external supporters of democratization. Voters in Afghanistan and Iraq, even women whose dress suggested that they were far from full participants in the modern world of gender equality, wanted to show that they had voted.

Elections are everywhere known and legitimated. Virtually every country in the world holds elections; there are only five or six countries that have not had a national election. The salience of elections has given support to the utopian vision that consolidated democracy is possible in any country, but elections are held not only in consolidated democracies but in many intermediate regimes and closed access states.[6]

From my own experience working at the National Security Council in 2002 and the State Department from 2005 until 2007, I can see that elections have had an irresistible appeal for American leaders. The attentiveness of domestic publics is fickle. Elections are events that are widely covered by the press. They are live demonstrations that a commitment to democracy is taking place even in troubled polities. No other single event associated with democracy has as much salience and visibility. For a leader in the OECD world committed to the promotion of democracy, election promotion is very hard to resist.

Elections, however, are neither guarantees of individual freedoms nor effective constraints on despotic elites. In practice, many elections do not come anywhere near meeting conventional standards for free and fair. Rational choice institutionalism suggests that in despotic orders, free and fair elections will be impossible. Money and power flow from the control of the political system. Rulers will not go quietly into the night. They will frustrate free and fair elections if they believe that such elections would remove them from office.

It is now commonplace to make a distinction between electoral democracies and liberal or consolidated democracies. In 1997 Fareed Zakaria published an article in *Foreign Affairs* entitled "The Rise of Illiberal Democracy."[7] Zakaria pointed out that liberal democracy means not only elections but also the rule of law, protection of property rights, separation of powers, and freedom of speech and assembly. Democracy—governments chosen through elections—might be more common, Zakaria pointed out, but constitutional liberalism, which requires respect for the basic rights of individuals, did not necessarily accompany elections. In fact, the number of illiberal democracies was growing.[8] Autocrats or populists who trample on property rights or on individual rights more generally can be selected through free and fair elections.

Supporting Elections

Even in the 1960s the United States allocated some resources to democracy promotion, but these early efforts failed, in large part because American leaders were more concerned with supporting anticommunist rulers, whether they were fairly elected or not, than with promoting democratic change, especially where the behavior of elected rulers could not be predicted with confidence.[9]

After the collapse of the Soviet Union, American democracy assistance increased to about 10 percent of the total aid budget, a significant commitment, even though the US aid budget overall declined. The core strategy for the United States has been to promote elections, support civil society, and press for a written constitution.[10] USAID (or at least one of its contractors), for instance, has developed detailed guides for improving electoral security. USAID's *Electoral Security Framework: Technical Guidance Handbook for Democracy and Governance Officers* includes a list of fifty-eight questions that can be posed to assess the state of security for elections. These questions are relevant for a wide range of government institutions, including legislatures, election monitoring boards, anticorruption commissions, national police, and local police. The questions that can be asked about local police, for instance, include the following: "What are their rules of engagement? How is election enforcement security coordinated with other agencies?"[11] The approach taken by USAID and other agencies is to identify a set of best practices that can help to lessen security threats around elections. External actors have supported many different kinds of programs, including cooperation with local partners, legal reforms, capacity building, diplomatic pressure, and even sanctions. In 2012, $500,000,000 was spent on support for elections.[12] This focus on elections, and the amounts spent, reflect a utopian vision that consolidated democracy is everywhere possible and could be helped along by external actors.

A large commitment of resources does not, however, guarantee good results. The United States committed more than $30 million to support three rounds of elections in Haiti that were supposed to culminate with the selection of a new president in February 2016. The opposition leader, however, rejected the first round of voting, which was held in October 2015, and refused to participate in the final round. Electoral violence was widespread despite the presence of UN peacekeepers, who had been in the country since 2004. Violent demonstrations took place in Port-au-Prince in the weeks before the scheduled vote. Electoral council offices were attacked, and in some more remote parts of the country balloting materials were stolen by armed gangs. On January 22, 2016, the Provisional Electoral Council postponed the presidential vote indefinitely because there was extensive violence throughout the country.[13] Over forty Haitian American groups and various community leaders wrote to US Secretary of State John Kerry criticizing the "unhelpful role the State Department has been playing in Haiti's election crisis."[14] Elections were held later in Haiti but there have been persistent accusations of fraud, and there has been widespread violence.

One new organizational form that has become highly institutionalized, and widely accepted, over the last two or three decades is the practice of election observation. This is a striking development, because elections had historically been considered to be entirely within the authority and jurisdiction of the state. International election observers, however, are now present in almost all elections.

The basic idea behind election observation is that international observers can reduce fraud, enhance the acceptance of election outcomes within a country, and validate a country's democratic credentials for external donors. The norm of using election observers has become universally accepted at least in part because refusing to invite such observers is taken by external donors as prima facie evidence that a regime is autocratic.[15]

There is considerable empirical evidence that the presence of election monitors does improve the quality of elections, the extent to which electoral outcomes actually reflect votes cast, but this varies across different types of regimes.[16] The quality of elections does not seem to be much affected in autocratic regimes even when election observers are present.[17] Autocrats or pseudo-democrats have many different strategies for frustrating international election observers. Election fraud or manipulation can take place at many different points both before and after the days in which votes are actually cast. The apparatus for election observation is now so widespread and accepted that autocratic regimes can pick and choose among organizations that provide election observers. There are many organizations that provide observers unlikely to criticize election results, such as the Commonwealth of Independent States and the Shanghai Cooperation Organization. Observers from the Organization of African Unity have also been reluctant to report that an election was fraudulent.[18]

The Azerbaijani election commission reported that there were 1,300 observers in the country from fifty different organizations for the country's 2013 presidential elections. Forty-nine of these groups praised the elections as free and fair. (Freedom House ranked Azerbaijan as a consolidated authoritarian regime.) Only one, the observer team from the Organization for Security and Co-operation in Europe (OSCE), demurred. Some of the observer teams that validated the elections were from credible institutions such as the European Parliament. Azerbaijan was better off having observers than not.[19] Election observers, however, did not change the autocratic nature of the regime. The Aliyev family has ruled Azerbaijan since 1993, first the father, Heydar Aliyev, and since 2003 the son, Ilham Aliyev.

Even when election observers deter fraud in one place, the governing party may simply engage in fraud elsewhere.[20] In Ghana, for instance, one of the African states most widely regarded as democratic, a group of scholars found that, on balance, election observers did reduce fraud but did not eliminate it. Political parties were able to move fraudulent practices away from polling places with observers to nearby sites that were under party control.[21] In the 2018 elections in Turkey the state-controlled mass media gave the most coverage to Erdogan. One opposition candidate had to conduct his election campaign from jail.[22]

Election observers have made a difference but that difference is most marked in regimes where there is already some commitment to honest elections. Autocrats who hold elections still have many mechanisms that can be used to undermine the integrity of election results.[23]

The effectiveness of external actors depends on the interests of national elites. In extractive regimes, national elites will not accept electoral practices that would deprive them of office. External actors do not, probably cannot, have a fine-grained understanding of local circumstances. Despotic elites have a better understanding of what they need to do to stay in power. Especially in closed access, extractive orders, national elites will, if necessary, frustrate efforts to promote free and fair elections that they might lose. The intimate understanding that despotic elites have of their own situation provides them with many tools to use to frustrate the good intentions of external actors.

Moreover, in situations where external actors are committed for security reasons to a particular country or regime, as was frequently the case during the Cold War and as was the case for the United States in Afghanistan and Iraq after 9/11, national elites understand that external actors will limit the pressure that they bring to bear. For the external actor, a national regime, even a despotic national regime, may be better than the alternative that might be produced by free and fair elections. Political elites in OECD countries will have an incentive to demonstrate to their own constituents that they are making progress with regard to security, service provision, and human rights, and this will undermine the credibility of threats that they might make to withdraw aid. In Liberia, to which few in the US electorate were paying attention, national actors had every reason to believe that external donors would withdraw aid if GEMAP were not accepted. In Afghanistan, Karzai had little reason to believe that the United States would crack down. External election observers have made a valuable contribution to improving democratic governance, but mostly in countries where important elements of the domestic elite were already committed to such changes. In intermediate polities external actors have at least some

chance of mobilizing members of the national elite that are supportive of more open access institutions; in closed access polities
such elites do not exist.

Elections Do Not a Liberal Democracy Make

Elections are often problematic with regard to the provision of
public goods and accountability, despite being regarded almost
universally as the only way that government authority can be legitimated. Rather than consolidate liberal progress, elections may
impede accountability and individual rights. Rather than increase
security, they may reduce it. Elections, even free and fair elections,
have not necessarily led to economic growth and better service
provision. Corruption is empirically worse in countries where elections are being held for the first time.[24] And despite the huge international apparatus designed to ensure election integrity, elections
are often corrupt.

Despots that are dependent on foreign assistance cannot avoid
elections. In sub-Saharan Africa, for instance, multiparty elections
have become the norm since the 1990s. Because of pressure from
aid-giving wealthy democratic states, it has become more difficult
for despots to maintain power by creating single parties whose rule
is never seriously contested. One observer notes that "virtually all
of Africa's post–Cold War autocrats govern with nominally democratic political institutions: presidential term limits, multiparty legislatures, and regular elections. Indeed, they have little choice. As
a range of scholars have observed, Western creditors have virtually
required nominally democratic institutions in exchange for foreign
aid and debt relief."[25]

Despots can minimize the chances that elections will remove
them from office. Single parties that had governed in African states
before multiparty elections were introduced usually won the first
multiparty election, and the party that won the first election was

and continues to be able to stay in power. The typical African party system was composed of one dominant party and a number of weaker parties. Dominant parties were able to use the resources of the state to marginalize their weaker opponents. Electoral districts have been gerrymandered, voting lists have been manipulated, and opposition parties have been harassed. Parties have been largely based on ethnicity rather than on electoral programs. Power has been concentrated in the presidency. Of the forty-five multiparty electoral systems in Africa only four are parliamentary regimes. Presidents control budgets. Presidential staffs can be enormous, numbering in the tens of thousands. The dominant party monopolizes or dominates mass media.[26]

In the Democratic Republic of the Congo, Joseph Kabila, for instance, refused to leave office even though the two terms to which he was limited by the Congolese constitution ended in December 2016. Kabila assumed office in 2001 when his father, who had been president before him, was assassinated. Rather than leave office, he blocked new elections for two years. The editorial board of the *Washington Post* described the elections that were held in December 2018 as "an enormous fraud perpetrated by outgoing president Joseph Kabila."[27] Even after he prevented new elections from being held and refused to leave office, Kabila said, "The source of legitimacy is only through the people at the ballot box."[28]

In the Republic of the Congo (Brazzaville), the president, Sassou Nguesso, kept himself in power for decades. After losing power in the 1970s he fled to Paris; engineered, with French help, a civil war; and returned to power in 1997. To satisfy external donors, on whom he heavily depended, he needed to maintain a facade of democracy. He created a parallel government whose core members were a close circle of confidants that he had developed while he was in exile in France. He fostered competition among potential rivals. He was able to weather revelations in a 2004 document that showed gross corruption. Nguesso owned many of the wealth-generating activities in the country, including major buildings; banks; and construction, transportation, and insurance companies. For most of his rule Nguesso avoided outright repression, fearing that Western donors would deny his regime foreign assistance because of corruption. Nguesso cultivated closer relations with China and increasingly relied on Chinese foreign assistance. He intensified repression after 2010, exiling journalists, shutting down opposition media, and killing opponents.[29]

Elections and Violence

In despotic orders, electoral violence is associated with situations in which elections might bring a significant shift in power within a country. Threatened incumbents are more likely to use violence than incumbents that are not threatened. Governments are the most important perpetrators of electoral violence. Eighty percent of elections over the period 1960 to 2010 experienced some violence. In this period there were 350 cases of electoral violence. The percentage of elections in which violence occurred increased after 1990 as the number of countries holding potentially contested elections increased.[30]

Almost all poor countries are dominated by despotic elites. Government office is a major source of wealth and power; the difference in security, wealth, status, and prestige between being in office and out of office is huge. Institutional constraints on the behavior of political elites is limited.[31] Paul Collier, a British economist who has popularized the term *the bottom billion*, concluded in a 2009 study that in countries where the world's poorest people live, elections are associated with higher levels of violence: "To date democracy in the societies of the bottom billion has increased political violence rather than reducing it."[32] Collier finds that the crossover point, the level of per capita income where elections decrease rather than increase violence, is $2,700. The most violent kinds of regimes are nominal democracies with factionalism and despotic executives. The next most problematic regime type with regard to instability is autocracies with some competition.[33] When executives are unconstrained, politics becomes a winner-take-all struggle, and the difference between controlling the state and its resources and not controlling it is huge. The most stable regimes are closed despotisms such as Saudi Arabia and North Korea, where there is no competition; and liberal democracies, regimes in which there is fully open electoral competition among well-developed political parties and in which executives are strongly constrained by legislatures.[34]

In autocratic or closed access regimes, elections are a focal point around which opposition groups can organize. Often they organize violently, since they know that a despot will not relinquish power based solely on election results.[35] In Colombia in the late 1980s, elections facilitated population displacements and expulsions, because elections served as information-revelation mechanisms. After local elections were held in 1988 the paramilitaries engaged in mass killings in areas that had shown sympathy for the left-wing Unión Patriótica (UP); UP sympathizers fled. Local elites threatened by UP electoral gains brought in paramilitaries to kill UP leaders.[36]

Even in countries where elections have a long history, they can become focal points for violence. The elections that took place in India in 2013 were accompanied by deadly rioting. In Uttar Pradesh, the country's most populous state, forty-four people were killed and forty-two thousand were displaced. Whole villages were sacked. The rioting was precipitated by a widely circulated video, fabricated by a member of the party of the man who is now prime minister, Narendra Modi, which purported to show two Hindus being lynched by Muslims. The violence helped to consolidate Modi's position in Gujarat and obviously did not prevent him from becoming the prime minister of India.[37]

For elites in the OECD world, elections in target recipient countries are attractive not only because they are a necessary condition for democracy, which almost all elites in the OECD world support, but also because they can be a graphic demonstration that the policies of external state-builders are succeeding. For elites outside of the world of consolidated democracies, elections can threaten to force them out of office and into the abyss, where they would be denied access to political power, material goods, and even their lives. Thus, external elites press for elections because they are a demonstration of success, but elections can lead to violence and instability.

Elections and the Provision of Public Goods

Elections do not necessarily improve the provision of public services. The assumption that elections will improve public services relies on a set of causal relations reflected in the responsible party government model. This model makes the following assumptions: voters have preferences over a range of issues, parties bundle issues, voters allocate their votes to competing parties, elected parties implement their programs, and in subsequent elections voters hold parties responsible for their actions. But the responsible party model works only in polities that are not despotic. In despotic polities, leaders want to hold on to power, not serve the people.

The responsible party model does describe how elections lead to accountability and the better provision of government services in consolidated democracies. In these polities, elections are free and fair, parties cannot monitor the behavior of individuals or small groups of voters, individuals have high levels of income, the state provides only a limited percentage of total jobs, the life prospects of individuals are not much affected by which party wins office, voters are reasonably well informed, and at least some voters care about the well-being of the polity as a whole. Political parties win elections by appealing to a large enough segment of the electorate to allow them to control the government. The only realistic appeals that parties can make involve the provision of public goods from which no segment of the electorate can be excluded.[38]

In many poorer countries, however, and in some richer ones, the assumptions of the responsible party government model do not hold. Even if elections meet explicit international standards, parties are able to monitor the behavior of individual voters. Powerful actors may be able to dictate how some citizens, such as employees, vote.[39] The government provides most of the jobs. The well-being of an individual can be dramatically impacted by which party holds power. Information is hard to come by. Voters are not necessarily well informed. Citizens live near the edge of poverty; they do not have the luxury of focusing on the well-being of the polity as a whole.

Even when elections meet international standards they may not have the kind of positive impact that would be expected from conventional theories of how democracies function. Elected officials, even voters, might be more interested in patronage than in service provision. Decentralization might actually worsen the provision of services, because local officials and their constituents are most interested in specific payoffs and rewards from supporting the winning party.[40]

A Transparency International study of the provision of education provides data for twenty-one countries on the absentee rates for teachers for the period 2004–2011. Higher, more democratic, Polity IV scores correlate with high absentee rates. The median shows that teachers are not in the classroom almost one-quarter of the time.[41] For this limited data set, higher democracy scores are negatively correlated with teachers actually showing up for class. Absent a full or consolidated democracy, elections do not necessarily result in higher service provision. Elections do not necessarily constrain all forms of corruption.

Clientelism can work only if political leaders are able to monitor the behavior of voters. Voters must know that if they defect, they will not receive benefits. In clientelistic systems politicians have many, often subtle, ways to observe voting behavior. The ballot may be organized so that voting a straight ticket is very easy and takes little time, while ticket splitting is complicated and requires more time. The amount of time the voter spends in the voting booth can be observed.[42]

In general, politicians and parties will prefer the clientelistic provision of private goods to the programmatic provision of public goods, if they provide private goods at all rather than simply steal public resources. Clientelism is a more secure way to get votes. If everyone knows that politicians can monitor voting patterns, no one has an incentive to defect, because defection can result in politicians withholding benefits. Parties are not organized around the programmatic delivery of services but around the ability to provide benefits to specific ethnic groups, castes, regions, or other voting groups. Voters are caught in a classic prisoners' dilemma. If they could coordinate their behavior and vote for the party that delivered programmatic public goods they would be better off. But since they cannot usually coordinate their behavior, they support the party that gives them clientelistic private goods because, in the absence of coordination, failure to support a clientelistic party would leave them even worse off.[43]

In India patronage predated independence; the British used patronage to maintain their hold on power by paying off key groups. After independence the Congress Party initially had no serious electoral competition. The level of patronage declined. With higher levels of electoral competition in the 1960s, however, Congress increased private payoffs to voters. Indira Gandhi dramatically enlarged the number of patronage jobs by nationalizing the banks and insurance companies. Borrowers from publicly controlled banks usually suffered no consequences if they did not repay their loans. Politicians in India have since directed their support to voters whose behavior they can monitor; nonsupporters are given as little as possible.[44] Similar developments have been reported in Africa, where more competition has simply reinforced voters' expectations of being paid off and politicians' commitment to clientelism as the most secure strategy for staying in office.[45]

Clientelism is far from the worst possible outcome. In many African states, prebendalism, in which officials steal public revenues for themselves, their supporters, or their ethnic kin, has persisted even in the face of multiparty elections. Prebendalism involves giving political supporters control over state resources that can then be turned into private income. Prebendalism is more corrosive than clientelism because it inescapably subverts the rule of law.[46] Widespread clientelism and patronage, which may be legal, have some benefits for the population; the more people on the patronage list the better. Prebendalism benefits only a very few and subverts any possibility that the state might act in the general interest.

One particularly compelling example of prebendalism involves the former home of the ousted Ukrainian president Viktor Yanukovych. The opulent villa that he owned on the outskirts of Kiev was supposed to be transformed into a museum of corruption. Instead, several months after Yanukovych was forced to flee the country it was taken over by Denys Tarachkotelyk, described by the *New York Times* as "a burly former businessman and now the self-declared 'commandant' of a 350-acre estate, nearly twice the size of Camp David." While claiming to protect the property from greedy and corrupt politicians Tarachkotelyk was himself collecting visitors' fees and concession revenues associated with the estate.[47]

Even if patronage is superior to prebendalism or gross mogul theft, democracy and clientelism have not been a path toward the reliable provision of public goods or of economic growth. There is no relationship between Polity scores and economic growth, although there may be some indirect paths through longer life expectancy.[48] Countries that hold elections do on average spend more money on education and health but this has not resulted in an aggregate improvement in infant and child mortality. Much of the additional expenditure goes to the middle and upper classes, not to the poor.[49]

In electoral democracies, as opposed to constitutional or liberal democracies, the competition for votes might not help the poor even when programs are ostensibly developed to reduce poverty. In the late 1980s, the PRI in Mexico launched Pronasol (National Solidarity Program). President Salinas announced with great fanfare that the program would reduce poverty in Mexico. It did nothing of the kind. Rather, under Salinas, Pronasol was used to pay off PRI supporters, many of whom were not poor. Pronasol had only a marginal impact on the provision of basic services such as water and electricity, things that the poor cared about. A great deal of money was spent on the national highway system, a collective good of little value to those without cars or trucks.[50] Mexico was hardly the only country in Latin America where ostensible poverty-reduction programs had little impact on poverty. Clientelism without poverty reduction can also be found in Venezuela under Chávez and Maduro; Ecuador under Correa; Peru under Fujimori; and Argentina under Peronista governments. All of these countries had elections.

Perversely, in democratic but clientelistic systems, politicians may have an incentive to keep the poor in poverty. Voters living on the very edge of impoverishment are particularly vulnerable and can be highly dependent on clientelistic payoffs. These benefits may be the difference between life and death. One astute observer has written, "In many developing-country democracies, including India, elected political leaders maintain structures and processes that foster the continuation of poverty. Indeed, there are apparently strong incentives for some politicians to ensure that the poor remain poor. The presence of a large class of impoverished people facing starvation and destitution in a particular area or region vulnerable to natural hazards . . . creates opportunities for political leaders to project themselves as 'saviors.' "[51]

Elections may encourage a move from prebendal politics or despotic politics, which benefit only a few, to a more clientelistic system, which has more beneficiaries. Elections can also provide the necessary but not the sufficient condition for movement from clientelistic politics to programmatic parties that provide public goods that improve the conditions of the poor in general and not just supporters of a specific party. In Mexico, the conditional cash-transfer program, Pronasol, organized by the PRI under Salinas (president of Mexico from 1988 to 1994), was transformed in the late 1990s under Salinas's successor Ernesto Zedillo, also a representative of PRI, to Progresa. Zedillo became president after the designated PRI candidate was assassinated. After leaving office, Zedillo became the director of the Center for the Study of Globalization at Yale University, not the highest-paying position to which a former Mexican president might have aspired and an indication that he was himself committed to a more open access order in Mexico. Pronasol gave grants to supporters of the governing party, the PRI. It did not in general improve conditions for the poor. Progresa allocated payments, such as for attendance at school and visits to doctors' offices, on the basis of objective criteria and not political support.[52]

This change in payments by the state was the result of unrelated events that undermined political support for the PRI. The revolt in Chiapas threatened both the economic and the political elites, who feared that the government's failure to maintain order in Chiapas could spread to other parts of the country. The financial crisis in 1994–1995 also undermined support for the PRI. The PRI, led by Ernesto Zedillo, adopted Progresa at least in part because the party anticipated that in 2000 it would lose the presidency for the first time in eighty years. Such a loss would not have been possible without elections, but elections had to be accompanied by specific circumstances and luck. Moving to a conditional cash-transfer program based on objective criteria rather than clientelism would deny the opposition party, the PAN, which did win the 2000 election, the opportunity to reinforce its position through the kind of clientelistic payoffs that had kept the PRI in power for so long.[53] More generally, the economic factors highlighted by modernization theory, especially a larger middle class and more wealth in general, make it easier to understand how an electoral system in which parties are able to maintain their support through clientelism might be supplanted by a party system in which success at the voting booth can be achieved only through programmatic parties that are focused on the provision of public, not private, goods for voters.

Still, the path from elections to the provision of public goods and higher levels of prosperity is uncertain. In 2018 Mexico elected a left-wing populist, who won because both the right-wing PAN, which won elections in 2000 and 2006, and the PRI, which won in 2012, had failed to bring peace, deliver services, and curb corruption. Without a large middle class and a well-trained, professionalized cadre of bureaucrats, clientelism may be the best that can be hoped for, even with elections. Clientelism is a second-best outcome. It rewards only some of the poor. Some resources will be stolen by the rich. But it is better than gross mogul theft, in which a small elite simply appropriates resources. Elections make clientelism rather than gross mogul theft more likely.

Uganda—granted, a very poor country, but one with elections—introduced many reforms under pressure from the World Bank. The marketing boards for coffee and cocoa, which had been a source of rents for the state, were eliminated. The number of parastatals was sharply reduced. Tariffs were cut. These reforms did improve conditions in the country. Uganda's president, Museveni, found new ways to pay off his supporters. He doubled the number of local districts. New districts meant many new jobs. New jobs provided a mechanism through which Museveni could reward supporters and keep himself in office even with multiparty elections that were validated as free and fair.[54]

Rwanda under President Paul Kagame is admired for the progress that it has made since the genocide of 1994. In 2016 it was ranked 50th out of 176 countries in Transparency International's Corruption Perceptions Index, the best ranking in sub-Saharan Africa. But at $1,720 per capita income, Rwanda is still a very poor country. Its Polity IV score in 2015 was −3. In a March 2017 story, *The Economist* magazine reported that two large para-statal enterprises, Crystal Enterprises and Horizon, one run by the governing party and the other by the Ministry of Defense, had been given many cushy projects.[55] Crystal, which provides many security services, funded half of the governing party's campaign in the 2010 election. Through the government itself and parastatals, the Rwandan government has many opportunities for rewarding its supporters. Clientelism has made Rwanda better off than it would have been under a completely prebendal regime or one of gross mogul theft, but it is not necessarily on the path to Denmark.

Establishing a system in which the expectations of the responsible party model are realized is a daunting task. Free and fair elections are not enough. Political parties must have an incentive to provide public rather than clientelistic private goods.

The ability to control taxation and more important expenditures must be lodged with the legislature, not just the executive. Many countries have budgetary processes that can be labeled executive-favoring revision rather than rule-of-law budgetary procedures.[56] In a rule-of-law budgetary procedure both taxes and expenditures are determined by parliamentary statute. If the parliament fails to pass a budget, then the government shuts down. This was the procedure adopted in England after the Glorious Revolution, at least for the military budget. It has not become the standard template. The third wave of democratization has been accompanied by executive-favoring budgets. Simply looking at elections does not reveal how government funds might be spent.[57] Even if elections are entirely free and fair, executive-favoring revisions give the executive the ability to pay off supporters and to undermine the independence of legislatures.

Reaching consolidated, or full, democracy—a Polity score of 10—has in almost every case been accompanied by a rule-of-law budget, which constrains the ability of the executive to act arbitrarily. However, a substantial proportion of countries, one-quarter to one-third, that Polity has classified as democracies with scores of 6 to 9 have executive-favoring reversionary budget processes.[58] Countries with elections that do not have shutdown provisions if the legislature does not pass a budget, that is, countries without a rule-of-law budget, share some of the same deformities as countries with no elections at all. Without shutdown provisions, parliaments may be less willing to authorize taxes, and executives will be more likely to concentrate power in their own hands.[59]

SINCE THE COLLAPSE of the Soviet Union, democracy has become the only universally understood mechanism for legitimating government authority. Elections are a necessary condition for democracy: no free and fair elections, no democracy. Elections are also a focal point for external and internal actors. No leading politician in the United States or Western Europe can reject elections. The conduct of a free and fair election is taken as evidence that democracy is moving forward.

Elections, however, are also a trap. In poor despotic polities, elections can impede rather than contribute to economic development and service provision. When holding the reins of political power is the most important source of money, status, and prestige in a polity, letting go is hard to do. Losing office can mean not only impoverishment but also exile or death. Elections can generate rather than dampen violence. Despotic leaders will do what they can, including using violence, to hang on to power.

Even when free and fair elections are held and even when they are not associated with violence, political parties will not necessarily compete on the basis of programmatic platforms that emphasize the provision of public goods. Clientelism is a much more efficient way for politicians to guarantee their hold on power. Clientelism may be the best that external actors can hope for in closed access orders. The alternative, prebendalism, where payoffs are limited to a very small number of supporters, is worse.

There is no guarantee that a country will transition from clientelism to an open access order, but clientelism may be consistent with conditions that make such a jump more likely. But getting to the OECD world of rich consolidated democracies is difficult. There is no automaticity. Luck matters. In Mexico and Brazil, both intermediate polities, scandals may or may not lead to inclusive orders.

Even when free and fair elections are held in poorer countries, political elites will try to maximize their discretionary control over public funds. Political elites in limited access or extractive polities will try to frustrate rule-of-law budgeting. Clientelism is the best that can be hoped for.

In despotic polities, the challenge is not to ensure free and fair elections but rather to manage relations among competing elites. Elections are more likely to provide stability if they ratify deals that have been made by competing elites rather than if they determine by themselves which elites will hold the reins of power. In 2014 James Dobbins, who was the US special representative in Afghanistan, observed that in Afghanistan "democracy is not sufficiently developed to the point where a winner take all system, in which the losers retire and organize for the next election but don't share any power following their loss, is really a workable solution."[60] In the 2014 Afghan elections, which were regarded by observers as much less corrupt than the 2009 elections, Abdullah Abdullah got the most votes in the first round. In the second round Ashraf Ghani got the most votes, an outcome that raised suspicions for many in the country. Secretary of State Kerry flew to Afghanistan and brokered a deal between the two leading candidates: the individual with the largest number of votes would become president and the runner-up would be appointed as principal executive official, a position that does not even exist in the Afghan constitution. Ghani was declared the winner, but the results of the election commission's audit were never made public.[61]

The 2014 Afghanistan election is not the only one whose outcome has been brokered. The 2007 elections in Kenya led to the deaths of more than one thousand people. After the voting, Kofi Annan, the former secretary general of the United Nations, brokered an agreement that included a role in the government for Raila Odinga, the ostensibly defeated candidate, and members of his party.[62]

Free and fair elections are an exceptionally demanding aspect of democracy. They are part of a utopian vision that will not work in closed access orders and will work in intermediate polities only if the circumstances are right. In closed access orders, peace, security, and opportunities for economic growth would be better provided without free and fair elections. This need not lead to the dystopian conclusion that there is nothing that can be done by external actors. External actors might help to broker deals among elites, which is better than violence. External actors might press elites in closed access orders to move from gross theft and prebendalism to patronage, which might benefit more people in the society. What external actors should not do is press for free and fair elections, which will not be accepted in closed access orders by local elites that control most of the means of violence.

CHAPTER 8

Historical Examples of Forcing Your Neighbor's Hand

SHORTLY AFTER THE FALL OF THE BERLIN WALL IN 1989, I WAS teaching at Stanford University. One of my colleagues was a visiting professor from the prestigious Freie Universität in West Berlin. He traveled back to Berlin after the wall fell and brought back for me a small piece of the wall. It was a cherished gift. As far as I could see, he was brimming with pride that his country, and his city, had been freed from the yoke of Soviet oppression.

That same German professor was subsequently arrested and convicted in Germany. He had been a spy for the Stasi, the East German secret police. He lost his position at the university and spent some time in jail. In his defense he stated that he had never given the East Germans anything of value and that he had worked for them only because his mother's refusal to reveal who his father was meant that he could not get public support from the West German state.

The Stasi employed more than one hundred thousand people in East Germany—on a per capita basis, many more than the Nazi Gestapo ever had. There were also many informers who were not official members of the Stasi. The Stasi had files on almost a third of the East German population. The Stasi tapped on a regular basis about one hundred thousand phone lines in West Germany and West Berlin. The organization was guided by the Soviet secret police, the KGB.

In East Germany and in other satellite states the Soviets were successful in putting in place a closed access order. A despotic state with ample military power can use its resources to create a regime in its own image. An external elite can successfully impose on another polity a closed access order. Moving other polities toward Denmark, toward consolidated democracy, is a much more challenging, often impossible, task.

Foreign-imposed regime change (FIRC) emerged in the international system as a prominent policy option only with the triumph of the sovereign state. Classical empires, which preceded sovereign states, often had ill-defined borders. Geographic noncontiguity was common. Territorial control was often hereditary. In the sixteenth century, the Hapsburg kings of Spain were accepted as the sovereigns over Spain, the Low Countries, parts of France, parts of Germany, territories in North Africa, and other parts of the Western Hemisphere. Imperial centers did not necessarily attempt to impose any kind of uniform institutional structures across all territories, if only because the centers lacked the administrative and military capacity to do so. Imperial centers demanded taxes, put down revolts, and suppressed ideologies or religions that might challenge their rule. But they did not demand institutional uniformity.

The Romans crushed the Jewish rebellions and scattered the Jewish population of the Levant in the first and second centuries because the Jews presented a set of beliefs that challenged Rome's preeminence and because they revolted against Roman rule. But so long as subject people were quiescent, Rome did not demand uniform institutions. The Romans were able to hold their vast empire with perhaps 250,000 members of the Roman legions because they did not necessarily challenge local practices.

The Mongols overran much of Eurasia and absorbed treasure

and technology where they could, but they had no institutional structure that they wished to impose on conquered territories.[1] In many cases the indigenous institutions displaced Mongolian practices. Ethnic Mongols became emperors of China but these emperors became Chinese. Kublai Khan, the grandson of Genghis Khan, became the first Yuan emperor after the Mongol conquest of China in 1271. The Yuan dynasty lasted for more than 150 years.

Colonial empires became a widely accepted international practice in the nineteenth century, although colonies had existed at earlier periods. Powerful states established colonies over which they could rule more or less directly because, by the nineteenth century, they had more administrative capacity than classical empires and technological changes in transportation and communication made it easier for home countries to oversee activities in their distant colonies. The extent to which colonial powers attempted to penetrate, replace, or pervert indigenous institutional arrangements, however, varied across countries. The British generally engaged in indirect rule in Africa, although the indigenous rulers through whom they ruled were often their own creations.[2] The French favored direct rule, imposing French institutions on their colonies. The highest Japanese official in Taiwan exercised, after a period of time, considerable autonomy, and adopted institutions that were compatible with indigenous Taiwanese practices because they made it easier for him to govern. The Americans in the Philippines, in contrast, attempted to impose American institutions and were much more constrained by officials in Washington, including members of Congress.[3]

Historically, any powerful state had several options, the most obvious being to conquer and absorb additional territory. When an enemy was defeated at least part of its territory could be hived off. Prussia/Germany was a larger state after the Franco-Prussian War of 1870–1871, resulting in the creation of the German Empire and the annexation of Alsace and Lorraine, which had been ceded to France after the Thirty Years' War, but Germany became a smaller state after the First and Second World Wars, losing not only Alsace-Lorraine to France but also East Prussia to Poland. For territory separated by distance the most obvious option, until the Second World War, was colonialism. However, both outright conquest and rule from the center require substantial resources or at least a very large power differential between conquerors and those subjugated. Colonialism was easy so long as the targeted areas' populations and indigenous political authorities had much less power than the colonizing states.

By the second half of the twentieth century, however, colonialism, direct responsibility for far-flung territories, was no longer an attractive option. The most powerful states in the world, the United States and the Soviet Union, opposed colonialism for ideological reasons. It had also become clear, even to colonizing powers, that keeping colonies did not pay. Leaders in different colonies, which had provided substantial numbers of troops (250,000 Indians fought for Britain in the Second World War, and a similar number of Africans fought for France), pressed for independence. Moreover, sovereignty, especially the idea that the inhabitants of a particular territory had the right to decide on their own institutions (known as Westphalian/Vattelian sovereignty), had become a widely legitimated norm by the second half of the twentieth century. National elites could use these norms to increase resistance to foreign rule. Forms of authority other than sovereignty, especially colonialism, were delegitimized. The original members of the United Nations in 1945 numbered 51 states (almost all of which were already politically independent); by 1963 the membership had grown to 113, primarily as a result of decolonization.

Very large power asymmetries remain in the world, but direct territorial appropriation and colonialism are only very rarely viable options. The payoff is too small, and changing norms, which applaud self-determination and castigate colonialism, provide focal points around which populations could organize against direct appropriation of territory. Russia's annexation of Crimea in 2014 is one of the few exceptions since 1945, and Putin legitimated Russia's claim by invoking self-determination.

In the contemporary world, foreign-imposed regime change, in which external actors for some limited period of time violate Westphalian/Vattelian sovereignty, is one option still available to the powerful. (The term *foreign-imposed regime change* can refer to both the leaders and the nature of the regime.) Even if only leadership change is involved, FIRCs are likely to be costly in terms of personnel or money. Extant leaders will resist. If they are displaced, the intervening state will have to commit resources to keep new leaders in place.

FIRCs are not common but they are not vanishingly rare either. John Owen (2010) has identified 209 attempts at foreign-imposed regime change in the period 1555–2010. Monten and Downes (2013) identify 96 cases of foreign-imposed regime change for the period 1816–2008. On average, a FIRC has occurred less than once a year.[4]

The most ambitious goal of a FIRC is to establish a consolidated democracy. Foreign-imposed regime changes initiated by democratic states, however, have not usually resulted in democracy or a path to democracy in target states. One obvious reason is that despite the liberal rhetoric accompanying many interventions, political leaders in democracies may be primarily interested in putting compliant leaders in place, especially if confronting an ideological rival.[5] Even if external interveners are well intentioned, foreign-imposed regime changes have usually been targeted at closed access polities, where the prospects for democracy taking hold are dim. Even where the United States used FIRCs to actively support democracy, it was rarely successful.[6]

External intervention can create consolidated democracy or put countries on that path, but only if domestic conditions are propitious. Higher levels of wealth, higher Polity scores, and a more homogeneous social landscape make it more likely that a state is in the intermediate category, in which the interests of national elites will be divided between open and closed access.

Efforts to implant or promote consolidated democracy will fail if they are opposed by the local political elite. Both democracy and higher levels of income are hostage to institutions that can maintain an open access order for at least a substantial part of the polity. In polities that are closed access or extractive, members of the political elite will oppose policies that are designed to promote greater accountability or that could change the economy, because such changes could threaten their ability to stay in office. Democracy promotion may be successful in intermediate polities, but as chapter 4 suggests, the number of such polities is limited. Operationally, intermediate polities are likely to be found in an income range between $7,000 and $17,000 per capita. There are not many countries in this range, about thirty-five.

Identifying intermediate polities, where FIRCs might actually contribute to the consolidation of democracy, is a major challenge. Per capita incomes can serve as a first approximate indicator, but an intimate knowledge of elite preferences is also essential. Only by betting on the right elites, those that would prefer an open access order, can external actors hope to use FIRCs to put countries more solidly on the path to full democracy.

A less ambitious objective would be to not engage in regime change at all but rather to bolster the regime in power and to maintain some degree of order and security regardless of regime type, an aspect of good enough governance. This is not the dystopian view in which nothing can be done, but it is not utopian either. Security is a good that external actors can help provide, even in despotic polities—or, at least, in some parts of despotic polities. Maintaining order or at least keeping a regime in power has been much easier than putting a country on a path to consolidated democracy.

External actors will find it difficult to establish their legitimacy if they have engaged in a foreign-imposed regime change.[7] When a polity has been riven by civil strife, individuals fall back on ascriptive groups—family, clan, tribe—because these are the only authority structures in which they have any confidence, so foreign actors will be suspect.[8] If external actors secure any legitimacy at all it will be through the better provision of services, and even then, legitimacy can be easily withdrawn.

External actors might secure output, as opposed to intrinsic legitimacy, if the policies that they support are successful.[9] Success is more likely if interveners stay for a longer period of time; success is impossible if there is opposition from local elites. However, if external actors stay for an extended period of time the performance legitimacy attributed to them might detract from the legitimacy of national actors. Finding the sweet spot, in which improved service delivery achieved primarily through the efforts of external actors is attributed to national actors, will be extremely difficult without intimate knowledge of the political and social environment. More-over, to satisfy their own domestic constituencies, external actors will want to demonstrate successes, and successes are more easily achieved if interveners act unilaterally.

In sum, achieving democratization is extremely difficult for external state-builders. Democratization efforts cannot be success-ful unless they are supported by at least some members of the indigenous elite. In despotic polities, however, accountability and free and fair elections will be antithetical to the interests of indig-enous rent-seeking elites. External actors might be more success-ful if their goals are more modest. The most salient objective of good enough governance is to establish security in a targeted pol-ity. Strengthening security forces in target states will strengthen rather than weaken indigenous rent-seeking elites. Greater secu-rity is an objective they are likely to support; strengthening the institutions of democracy, including free and fair elections, an active civil society, internationally oriented NGOs, and an inde-pendent judiciary, is something that elites in rent-seeking states will oppose.

The Soviet Union and Eastern Europe

In Eastern Europe after the Second World War, the Soviet Union established satellite states dominated by communist regimes whose leaders were beholden to the Soviet Union. This project succeeded from the late 1940s until the late 1980s. As an example of foreign-imposed regime change, the Soviet Union was successful for more than forty years. Democracy was not one of the USSR's objectives.

From the formation of the Soviet Union in 1917 the leadership of the country, the members of the politburo, were "realists in terms of means, though utopians in terms of ends."[10] They viewed themselves, following Marxism-Leninism, as the conduits through which a Marxist teleological vision of history would be realized. Human society, according to Marx, progressed through a series of stages, culminating in communism. Each stage, except the final stage of communism, held both the seeds of its own destruction and the factors that would lead to the next step on the path to a communist utopia.

The Soviets were never reckless. Stalin, for instance, recognized in the late 1940s that the Greek communists would be defeated and did little to help them. The Soviet leadership in the 1960s and 1970s did not support third world movements in any vigorous way. Nevertheless, Marxist ideology made the protection of communist regimes and the promotion of world revolution an imperative. The rationalist fallacy "assumed that the commitment to international revolution was merely a matter of choice for Soviet leaders and in so doing underestimated the very point that Trotsky insisted upon; namely, that however reactionary in preferences, Soviet leaders were driven by the nature of the system to pursue the expansion of the revolution."[11]

At the end of the Second World War the Soviet Union created satellite regimes in Eastern and Central Europe. This project involved foreign-imposed regime change in almost all of the target states.

There were no communist regimes in Eastern or Central Europe before the Second World War. By the late 1940s there were seven: the German Democratic Republic, Czechoslovakia, Poland, Hungary, Romania, Bulgaria, and Yugoslavia. Only one of these, Yugoslavia under Tito, had emerged out of an indigenous resistance movement against the Nazis. Stalin believed that in the medium term the presence of the Soviet army would guarantee a transition to socialism and ultimately communism.[12]

The extent to which the Soviet Union was able to impose its institutional structure on the conquered states of Eastern and Central Europe varied, primarily as a result of the ability of the target state, its population and extant authority structures, to organize and resist Soviet initiatives. In Poland, the Catholic Church and small landowners maintained some autonomy. About 75 percent of the Polish population was agrarian after the First World War. The newly independent Polish government undertook substantial land reform programs in the 1920s, strengthening the position of smallholders.[13] For the Soviet Union, collectivization of agriculture in Poland after the Second World War was too risky, too likely to encounter organized resistance. The Polish communist leadership abandoned collectivization in the mid-1950s because of anxiety about peasant resistance. The communist regime in Yugoslavia abandoned efforts to collectivize agriculture even earlier and for the same reason. The Yugoslav peasants had supported the party. Forced collectivization could have ended this backing.

Although there was variation across the satellite states with regard to the organization of agriculture, property ownership, secret police activism, and levels of repression, all of these countries conformed with the core elements of communism as understood by the Soviet leadership. The economy outside of the agrarian sector was at least formally directed by the state; market exchange was severely restricted. The Communist Party was the key political institution. The secretary general of the party was the most important political actor in the state. Following Leninist dictums, the decisions of the party could not be challenged. Party commissars oversaw activities in all important political, military, and economic sectors. The Soviet Union was able to mirror its own political structure in the satellite states.

The Soviet Union made it clear that it could use force to suppress efforts that threatened communist rule. In June of 1953 there was a revolt against the communist regime in East Germany, which began with workers' riots in Berlin and then spread to several hundred East German cities. The protests were spurred by government demands for higher output and more work hours with no increase in pay. The Soviet leadership acted decisively. A Soviet armored division was sent into East Berlin. The protesters were scattered. Scores were killed. This pattern, using force to prevent changes that were seen as a threat to the communist ruling structure, was repeated in Hungary in 1956 and Czechoslovakia in 1968 and did not end until Gorbachev became the general secretary of the Communist Party of the Soviet Union in 1985.

Repression, including the use of Soviet troops, was essential to maintaining the communist systems in Eastern and Central Europe because disaffection was endemic. The Soviets and their national allies used coercion effectively. "Brutal police and military actions were ordered and performed under the authority of individual states; however, in more serious cases, where the coercive capacity of the party-state was significantly weakened or its willingness to use force against the population was in question, the Soviet military and police forces were promptly employed, as was the case in East Germany in 1953, Hungary in 1956, and Czechoslovakia in 1968. The direct and massive use of the Soviet army in several situations clearly indicated the limited sovereignty of these countries and the imperial nature of Soviet domination in the region."[14]

By 1947 the Soviet Union had completely subjugated Hungary and imposed a Stalinist system. Rákosi, the communist leader, followed Stalinist policies. Noncommunist parties and a free press were eliminated. The bureaucracy was purged. The education system was centrally controlled. Independent churches were suppressed. All companies with more than ten employees were nationalized. In elections in 1949 the Communist Party won more than 95 percent of the vote.[15]

These Stalinist policies, however, had disastrous consequences for the Hungarian economy. Unrest grew. In the same year that Khrushchev condemned Stalinism, 1953, the Soviet Union leadership, anxious about potential unrest in Hungary, pressed their Hungarian counterparts to introduce reforms. These reforms did not prevent the widespread spontaneous uprising that occurred in late 1956.[16] In September 1956 many attendees at the Hungarian writers' convention called for full freedom of expression. In October, demonstrations that included off-duty soldiers called for the withdrawal of Soviet troops. Street demonstrations escalated. Armed groups attacked the main radio station. The Ministry of the Interior was seized.[17]

The new Hungarian leadership had announced Hungary's neutrality and withdrawal from the Warsaw Pact, and appealed for help from the West. The Hungarian leader, Imre Nagy, announced the end of one-party rule on October 30. A new government was formed that included representatives of peasants and smallholders as well as communists.

Allowing these changes would have meant the end of communism in Hungary. For the Soviet leadership this was intolerable. But because Hungarian security forces did not actively resist the revolutionaries, and in some cases just melted away, Soviet troops had to be used to crush the rebellion. Active fighting lasted for several days and unrest continued into early 1957. Nagy was replaced, then executed. The communist regime led by János Kádár was initially entirely dependent on Soviet tanks. Over time, however, Kádár implemented some reforms, but he did not challenge the basic character of the communist system.[18]

The Soviets made the control of the security forces their first priority after the Hungarian uprising, and the Soviet leadership reimposed tight control over the military. "Soviet advisers were allocated down to the level of regiment; the army command structure was revamped and fully integrated into the Warsaw Pact command structure. The reorganized army was more rigidly ruled by Soviet military organs than it had ever been before."[19] Once security was established the Soviets strengthened the party and moved to establish full control over the political and economic authority structures. Social and political organizations outside of the state were brought under party control.[20] The Soviets aimed at the control of force first, and once that was firmly established moved on to other goals; consolidated democracy was not one of their objectives.

The Communist Party enjoyed substantial support in Czechoslovakia after the Second World War. The bourgeois parties had been in power in 1938 when that country committed suicide by accepting Hitler's demands at Munich. After the war the Communist Party in Czechoslovakia did win a plurality of votes in a free and fair election. As opposed to the other satellite states, communism did have indigenous support there.

In the Prague Spring of 1968 the old-line Stalinist leader, Novotný, was replaced by Dubček. Dubček himself did not have a radical reformist agenda but he was not able to control developments. Elements outside of the party pressed for reform. Censorship was ended in March. The National Assembly selected a new president with a secret ballot, an unprecedented step for a communist regime. The Czech leadership was hoping to thread a needle, by keeping the external alliance with the Soviet Union but introducing domestic reforms that would weaken some of the prerogatives of the Communist Party. The proposed changes, however, were unacceptable to the leadership in Moscow despite Czech pledges of loyalty to the Warsaw Pact. In the summer of 1968 party leaders from other communist countries and the Soviet Union criticized the Czech reforms. Warsaw Pact troops massed on the Czech border.[21] "The emergence of the reform movement in Czechoslovakia was viewed as a serious threat to the internal stability of other state-socialist regimes that, like Poland, were experiencing economic difficulties and growing internal dissent among intellectuals and students."[22]

The Soviets began planning for a military invasion of Czechoslovakia as early as February or March 1968, although the final decision to invade was not made until August. In the end the decision to intervene reflected the belief among Soviet decision makers that the regime in Czechoslovakia was unstable and unreliable.[23] On the night of August 21–22, 1968, Warsaw Pact forces invaded Czechoslovakia. It was the largest military operation that had taken place in Europe since the Second World War, initially comprising more than two hundred thousand troops and 6,300 tanks. Casualties were very low.[24] Soviet commanders kept tight control over the Czech military, which was, in any event, deeply enmeshed with the Warsaw Pact. The Czech army, on orders from the Czech government, did not resist the invasion.[25]

Dubček and other reformist leaders were taken to Moscow immediately after the military occupation. There was no widespread popular reaction. When Dubček and his compatriots returned in August and were restored to their previous positions, they urged the population not to actively resist.[26] Opposition continued sporadically into the early months of 1969, but it was weak.

After Czechoslovakia in 1968, the Soviet Union used military force in only one other country, Afghanistan. Unlike their previous interventions in East Germany, Hungary, and Czechoslovakia, the Soviets failed. Force alone was not enough to establish a stable communist regime in Afghanistan. Afghanistan had been riven by internal rivalries for decades. Iran, Pakistan, the United States, and the Soviet Union were all involved with one faction or another. The American ambassador was abducted and then killed in February 1979 in a shootout with the Afghan police. Soviet military advisors and their wives and children were killed in a revolt in Herat in March 1979.

Initially the Soviet leadership refused to send troops into

Afghanistan, given the country's internal rivalries, backwardness, and lack of development. Conventional Marxist analysis did not suggest that communism would succeed in Afghanistan. Different Afghan factions actively tried to influence the Soviet Union.[27]

The loss of communist control of a country, once that control had been established, posed a grave problem for the Soviet leadership. For Marxist ideology, such a reversal was anathema. Marxism is a teleological theory. Should a socialist or communist regime be overthrown, the hollowness of the legitimating myth for the regime in the Soviet Union itself would be manifestly obvious. Thus, even in Afghanistan, the Soviet leadership was acutely concerned about the durability of Afghanistan's communist government.

At the end of 1979, the Soviet Union dispatched troops to Afghanistan in an effort to save the newly established Democratic Republic of Afghanistan. Despite the dramatic differences in location, culture, and level of development, the fundamental challenge for the Soviet leadership was the same as had been the case in Eastern Europe: the danger that a communist regime would be displaced by some other form of government that would be anti-Soviet and noncommunist. The Khalqi government of Afghanistan espoused communist ideology but was riven by internal rivalries, often along tribal lines. This regime was hardly a conventional example of communism, but it was communist nevertheless.

East Germany, Hungary, Czechoslovakia, and Afghanistan are the four examples of the Soviets' use of force to ensure that a communist regime, once established, did not revert back to some kind of capitalist or primitive order. The Soviets were not successful in Afghanistan, where they were never able to identify reliable local actors that had credibility with the Afghan population. But they were very successful elsewhere.

Eastern Europe during the Cold War is an example of the fact that foreign-imposed regime change can work provided that external actors focus on providing the security support that is needed to keep their preferred regime in power. Using force was costly for the

Soviet Union, but not as costly as the loss of communism in Eastern Europe ultimately proved to be.

Moreover, the Soviets were always able to rely on local allies, although the best electoral showing by the communists was in Czechoslovakia in the 1947 elections, where the party got 38 percent of the vote. The communist leaders that came to power in Eastern Europe came from the societies that they governed, including Gottwald in Czechoslovakia, Ulbricht in East Germany, Hoxha in Albania, Rákosi in Hungary, Dimitrov in Bulgaria, and Tito in Yugoslavia. They were not Russians, not outsiders to their own national cultures. The Soviets were able to identify local allies, many of whom had spent at least part of the war in the Soviet Union.

Some of the satellite regimes were able to follow policies that defied some of the preferences of the Soviet leadership, but they did not challenge the primacy of the Communist Party. Communist regimes in Yugoslavia in 1948, Poland in 1956, Romania in 1960, and Albania in 1961 challenged Soviet dictates with regard to foreign policy. In all of these cases, however, the basic structures of the communist system remained intact. Policies might not have conformed perfectly with the preferences of the Soviet leadership, but leaders in Eastern Europe were displaced if they threatened the legitimacy of the communist system itself.

In Poland in the mid-1950s, for instance, there was unrest and disorder. Workers rioted. Władysław Gomułka, a communist who had been secretary of the party from 1943 to 1948 and was then imprisoned in 1951 by hard-line Stalinists, became the prime minister. Gomułka did not threaten communist rule in Poland or suggest that his country would end its ties with the Soviet Union. He did succeed in renegotiating Poland's relationship with the Soviet Union. Efforts to collectivize Polish agriculture ended. Russians were removed from direct positions of authority. Gomułka never, however, challenged the fundamentals of the communist system. The Soviets accepted these changes. The use of force was unnecessary.

Yugoslavia under Tito was always able, to some extent, to go its own way in foreign affairs. Tito became a self-styled leader of the third world. The nonaligned movement was founded in Belgrade in 1961, with Tito as one of its five leaders. The others were Kwame Nkrumah of Ghana, Gamal Nasser of Egypt, Jawaharlal Nehru of India, and Sukarno of Indonesia. Tito had led a successful partisan movement during the Second World War. The Soviet Union and Yugoslavia did not have a contiguous border, making invasion more complicated, although communist satellite states did border Yugoslavia. Tito, however, never questioned or challenged the communist system within Yugoslavia itself.

Nicolae Ceaușescu made Romania a rigidly Stalinist country after he became the country's unchallenged leader in the mid-1960s. But at the same time he defied the Soviet leadership on some international questions. He condemned the invasion of Czechoslovakia. Romania became the first Eastern bloc country to recognize West Germany and join the IMF. Nixon visited Romania in 1969, the first visit by an American president to a Soviet bloc country. Ceaușescu irritated the Soviet leadership but he never challenged the communist system within his own country. The Soviets never used force to bring him to heel.

The Soviet empire collapsed with the end of communism. Nevertheless, during the Cold War the leaders of Russia were able to impose and preserve, through the threat or actual use of force, their preferred regime type in the satellite countries in Eastern Europe. They were able to identify reliable local allies, which they were never able to do in Afghanistan. Communist rulers in Eastern Europe were able to rely on their own repressive apparatuses and the backing of the Russian army to keep themselves in power. Foreign-imposed regime change that focused on maintaining control over the instruments of violence did work in the Soviet bloc in Eastern Europe during the Cold War.

Not only were the Soviets able to maintain communist regimes in Eastern Europe, they also provided security. Internal conflicts were common in the Middle East and North Africa, Asia, and sub-Saharan Africa during the Cold War period. In contrast, in Eastern Europe conflicts within states were virtually absent. With regard to security, foreign-imposed regime change worked in Eastern Europe. Conflict levels in Latin America and the Caribbean, an area where American influence was strong, were lower but hardly trivial.[28]

The satellite states of Eastern Europe also experienced other aspects of good enough governance. Their gross national income more than doubled between 1950 and 1970.[29] Like the Soviet Union, the states of Eastern Europe were able to increase productivity by moving workers from rural to urban areas. Health conditions in the Central European satellite states also improved; life expectancy approached that in high-income OECD countries.[30]

In sum, although the Soviet Union failed in Afghanistan, it did succeed in establishing good enough governance in the satellite states of Eastern Europe, until the Soviet Union itself collapsed. There was security. There was economic growth. Health improved.

The United States during the Cold War

During the Cold War, the record of the United States in installing or supporting regimes that reflected the American model of governance was much more problematic than that of the USSR. Americans had a utopian vision of consolidated democracy; the Soviet vision was much closer to good enough governance. Putting in place political orders that reflected American values and institutions was a much more ambitious project than that of the Soviet Union because the United States favored, at least rhetorically, an open access order in which there was a market economy and consolidated democracy. A consolidated democracy requires checks and balances; a robust civil society; the rule of law, including an independent judiciary; and rational-legal control of the instruments of violence. This is an extremely demanding project and American policy makers, especially during the Cold War, largely settled for the much less demanding goal of keeping in place autocratic rulers that supported the United States or at least did not explicitly support the Soviet Union. Exceptions to this were Japan and a few countries in Western Europe, where the kinds of conditions suggested by modernization theory were propitious (high levels of per capita income, a middle class, some experience with democracy) and where there were local allies in the political elite. After and even during the Cold War the United States usually failed, sometimes spectacularly, as in Vietnam, Afghanistan, and Iraq.

In Italy and France in the late 1940s, American policies and resources frustrated the electoral efforts of communist parties. Absent support for noncommunist political leaders, communists with ties to the Soviet Union might have won elections and dominated governments, especially in Italy. Despite its ambitious rhetoric about promoting democracy, the United States during the Cold War was focused on maintaining, at least nominally, pro-Western leaders rather than on implanting democratic practices.[31]

Germany and Japan

In Japan and Germany the United States was spectacularly successful in supporting a transition to consolidated democracy. Both countries were relatively rich and developed. Autocratic regimes had been discredited by the losses of the Second World War. In both countries the United States found local allies that supported an open access order. In Japan an open access order was the best among a set of bad outcomes that confronted the national elite, including the emperor.

Germany had been at the cutting edge of technology in the Western world from the latter part of the nineteenth century until the Nazi takeover of power, dominating the world's chemical and electrical industries before the First World War.[32] State intervention to promote economic development in Germany had been impressively effective in the nineteenth century.[33]

Japan was the only non-Western power to modernize itself and to successfully resist European and American encroachment in the nineteenth century. In 1905 Japan became the first Asian state to defeat a European power, Russia, in the Russo-Japanese War.

Both Germany and Japan also had some experience with democracy. The Weimar Republic, although torn by internal dissent, including the assassination of the foreign minister Walther Rathenau in 1922 and Hitler's failed Nazi *putsch* in Munich in 1923, was a reasonably functioning democracy from the end of the First World War until the burning of the Reichstag and the Nazi assumption of full power in 1933. Japan has always been formally an imperial system with a hereditary emperor, but there was democratic contestation in the 1920s, ultimately stifled by violence and a wave of assassinations carried out by ultranationalist leaders.

Thus, for reasons suggested by modernization theory, Germany and Japan were unusually well suited to move along the path to consolidated democracy after the Second World War. They were intermediate polities.[34] Of course, the elevated levels of development that both of these countries had enjoyed before the 1930s had not produced a consolidated democratic regime. High per capita income does not automatically lead to democracy.

Both Germany and Japan were devastated in 1945. Hitler had committed suicide along with his wife and children in his bunker in Berlin, declaring that the Germans were not worthy of victory. Berlin and many other major cities in Germany were smoldering piles of rubble. There were fifteen million refugees in Germany at the end of the war, most of them ethnic Germans who had fled the fighting in East Prussia and elsewhere.[35] Hitler's reign had brought death and destruction to Germany and to many individual Germans, not only to Jews. In Japan, 3–4 percent of the prewar population had been killed. Sixty-six major cities had been heavily bombed, including Hiroshima and Nagasaki, which were destroyed by nuclear weapons.

The dark underside of militarism was manifest to ordinary Japanese and Germans after the war. In Japan, the officer corps, the supposed highest reflection of the imperial system, which emphasized racial unity and self-sacrifice, engaged in theft and pillaging while ordinary Japanese, including returning servicemen, starved.[36]

Democratic developments in Germany and Japan can also be explained from a rational choice institutional perspective, which emphasizes the importance of national elites. In both countries, American plans for large-scale and lengthy occupations were quickly shelved because of pressures for demobilization. The Americans wanted to transform the domestic political structures of the defeated Axis powers, but they could not do this by relying on American resources alone. They had to identify national elites with whom they could engage, national elites that would see it as being in their own interests to embrace a vision for their country that at least complemented that of their American conquerors.

American officials had ambitious plans for Japan. Their objective was to transform the country; they wanted to be sure that the Second World War would be Japan's last war. They believed that they could accomplish this by making Japan a genuinely democratic country. They quickly realized, however, that they could not govern without the cooperation of members of the Japanese elite. The first postsurrender directive issued in Japan stated that the United States would work through "Japanese governmental machinery and agencies, including the Emperor, to the extent that this satisfactorily furthers United States objectives."[37] The support of Emperor Hirohito was essential. He was a revered figure in Japan, the supposed living descendant of an unbroken dynasty that was believed, at least by most Japanese, to stretch back beyond recorded history to the sun goddess Amaterasu. Hirohito was the only political leader who had been in a position of power and authority throughout the entire period of Japan's military buildup;

the invasions of Manchuria, China, and Southeast Asia; and the attack on Pearl Harbor. Hirohito could have been tried as a war criminal but doing so could have not only precipitated nationalist resistance but also strengthened the position of leftist and communist groups in Japan.

The Americans had to find a way to separate the emperor from the wartime government if they were to use him for their own purposes. The American occupiers never seriously investigated the emperor's role in the war, and they persuaded Hirohito to neither abdicate nor apologize to the Japanese people.[38] Rather, the Americans represented him as acting under duress. Hirohito remained the head priest of the Shinto religion. After the war, the emperor visited all of the prefectures in Japan with a security detail that was provided by the United States military. He was transformed from a god to a man under American tutelage, but he kept his place as the formal head of the Japanese government and people.[39]

General MacArthur, in particular, cultivated Hirohito's cooperation. In an iconic photograph taken shortly after the American occupation began, MacArthur, six feet tall, in shirtsleeves with an unbuttoned collar, stands to the right of and towers over the five-foot, five-inch emperor, who is dressed in a formal cutaway coat. The message is unmistakable: the Americans are in charge but are working together with Japan's traditional leadership.[40]

The American occupiers also relied on the Ministry of Commerce, reconstituting it as the Ministry of International Trade and Industry (MITI), which played a key role in Japan's postwar economic miracle by encouraging the international competitiveness of Japanese companies and, along with the Ministry of Finance, providing capital for companies that demonstrated their ability to compete in foreign markets.[41]

The number of Japanese convicted of crimes was not large: 5,000 and 700 people, respectively, were accused of Class C (crimes against humanity) and Class B (war crimes); of these, 1,018 were acquitted and another 279 were never brought to trial or never sentenced. About 920 were executed. The Tokyo tribunal for Class A (crimes against peace) criminals sent only 7 people to the gallows. The actual prison terms served by many others were relatively short. The former prime minister, Shigemitsu Mamoru, for instance, was released from prison in 1950 and reentered politics. In 1958, the ten men still in jail were granted clemency.[42]

That the Americans would succeed was hardly a foregone conclusion. Japan experts in the United States, such as Joseph Grew, who had been the ambassador before the war, believed that Japanese cultural values, especially the emphasis on hierarchy, precluded a democratic transformation. But these experts were shunted to the side. American policy was dominated by social scientists and others who were committed to the idea that Japan could be fundamentally changed.

The American occupiers moved to alter many aspects of Japan's society and polity. Within months, the Americans had issued directives breaking up the *zaibatsu* (Japanese corporate conglomerates), requiring land reform, opening the school system, mandating equality for women, and calling for free speech.[43] A small group of Americans, most with no detailed knowledge of Japan, wrote the new constitution and included provisions for equality of women that were introduced by Beate Sirota, the Austrian-born daughter of European parents who had lived in Japan during the 1930s and was one of the few individuals on the American team that was fluent in Japanese. The members of the traditional elite were not sympathetic to American values or aspirations for Japan but were persuaded to accept the new constitution because they feared that any alternative would, for them, be worse.[44]

In sum, in Japan the American occupiers were able to take advantage of a country that was already relatively rich and developed. Rather than replace the existing Japanese elite they appropriated parts of it, most notably the emperor, some industries, and some government ministries. Members of the Japanese elite accepted the conditions of the American occupation, indeed played critical roles in supporting that occupation, because the alternative, a lurch to the left that would have displaced the old elite entirely, looked far more troubling. Japan was a place ideally suited for a utopian American vision; because the indigenous elite was willing to cooperate with the Americans even if they did not share American values, because Japan was relatively well developed, and because traditional values had been delegitimized by the war, Japan was ideally suited to achieve consolidated democracy.

In Germany, initial American plans to keep more than three hundred thousand US troops in the country were quickly dropped because of domestic demands for demobilization. Denazification programs were scaled back. More than 3.5 million people were chargeable under occupation laws covering involvement with the Nazi regime; of these, almost 900,000 were charged by the *Spruch-kammern*, which were run by German officials; and of these, 117,000 were convicted.[45] By 1947 or 1948 the denazification program, which had been viewed as a crucial aspect of the occupation immediately after the war, was seen as being counterproductive.[46] Approximately 6,500 SS members served as guards at Auschwitz; only 29 were tried in West Germany and 20 in East Germany.[47]

As in Japan, the United States could not administer Germany after the war without relying on local officials, some of whom, though not the most prominent figures, had been complicit in the Nazi regime. Unlike in Japan, however, the United States did not try to rehabilitate any of the leaders of the old regime. Hitler had committed suicide. Goering killed himself one day before he was to be hanged. Most other Nazi high officials were sentenced to death. There was no figure like Hirohito who could be resurrected after the war.

The United States, along with Britain and France, allowed elections in the western zone in 1949. Konrad Adenauer was elected as the first chancellor of the German Federal Republic, although the allies retained ultimate authority until 1991. The quasi-sovereign German government moved immediately in 1949 to limit the prosecution of accused Nazis and to facilitate the rehabilitation of those that had already been convicted. As early as 1947 and 1948 the western occupying powers issued limited amnesties. The effort to purge those who had been officials in the Nazi regime ended in 1949 with the election of the first West German government.[48]

The outcome in Germany, primarily as a result of the values and identity that have been embraced by Germans, was even more successful from an American perspective than was the outcome in Japan. Contemporary Germany is a radically different polity than the one that existed before the end of the Second World War. Germany has come to terms with its past much more fully than Japan, a reckoning that has been carried out by Germans themselves. Japanese elites are still divided about responsibility for the Second World War and the way in which the war was conducted. The main Holocaust memorial in Berlin, just south of the Brandenburg Gate, covers a large area; it is highly abstract, consisting primarily of many large but variegated rectangular concrete blocks. There are, however, many more personal and compelling Holocaust memorials scattered throughout Berlin's many neighborhoods, including a transparent wall in Steglitz with the names of Jews who lived in the area before the Second World War; a signpost at the Wittenbergplatz U-Bahn station opposite Berlin's most famous department store, KaDeWe, showing the direction and distance to German concentration camps; and a set of bricks in the platform of the S-Bahn station Grunewald, showing the number and dates of Jews who were deported to the east from that station during the war.

Most of the German population has fully accepted responsibility for Nazism and its genocides. Most Germans have redefined their identity as Europeans. Germany has been a major advocate of the European Union.[49] German leaders have tried to constrain German power in Europe by embedding it in multilateral institutions. German, French, and European flags fly over Verdun, the site of one of the most costly battles of the First World War. At least one of the motivations for Angela Merkel, the long-serving prime minister of

Germany, to so warmly offer Germany as a place for refugees in 2015, for those fleeing civil wars in Syria and other parts of the Middle East, was to show Germany as a humanitarian power, one that had radically broken with its Nazi past.

In contrast, there are no such prominent memorials in Tokyo. The Japanese have come to see themselves as victims of the war. Formally, the Japanese have apologized for forcing Korean women into prostitution during the Second World War, but, informally at least, some Japanese still believe that this was a justifiable policy that contributed to preventing more widespread rape. Right-wing sound trucks have continued to blast away their messages in Tokyo. Among Japan's neighbors, especially South Korea and China, suspicion runs deep.

Japan and Germany are impressive illustrations of the ability of an external actor, in these instances the United States, to impose democracy where before it had only a toehold. Japan and Germany seemed to vindicate America's utopian aspirations. Japan and Germany, however, were relatively rich countries. They both had a significant middle class. In both countries, the United States was able to identify members of the local political elite who were willing to work with the American occupiers. The devastation resulting from the war had delegitimized those who had brought the Axis powers into conflict with the United States and its allies. Germany was an intermediate polity, one in which there were members of the political, social, and economic elite that were committed to an open access order. In Japan most of the traditional elites, including the emperor, had supported the war, but they were willing to lend their status and prestige to the American occupiers. The alternatives, especially the creation of a communist regime, would have been worse for the Japanese elite than the democracy supported by the United States.

IN SUM, ambitious foreign-imposed regime change can work, provided the regime that external actors are trying to create has the support of local elites. It is much easier to create good enough governance, with security and some service provision—the path chosen by the Soviet Union—than to put countries on the path to consolidated democracy. National actors will accept the path to consolidated democracy only if at least some members of the elite see their own interests being furthered by an open access order. This will be the case only in intermediate orders.

The Soviet Union was successful for forty-five years in Eastern and Central Europe. The Soviets were not interested in creating a democratic regime; they were content with communist despotisms. Once communist regimes were in place, the Soviets supported them. They were able to draw on indigenous actors who were committed to communism for either ideological or instrumental reasons. They failed in Afghanistan not only because it was a poor country but also because their local allies could not command domestic support.

Keeping communist regimes in power did not require winning popular support, but it did require an effective security apparatus. After the repression of the Hungarian uprising in 1956, it was evident that the West would not come to the aid of dissidents that took up arms against the Soviet imposition of communist rule. The Soviet army would have preponderant power in the satellite states. The militaries of satellite states could not operate independently. With the Soviet military as the final arbitrator, local forces, both police and military, could maintain communist regimes in power. In this aspect of good enough governance and in others, including the provision of some services such as health and education, the Soviet Union was successful in Eastern and Central Europe.

The United States did help to create democratic regimes in Germany and Japan, the two Axis countries that were defeated and devastated by the war. Democracy was an ambitious goal. This achievement was fully consistent with the utopian vision that consolidated democracy could exist anywhere. The creation of democratic regimes in the conquered Axis powers is consistent with both modernization theory and rational choice institutionalism. Germany and Japan were relatively rich countries before the war. They had both had some experience with democracy in the interwar period. But experiences in Germany and Japan are also consistent with rational choice institutionalism. The United States secured the support of some parts of the indigenous elites. This effort was particularly striking in Japan, where the Americans rehabilitated the emperor, relied on key prewar ministries, and, while formally breaking up the prewar *zaibatsu*, essentially allowed Japan's industrial organizations to persist after the war. Once the formal peace treaty was signed in 1951, Japanese companies again coalesced into *keiretsu*, which allowed coordination through joint stock ownership and other mechanisms. In Germany, the top echelons of the Nazi regime were too discredited to rely on and either committed suicide or were tried at Nuremberg and hanged. The United States did, however, rely on Germans, such as Konrad Adenauer, who had managed to avoid any close association with the Nazi regime. By the late 1940s the Americans were focused on opposing communism, not denazification. In Germany, as in Japan, the Americans were able to find members of the local elite (Adenauer had been mayor of Cologne during the Weimer Republic) on whom they could build a new democratic regime. The circumstances that allowed the Americans to be successful in Germany and Japan were not, as will be evident in the next chapter, replicated in many other areas of the world.

CHAPTER 9

What Happened in Afghanistan and Iraq?

ON 9/11, I WAS IN MY OFFICE AT THE POLICY PLANNING BUREAU of the State Department. I had arrived a couple of weeks earlier. I was hoping that a stint in Washington would give me a different perspective on topics that I had been studying as an academic for most of my life. Neither I nor my colleagues expected the administration of George W. Bush to focus on foreign policy. These expectations changed on September 11, 2001.

The staff at the State Department was dismissed within a couple of hours of the attack. I was commuting by bicycle and took the short ride over to the Potomac. Smoke was rising from the Pentagon on the other side of that river. Memorial Bridge was already closed. I encountered one other person on the river overlook. He might have been in the military. And his comment was completely Jacksonian. He said something to the effect of "Now we are really going to kick some ass."

The response of the administration was, however, very different. The president and some of his close associates were determined to put Afghanistan and Iraq on the path to Denmark. Very utopian. They believed that transnational terrorism could not be dealt with unless the root causes of violent actions were addressed and they identified these root causes with repressive regimes in parts of the

Islamic world. Many officials in the Bush administration, although not all, deeply believed in this policy prescription.

In Afghanistan and Iraq, however, democracy or even the path to consolidated democracy was not a realistic objective. If Germany and Japan are one bookend, along a success-to-failure continuum of American efforts to impose consolidated democratic regimes on other states through the use of force, Afghanistan and Iraq are the other. Foreign-imposed regime change occurred in Germany and Japan at the beginning of the Cold War. The efforts in Afghanistan and Iraq began more than a decade after the Soviet Union had collapsed. On every dimension, and from every theoretical perspective, Germany and Japan were countries in which the United States was likely to be successful, and Afghanistan and Iraq were countries where the United States was likely to fail. Neither modernization theory nor rational choice institutionalism would suggest that Afghanistan and Iraq were likely to become consolidated democracies or to find the path to Denmark.

Afghanistan and Iraq were as problematic for consolidated democracy as Germany and Japan were propitious. Both countries were poor—in the case of Afghanistan, very poor. Afghanistan's per capita income in 2004, the earliest date for which World Bank figures are available, was $240. Iraq's per capita income in 2006 (again the earliest date for which World Bank figures are available) was $2,040.[1] The institutional capacity of both states had been gutted, in Afghanistan's case through years of civil war, in Iraq's case through Saddam Hussein's dismantlement of any institutions that might challenge his rule, and in both cases by the misguided policies of the United States. Both countries were more than familiar with despotic rule.

In both Afghanistan and Iraq, the United States began with the ambitious objective of putting both of these countries on a path that would lead to consolidated democracy. The administration of George W. Bush was committed to this objective. Recent history, especially the collapse of the Soviet Union and the evolution of Eastern and Central Europe from Soviet satellite states to membership in NATO and the European Union, seemed to confirm this optimistic assessment. The president did not believe that democracy and democratic values were, as he put it after he left office, the exclusive preserve of white Methodists. The academic finding that democracies did not fight among themselves was widely known by key officials. A democratic Iraq would, they believed, transform domestic regimes in the Middle East, including the country that was a mortal enemy of the United States and with which Iraq had fought a painful war for a decade, Iran. The first paragraph of President Bush's preface to the 2002 *National Security Strategy of the United States of America* reads as follows:

> The great struggles of the twentieth century between liberty and totalitarianism ended with a decisive victory for the forces of freedom—and a single sustainable model for national success: freedom, democracy, and free enterprise. In the twenty-first century, only nations that share a commitment to protecting basic human rights and guaranteeing political and economic freedom will be able to unleash the potential of their people and assure their future prosperity. People everywhere want to be able to speak freely; choose who will govern them; worship as they please; educate their children—male and female; own property; and enjoy the benefits of their labor. These values of freedom are right and true for every person, in every society—and the duty of protecting these values against their enemies is the common calling of freedom-loving people across the globe and across the ages.[2]

In reality, the number of national elites in Afghanistan and Iraq with whom the United States might align itself, or whose interests might have been complementary to those of American leaders, was vanishingly small. Afghanistan was and is basically a tribal country. The dominant ethnic group is Pashtun, and anyone who has sat in a room with a group of tribal leaders, as I have, could not fail to recognize two things: first, the physical characteristics of these individuals are striking, including, for many, green eyes that can probably be traced back to the soldiers of Alexander the Great, who conquered parts of Afghanistan in the third century BC; and second, language issues aside, the life experiences, norms, and values of these traditional leaders were completely different from those of any Westerner. The Pashtuns, in particular, are guided by Pashtunwali, a system of internalized norms that rests on proportionate revenge mitigated by the possibility for negotiation and hospitality. The Pashtuns have maintained their independence not only because of the rugged mountainous territory in which they live but also because of their essentially stateless legal system.[3]

In Iraq, the Coalition Provisional Authority under Paul Bremer dismantled what was left of the Iraqi civil service and military. If there was a Hirohito in Iraq or even an effective minister of the economy he was delegitimized by Bremer's decision.

Iraq was complicated, or at least difficult for Americans to understand. It was not a Western country. Most American officials were unfamiliar with its mixture of tribes; its Islamic sects, notably Sunni and Shia; and its ethnic and language divisions, including the Kurds in the North who, thanks in large part to American airpower, were able to govern themselves with little interference from Baghdad. Nevertheless, a modernization theory approach would have held out some hope, if only because the country had some pockets of prosperity thanks to oil and because, compared to other developing countries, it was relatively well educated. A rational choice perspective, in contrast, would have suggested that the first objective of the occupation should have been to identify potential allies among the Iraqi population, recognizing that the individuals who might share American values and command support within Iraq might be a null set.

The American administration instead relied on exiles like Ahmed Chalabi, who had fled Iraq in 1958 and did not return until after the American invasion. These individuals were familiar with the West and usually spoke fluent English. They could tell the Americans what the Americans wanted to hear. At a meeting of the Council on Foreign Relations in Washington, DC, before the American invasion of Iraq, a prominent neoconservative closely aligned with the Bush administration unabashedly sang the praises of Chalabi and his associates. To have any chance of being effective, a rational choice institutional approach suggests, the United States should have tried to replicate the practices that had been so successful in Germany and Japan after the Second World War and identified individuals, even individuals whose past behavior had been highly problematic, whose interests after the invasion might have complemented those of the United States.

There would have been no guarantee that the American occupiers could identify the individuals that might help them. Moreover, the best that could have been hoped for would be good enough governance, not consolidated democracy. The American occupiers, however, tacitly relied on modernization theory, which suggested that Iraq, with its substantial (if only in absolute numbers) middle class, would embrace and defend democracy; they did not attempt to identify potential local allies who might have supported some American reform efforts even though they would have fallen short of consolidated democracy. The best became the enemy of the good. There was something in between the utopian vision of consolidated democracy and the dystopian view that nothing could be done, but American policy makers were not searching for this middle ground.

The results of American efforts at foreign-imposed regime change have been unfortunate in both Afghanistan and Iraq. By hoping to accomplish too much, and by relying too heavily on the appeal of democracy, the Bush administration destabilized both countries and strengthened the position of Iran in the Middle East. By failing to see the possibilities for good enough governance in Afghanistan and Iraq, the Obama administration did too little.

The Trump administration has no strategy at all. Good enough governance would have furthered the interests of the United States and the peoples of those two troubled countries.

Problematic Outcomes: Afghanistan

Governing Afghanistan has always been a challenge for external actors, and for internal actors as well, for that matter, who sought to establish a strong central government. During the nineteenth century the British were able to maintain control over Afghanistan's external affairs, but not the country's internal affairs.

In Afghanistan, the Americans began with unlimited ambitions but limited resources. President Bush and some of his closest advisors wanted to transform the country. The secretary of defense, Donald Rumsfeld, and the vice-president, Richard Cheney, had less ambitious goals. They wanted to focus on American national security and destroying al-Qaeda. The only way to square the circle of constrained resources and aspirational goals was to believe that if the yoke of oppression were removed, Afghanis would be committed to an open and democratic polity. This proved to be a hollow expectation. The utopian vision could not be sustained.

The dramatic American victory following 9/11 provided a false sense of optimism that the United States could not only prevail in but also transform Afghanistan. An international agreement, quickly concluded at Bonn in December of 2001, provided for the establishment of an interim Afghan authority headed by Hamid Karzai (who was elected president in 2004) and the convening of, first, an Emergency Loya Jirga and, then, a Constitutional Loya Jirga that would determine permanent institutions. The Bonn agreement was signed by most of the major figures in the Northern Alliance, which had opposed the Taliban and al-Qaeda and fought with the United States, and by Lakhdar Brahimi as the special representative of the secretary general of the United Nations for Afghanistan.

The language of the agreement called for free and fair elections, an impartial judiciary, an independent civil service commission, an autonomous human rights commission, and cooperation with the international community in the fight against drugs, terrorism, and organized crime; it also noted that the interim agreement was "intended as a first step toward the establishment of a broad-based, gender-sensitive, multiethnic and fully representative government." This agreement could only have warmed the hearts of those who expected Afghanistan to put itself on the path to consolidated democracy. The agreement called for the participation of women and for the equitable representation of all ethnic groups and religious communities. Article 4 of the agreement states that "the Emergency Loya Jirga shall decide on a Transitional Authority, including a broad-based transitional administration, to lead Afghanistan until such time as a fully representative government can be elected through free and fair elections to be held no later than two years from the date of the convening of the Emergency Loya Jirga."[4]

The Bonn agreement and its immediate aftermath were not the first steps on the road to consolidated democracy but more a high-water mark of the American effort to achieve this laudable goal. Virtually everything deteriorated quickly. The Afghan elite was riven by internal rivalries. The Pashtuns, in a government led by Hamid Karzai, never reconciled with the minority groups that had joined together in the Northern Alliance. Cooperation, where it occurred, was no more than a marriage of convenience. Karzai was able to accrue power because as head of the government he had access to foreign assistance, which provided most of the government's resources. Politics were dominated by oligarchs and clans through patronage networks that primarily benefited a narrow elite, including various warlords.[5] The Taliban filled vacuums created by the absence of central authority. Pakistan played a double game from the beginning, providing the Taliban with a safe base of operations while allowing the United States to ship military equipment through the country in exchange for large payments. Afghan government ineffectiveness would have been enough to doom American efforts to democratize the country. Pakistani involvement made the problem insoluble.

In the first year of the occupation, the United States consciously adopted a light footprint in Afghanistan. This tactic was supported by Afghan leaders and by the very experienced special representative of the secretary general of the UN, Lakhdar Brahimi. This approach failed. The Afghan national government was unable to provide basic services, including security, in many parts of the country. The vacuum left by Kabul's poor governance fueled the insurgency and support for the Taliban.[6]

Although it was clear to the highest officials in the Bush administration by the beginning of his second term that the goals of the administration would be harder to reach than was originally thought, democracy promotion remained a prominent feature of American policy. The performance management plan adopted by USAID for Afghanistan in May of 2006, for instance, still had very ambitious objectives. The plan stated that "the strategy aimed to support the rapid transition of Afghanistan to a more stable and productive state through the promotion of democracy, rule of law, and sustainable economic and social development responsive to citizens' needs."[7]

In Afghanistan, the temptations from illicit and rent-seeking activities were difficult to resist for both farmers and members of the elite. The production of poppies used to make opium remained an important source of income for farmers in many parts of the country. Poppy production increased under American occupation. The financial returns to the narcotics trade were largely appropriated by middlemen rather than the farmers themselves, but the farmers still made more money than they could make growing other crops. These middlemen needed, at a minimum, cover from the state if they were not themselves part of the state.

On my first visit to Afghanistan as a government official in 2005

I had a breakfast meeting with some mid-level Afghan officials to discuss the illicit narcotics trade. All of the people that I met with were completely insistent that they were utterly opposed to drugs. They offered to an American official what they thought an American official would want to hear, although the message was not delivered in a credible way.

The value of illicit drugs was too great, in a basically closed access rent-seeking economy, for external actors to effectively control. The importance of illicit drugs did fall after the US-led invasion. In the southern areas of the country, however, where much of the poppy was grown, the income of poppy-growing farmers was almost twice that of non-poppy-growing farmers in 2006. From 2003 to 2009 the number of people involved in poppy cultivation and trade increased from 1.2 million to 1.8 million. Narcotics remained a major source of economic activity in Afghanistan, despite American counternarcotics expenditures of several hundred million dollars.[8] A UN report that appeared in late 2013 stated that the amount of acreage being used for poppy cultivation had reached an all-time high in that year. Between 2005 and 2014 poppy cultivation more or less doubled in Afghanistan. Between 2015 and 2016 the number of hectares committed to poppy production increased by 10 percent.[9]

Major drug dealers were able to bribe their way out of jail even if they were arrested. Haji Lal Jan Ishaqzai was on the US list of major drug kingpins. He was arrested in 2012 by the antinarcotics police force that had been established with American assistance, after his protector, the governor of Kandahar Province, Ahmed Wali Karzai, the half brother of the president, was assassinated in 2011. Ishaqzai, however, bribed his way out of jail, reportedly for as much as $14 million. The release was covered over by appropriate paperwork signed by as many as ten Afghan judges. Ishaqzai had been transferred from a prison in Kabul to a smaller facility in Kandahar under orders from the interior minister and a judge of the supreme court. After bribing his way out of jail he fled to Pakistan. Even if the figure was far less than $14 million, the sum is astronomical in the Afghan context.[10] The *New York Times* quoted one unnamed Western official as saying, "We have failed, we have lost—that's all there is to it."[11]

Not only did coalition efforts to end the illicit drug trade fail but these programs almost certainly undermined efforts to weaken the Taliban. The local populations resented eradication programs. There was no other crop that could provide farmers with the same level of income as poppy. Eradication efforts produced economic refugees who supported the Taliban in either Afghanistan or Pakistan. The Taliban was able to mobilize backing from farmers who saw their livelihood threatened by the Kabul government's or local elites' support for eradication efforts, support driven by pressure from the United States and its allies. The incentive for the local population to provide intelligence to coalition forces was undermined when these forces supported programs to kill off poppy production. Recognizing the negative impact of the counternarcotics campaign, the Obama administration defunded these activities in 2009.[12]

The narcotics trade was only one example of the persistence of corruption in Afghanistan despite the billions of dollars that were ultimately spent by the United States and others to put in place a more accountable, open government. The highest officials in the Kabul Bank looted almost $900 million from that institution, equal to about 5 percent of Afghanistan's economic output, much of which went to individuals closely associated with President Karzai and his vice-president, Muhammed Qasim Fahim. The bank took in money, much of it originating from foreign donors, and skimmed the proceeds through fraudulent loans and kickbacks. More than $800 million, equal to about 5 percent of the national output of Afghanistan, had gone to just nineteen individuals and firms. Loans were made to fictitious companies. Expensive villas were purchased in Dubai. Brothers of the president and vice-president, who benefited handsomely from the scheme, were never charged with any crime. Afghan bank regulators who moved against the bank were themselves prosecuted. Karzai's inner circle constructed the list of those to be tried. The full scope of the corruption was revealed only because the president of the bank in 2010, Sherkhan Farnood, was enmeshed in a dispute with other Afghanis over control of the bank. He found revenge more attractive than silence and spoke with investigators from the United States. Some honest Afghan officials, bank regulators in particular, were, at the insistence of individuals close to the president, sentenced to jail and fined. Siblings of the president and vice-president, who stole millions, were never prosecuted.[13]

Less prominent but equally disheartening has been the fate of a lapis lazuli mine in Badakhshan Province. The contract to develop the mine was initially awarded to an Afghan family that had been involved in the lapis business for generations. Within a month of being awarded the contract, the family lost control of the business to a local militia leader who was supported by members of the ruling elite in Kabul. Eventually the proceeds from the mine were split with the Taliban, giving it a strong foothold in an area where it had previously had little presence. The new president, Ashraf Ghani, at least initially gave no support to the formal owners of the mine, perhaps showing the limitations of even a political leader whose intentions are much more complementary to those of foreign donors.[14]

Afghanistan ranked 172 out of 180 countries in Transparency International's 2018 survey.[15] Half of all Afghanis report paying bribes in 2015. The percentage of Afghanis who view corruption as a serious problem increased from 42 percent in 2006 to 62 percent in 2014. Survey results identify judges as a particularly corrupt category of officials. A 2008 law required that high Afghan officials reveal their assets to the High Office on Oversight; few complied, and even when some did, their reports were not verified.[16]

American efforts to wipe out corruption in Afghanistan have been doomed to fail. Afghanistan is a basically closed access, rent-seeking state. Corruption is a mechanism to enhance personal wealth and to stay in power. Rather than attempting to entirely eliminate corruption, American and coalition efforts might have been more effective if they were focused on making clientelism and patronage rather than gross mogul theft the most significant kind of corruption. This would have meant accepting corruption that benefited at least part of the population and attempting to eliminate corruption that enriched only the few at the top, as was the case for the Kabul Bank scandal.

Corruption is only one indicator of how badly the American effort has failed in Afghanistan. The United States always needed Karzai too much. To maintain his own power, Karzai had to cater to his own domestic constituents. He believed that the Americans needed him as much as he needed the Americans, perhaps more. In March of 2014 Karzai essentially recognized the Russian annexation of Crimea, perhaps to show his independence, perhaps because Russian annexation of an area with many Russian speakers resonated with Afghan aspirations to incorporate the Pashtun population allocated to Pakistan by the Durand Line. Still, the Afghan president's acceptance of a policy that had been roundly condemned by the United States was an indication of how little control the United States had over Karzai.[17] Ashraf Ghani, who succeeded Karzai, may be more responsive or may simply care more about the debilitating impact of corruption, but he is enmeshed in a closed access order that makes the elimination of corruption impossible.

By the end of 2015 the Taliban held more territory than at any time since the American invasion in 2001. In May 2017 radical Islamists killed 150 people in a bomb attack in Kabul. In November of 2017 they seized an area in northwestern Afghanistan. Planning for attacks against the United States continued in Afghanistan. In 2018 civilian casualties in Afghanistan were at or near record levels.[18]

The various strategies that have been used by the United States—perhaps better thought of as tactics that sometimes summed up into strategies—have all failed. The light footprint but heady ambitions of the early years of the intervention was followed by more modest goals but a larger commitment of civilian resources and foreign aid and then by the military surge that was authorized by President Obama in 2010 and informed by the counterinsurgency (COIN) doctrine. President Trump has offered no coherent policy.

COIN, which became the reigning orthodoxy for the United States, had many elements of good enough governance but was still excessively ambitious. Under Obama, the COIN doctrine, articulated in Army Field Manual (FM) 3-24, published in December of 2006, became the reference point for how to move forward in Afghanistan.[19] General Stanley McChrystal, a strong proponent of COIN, was appointed as the commander in Afghanistan but had to resign in July 2010 because of intemperate comments made by his staff at what they thought was an off-the-record occasion in Paris. McChrystal was replaced by General David Petraeus, the principal author of FM 3-24. COIN maintained that the civilian population be provided with security, the enemy degraded, and the government accepted as legitimate by most of the "uncommitted middle" of the population. "The primary objective of any COIN operation is to foster development of effective governance by a legitimate government." Legitimacy, the manual goes on to argue, depends on "the ability to provide security for the populace (including protection from internal and external threats)," the "selection of leaders at a frequency and in a manner considered just and fair by a substantial majority of the populace," a "high level of popular participation in or support for political processes," a "culturally acceptable level of corruption," a "culturally acceptable level and rate of political, economic, and social development," and a "high level of regime acceptance by major social institutions."[20]

Governments, the manual argues, do not have to score high on all of these indicators, but they do have to provide security, which is a necessary condition for moving forward on other dimensions. Moreover, the manual goes on to state that "the presence of the rule of law is a major factor in assuring voluntary acceptance of a government's authority and therefore its legitimacy. A government's respect for preexisting and impersonal legal rules can provide the key to gaining it widespread, enduring societal support. Such government respect for rules—ideally ones recorded in a constitution and in laws adopted through a credible, democratic process—is the essence of the rule of law."[21] For counterinsurgency to be successful the host nation has to be regarded as legitimate, and for the host nation to be regarded as legitimate it has to provide good governance.[22]

Thus, while put in very different language from the Bush administration's focus on democracy, COIN offered a very similar set of policy prescriptions. Where COIN did differ was in its focus on the need for long-term commitment, local knowledge, and intelligence, all of which are necessary, the manual argued, to overcome the insurgents' inherent advantage conveyed by their knowledge of local conditions.

COIN failed. It was too ambitious, both in its objectives and in its demands on American forces, civilian and, especially, military. The Americans charged with implementing COIN, often young officers operating at the village level, had neither the background nor the time to acquire intimate knowledge of local conditions, despite their often very impressive personal characteristics. They were usually deployed for one year, not enough time to understand the intricacies of Afghan society or the individuals they were interacting with. Some initiatives, such as female-engagement teams—American female troops charged with engaging Afghan women—were painfully naïve, reminiscent of early efforts in Iraq such as the expectation that a modern stock exchange could be created with a little advice from twentysomethings and some new electronic equipment.

A deeper problem, however, was that the top leadership in Afghanistan had no incentive to implement the COIN strategy. President Karzai ostensibly thought that the basic premises of the American effort were incorrect. He said that the insurgency was a product of Pakistani extremism, not the failings of his own government. The successful implementation of COIN—instituting the rule of law, reducing corruption, increasing transparency—would have undermined the ability of the political elites, including Karzai, to engage in personal plunder or to pay off their key supporters.[23] Although somewhat more modest in its immediate ambitions than consolidated democratization, COIN suffered from the same fundamental flaw: its successful implementation would have undermined the position of political elites in the host state whose cooperation was essential if the strategy was to succeed.

President Obama's objectives in Afghanistan were much more focused on defeating al-Qaeda and terrorist threats to the United States than on regime transformation in Afghanistan and Iraq. In his December 2009 speech at West Point he noted that on coming to office he "then announced a strategy recognizing the fundamental connection between our war effort in Afghanistan and the extremist safe havens in Pakistan. I set a goal that was narrowly defined as disrupting, dismantling, and defeating al-Qaeda and its extremist allies, and pledged to better coordinate our military and civilian efforts."[24] Under Obama, US foreign assistance programs focused more on capacity building than on democratization. USAID's performance plan for Afghanistan for the time period was focused much more on specific objectives, including improved government accountability, improved health, better education, a more welcoming climate for business, better infrastructure, and greater security.[25]

A major rationale for a departure of the Americans and their allies, which was one of Obama's primary objectives, was the ability of the Afghan National Army to assume responsibility for security. In every visit that I made to Afghanistan while I was in the government from 2005 to 2007, before Obama assumed office, I was briefed by a flag-rank officer on the progress that was being made in training the Afghan National Army.

At the end of Obama's second term, the American military concentrated on creating national capacity to maintain domestic order and cooperate with the United States on countering transnational terrorism. US forces emphasized programs that were designed to increase the competence of the Afghan National Army. The small number of American troops remaining in the country would emphasize training and support of Afghanis, not combat. The International Security Assistance Force (ISAF) mission led by the United States was very clear about the essential functions that would have to be carried out by Afghan security forces. These included planning, programming, budgeting, and execution (PPBE); transparency, accountability, and oversight (TAO); civilian governance of the ASI, including adherence to the rule of law (RoL); sufficient intelligence capabilities; and strategic communication (STRAT COMM). These are classic institutional capacity objectives. This emphasis on the competence of the Afghan army, at least implicitly, reflected an institutional capacity understanding of how development could take place. The tacit assumption was that an island of excellence could be created in the Afghan military through training by American forces.

The American military was not, however, naïve about the impediments to instantiating these functions in their Afghan counterparts. A December 2014 ISAF command brief noted the challenges posed by disagreements among leaders within the new government, relations between Afghanistan and Pakistan, corruption, nepotism, narcotics, and dependence on foreign assistance.[26]

The focus on training a competent Afghan military reflected the resources available to the Department of Defense. Training foreign militaries, including providing foreign officers' training in US military centers, such as the Army War College, and even in the service academies, is something that the American military knows how to do. While the American military is very well prepared to train foreign forces, it cannot create a relationship between security forces and civilian authorities. It is much easier to train an individual, even a poorly educated individual, to shoot a weapon than it is to create a set of common purposes across a government.

In Helmand Province, Mazar-e Sharif, and elsewhere, American-trained Afghan forces—with more men and more firepower than their Taliban opponents—melted away when they came under attack. Near the end of Obama's presidency several hundred Taliban forces captured Kunduz, a major city in the North; about seven thousand Afghan government troops fled. The city was retaken only with the assistance of American air strikes and special forces.[27]

Troops have to be willing to die, and many Afghan troops are not willing to die for the government in Kabul. American efforts to build a competent state in Afghanistan, much less to put the country confidently on the road to consolidated democracy, have failed. Almost all American policy initiatives have been implicitly informed principally by modernization or institutional capacity approaches. American leaders have assumed that all countries could become just like America. COIN, with its emphasis on gaining the support of local elites, was perhaps closest to rational choice institutionalism, but COIN had no plan for how the incentives of officials in the central government in Kabul under Karzai might be altered to make these officials more responsive to a broader segment of the population. In fact, the explicit objectives of COIN were inconsistent with the interests of the political elite in any closed access order.

In President Ghani's first year in office the Taliban gained ground in many parts of the country, including areas in the North from which they had previously been excluded. President Obama, who clearly wanted to end American involvement in Afghanistan, had to announce that eight thousand Americans would remain in the country. Jeffrey Goldberg wrote in the March 2016 issue of the *Atlantic*, based on numerous interviews with President Obama, that "Obama generally does not believe a president should place American soldiers at great risk in order to prevent humanitarian disasters, unless those disasters pose a direct security threat to the United States."[28] Complete withdrawal would have risked a Taliban takeover.

In Afghanistan the Taliban continued to exert influence in many parts of the country more than a decade after the American intervention. Relations between American officials and Hamid Karzai, the president from 2001 to 2014, were strained, if not poisonous, by the end of his term in office. In a November 2009 classified cable the American ambassador in Afghanistan, Karl Eikenberry, described Karzai as "not an adequate strategic partner," as someone who shunned "responsibility for any sovereign burden whether defense, governance, or development."[29]

Ashraf Ghani, who took office in 2014, was a more promising partner for the United States. Ghani had a PhD from Columbia University. He had worked for the World Bank for many years. His children had graduated from elite universities in the United States. His wife, a Lebanese, had attended the American University in Beirut. Ghani offered much more than just language skills.

Ghani, however, became president of a very poor country. In 2015 the per capita income in current US dollars was just under $600.[30] The warlords and other leaders on whom Ghani depended relied on rent-seeking practices and closed institutions to maintain their own bases of domestic political support. Ghani's first vice-president, Abdul Rashid Dostum, an Uzbek warlord from the North, had been accused of human rights violations. In early 2017 nine members of his security guard were accused of kidnapping and sodomizing with a rifle one of Dostum's political rivals.[31]

Ghani needed Uzbek votes, and Dostum could deliver them. Ghani's election was contested and he assumed the presidency only after a brokered deal with his major rival, Abdullah Abdullah. The American secretary of state, John Kerry, did the brokering.

Rational choice institutional perspectives suggest that Ghani would be a more effective partner for the United States, since he lives in both the modern, open access West and the traditional, closed access Afghan political environment. Before Ghani became president he explained how, as Karzai's representative for the 2014 transition, he had been able to visit every area of Afghanistan with a limited security guard. Ghani said that he was safe because if any warlord killed him that warlord would be involved in a feud with Ghani's clan for decades. Ghani is truly a man of both worlds, the modern World Bank West and traditional Afghanistan, and the modern West does give him options that were not available to his predecessor.

Basic conditions in Afghanistan, however, did not change just because Ghani became president. The country is desperately poor and dependent on foreign aid. Modern institutions remain fragile. Most members of the Afghan elite stay in power because they can exercise despotic or arbitrary power. After leaving the presidency Karzai did not go quietly into the night. His ties with leaders in Afghanistan remained strong. He criticized American policy. In an interview with the *New York Times* in the summer of 2016 he stated that "the Americans, whose primary slogan is democracy, are making a sham of democracy in Afghanistan." After the United States used the most powerful nonnuclear bomb in its arsenal against an Islamic State cave complex in Afghanistan, Karzai accused his successor of being a traitor. While Ghani has consistently supported changes that would move Afghanistan along a path with less corruption and more effective state institutions, he is only one part of the Afghan system.[32]

Neither modernization theory nor institutional capacity approaches can provide policies that might be promising in the Afghan environment. Rational choice institutionalism suggests that there are at least some deals that Ghani would find attractive, if only because he would be more risk acceptant, given the option of an alternative future in, say, a suburb of Washington, DC. There is, however, no way in which Afghanistan can be put on the road to consolidated democracy.

Before Ghani came to power, American options were limited and unattractive. Even good enough governance was not a realistic option. Despite the American and later NATO invasions and substantial resources targeted at creating a more honest and

accountable government, corruption remained rampant throughout the country. According to World Bank figures, corruption
became marginally worse from 2002 to 2011, hardly a surprising
outcome from a rational choice institutional perspective: foreign
assistance was just one more source of funds that Karzai and his
associates could pillage. Government effectiveness, voice, and
accountability improved only marginally in the same period.[33] In
2017 Afghanistan rated in the lowest 5 percent among all countries
in the Transparency International Corruption Perceptions Index.[34]

Social indicators were not quite so bleak: Life expectancy
increased from 45.6 years to 48.7 years from 2001 to 2011, and
increased further to 63.7 years by 2016. Per capita income, while
still below $400 in 2011, had grown by one-third from 2002, and
grew to $610 by 2017. Immunization rates for the measles vaccine
increased to 62 percent in 2016, below the world average but way
above the 11 percent that it had been in 1980.[35]

The successes in Afghanistan under Karzai involved social services that did not threaten the rent-seeking opportunities of the
political elite. The Ministry of Health provided basic health services. The number of health-care facilities in the country more
than doubled from 2002 to 2007. The number of outpatient visits
increased 400 percent from 2004 to 2007. The Ministry of Health
achieved these improvements by contracting services out to NGOs
and monitoring the results. External actors were able to improve
health-related service provision for at least some specific services.[36]
However, even in the health arena, successes were limited. Afghanistan has the highest under-five mortality rate in Asia, and many
children, especially in contested areas of the country, notably the
South, were malnourished.[37]

A second area in which the government functioned more or
less effectively, even under Karzai, was in the provision of services
through local government councils. The National Solidarity Program started in 2003. Ashraf Ghani was a moving force behind
the creation of this program. It operated in all thirty-four prov-

inces and in 361 districts within these provinces. The program supported more than fifty thousand development projects that were selected by community development councils. Formally, the members of these councils had to reflect gender balance; in practice this was generally but not always the case.[38] More than six thousand latrines were improved, and more than 171,000 hectares were provided with irrigation and drainage ditches.[39]

This National Solidarity Program had substantial input from external actors, who not only provided funding but also constructed, implemented, and reported on specific activities. The German Development Agency, GIZ (Deutsche Gesellschaft für Internationale Zusammenarbeit), helped to manage the allocation of funds that came from the multidonor Afghanistan Reconstruction Trust Fund. NGOs, such as the Aga Khan Foundation, BRAC, CARE, Oxfam, and the International Rescue Committee, were involved in convening meetings, working with villagers to determine priorities, and providing technical assistance for writing proposals and reporting on outcomes. The National Solidarity Program councils sometimes found that their work was undermined or sidelined by Provincial Reconstruction Teams (PRTs), civilian-military units staffed by ISAF countries, which could often pump money much more quickly and in larger amounts into local villages. World Bank forms were often so complicated that they had to be filled out by international facilitators rather than villagers; the capacity of local actors did not necessarily grow. It was difficult for the National Solidarity Program to work in insecure areas, especially after the Taliban stepped up attacks in 2006. One World Bank report found that while the National Solidarity Program did well in providing specific projects, it did not have a lasting impact. The structure of the program, with its focus on community councils and grants made directly to villages, was in tension with the Afghan government itself, which was organized in a highly centralized way.[40] The National Solidarity Program could function effectively only so long as it did not threaten political leaders in Kabul.

A third area that has experienced some success in Afghanistan has been the Ministry of Finance. Ashraf Ghani was the first minister of finance. He was interested in creating a well-functioning bureaucracy. The Open Budget Index score for Afghanistan went from 8 in 2008 (earlier figures are not available online) to 21 in 2010, rose to 59 in 2012, and then fell to 49 in 2017. The scale for the index ranges from 0 to 100. In 2008 Afghanistan was bracketed in the ratings by Bolivia, the Kyrgyz Republic, Yemen, Vietnam, and Chad—poor company; in 2012 it was bracketed by Italy, Poland, and Colombia, much better company. In 2017 the countries whose scores were closest to Afghanistan's were Ecuador and India. Still, the improvements in the Open Budget Index for Afghanistan were dramatic. Even after Ghani left his ministerial position, he continued to advocate for reforms and greater transparency in the public financial management system.[41] Ghani is an exceptional Afghan leader. He has been able to work in both the traditional environment and in the cosmopolitan environment of the World Bank. His work in the Finance Ministry facilitated the flow of foreign assistance on which the Afghan elite, including President Karzai, feasted.

Foreign donors put significant pressure on the government with regard to the official budget. In 2010–2011, Afghanistan was the most aid-dependent country in the world. In that year, aid accounted for 71 percent of GDP. Much of this aid was distributed directly by donors to implementing agencies, often foreign, but some did go through the government budget, and foreign donors insisted on some transparency and accountability.[42] The leverage of external donors was limited because they needed Afghanistan to succeed and could not make a credible threat to precipitously withdraw funds, but it was evident by 2011 that the United States was anxious to limit its exposure in Afghanistan. Under Trump the United States made it clear that it was leaving. The government in Kabul saw improvements in budget transparency as one way to soothe critics in Afghanistan, both civil society organizations and some members of the legislature, without necessarily compromising the rent-seeking opportunities available to the political elite.

Despite some improvement in basic social indicators and some specific programs that worked reasonably well, the huge American expenditure in Afghanistan, in terms of troops and resources, along with the contributions of many NATO allies, had limited results. Afghanistan has been America's longest war and after more than a decade and a half of foreign involvement the country remains poor and unstable. Osama bin Laden was killed in Pakistan but there is no guarantee that Afghanistan, or at least parts of it, will not again become safe havens for transnational terrorists.

Iraq

In Iraq, as in Afghanistan, President Bush and some of his closest advisors began with an ambitious set of objectives. The leaders of the administration did not believe that American efforts should be focused solely on defeating the immediate security threat. The grand strategy of the Bush administration enunciated in the 2002 *National Security Strategy* emphasized that the root causes of transnational terrorism had to be extirpated. Al-Qaeda had to be degraded and destroyed through military action, but the conditions that had nurtured al-Qaeda also had to be changed. This would require altering the trajectory of political developments in Iraq and ultimately in the broader Middle East. For the Bush administration, the United States would have to pursue a set of policies that would ultimately lead these countries to consolidated democracy. American leaders accepted a utopian vision for the future of Iraq.

This very ambitious goal reflected Bush's embrace of Wilsonianism after 9/11. The idea of the United States as the global supporter of democracy was one that the American public could readily grasp. The overweening power of the United States in the decade following the collapse of the Soviet Union had not only afforded resources for such an ambitious agenda, but also sustained the belief that the global embrace of American values was inevitable.[43]

The United States committed more troops, matériel, and resources in Iraq than in Afghanistan but these levels were unimpressive compared with the resources provided to other state-building projects, especially those that had been going on in the Balkans since the 1990s. For Republicans, democratization had to be both possible and inexpensive. The administration believed that it could quickly transition formal authority back to Iraqis. Military briefings before the war estimated that the United States would have only about five thousand troops in the country by 2006, a wildly optimistic assessment. The military initially focused on combat, but not on Phase IV, postwar planning. Civilian authorities failed to develop adequate plans for how Iraq would be governed after the war.[44]

The American invasion of Iraq did not, unlike that of Afghanistan, lead to much in the way of social welfare improvement for the population as a whole, at least compared with 1990, the year before the first American invasion following Iraq's occupation of Kuwait, and subsequent sanctions. At least in part this was because Iraq was not doing all that badly. The percentage of individuals enrolled in primary school in 1991 was the same as the percentage enrolled in 2007; in both cases the numbers were very high. Life expectancy did increase from 66 in 1990 to 70 in 2016, but per capita income fell from $7,020 in 1990 to $5,429 in 2016. The high after the American invasion was $6,850 in 2013.[45] Iraq first appeared on the Transparency International Corruption Perceptions Index in 2003, when it ranked 113 out of 133 countries. Things did not get better. In 2010 it was ranked 175 out of 178; and in 2017, 169 out of 180.[46]

Some of the decisions made by the Coalition Provisional Authority led by Paul Bremer, especially the dismissal of thirty thousand members of the Ba'ath Party from the civilian administration, and the dismantling of the Iraqi army, or at least its higher echelons, seem woefully misguided in retrospect and were questioned at the time. When Bremer arrived in Baghdad he quickly issued an order, CPA Order Number 2 (Dissolution of Entities), disbanding the Iraqi army, the Ministry of Defense, and the Iraqi security services. All former members of the Iraqi military were dismissed. The order left 230,000 members of the military unemployed. They demonstrated around the country.

Walter Slocombe, Bremer's deputy, announced that the first division of the new Iraqi army, twelve thousand troops, would be created within a year. The CPA also announced that some payments would be made to former members of the military but that the top six thousand officers would get nothing.[47] The number of members of the old military elite that could hope for service in the new military was initially de minimis. Bremer and Slocombe reported that the Iraqi military had already disbanded itself.

Bremer believed that it would be necessary to convince the Iraqi people that the United States had brought a truly different regime to the country. Bremer wrote in his memoir *My Year in Iraq*:

> It's absolutely essential to convince Iraqis that we're not going to permit the return of Saddam's instruments of repression— the Ba'ath Party, the Mukhabarat security services, or Saddam's army. We didn't send our troops halfway round the world to overthrow Saddam only to find another dictator taking his place.[48]

DDR—disarmament, demobilization, reintegration—had become part of the standard toolkit for addressing post-conflict situations. Bremer ignored what was widely understood about dealing with former combatants. He demobilized Saddam's army, but soldiers still had their weapons and he failed to promptly address questions of reintegration. Payments for former soldiers took several months. Efforts to retrain former soldiers for civilian jobs failed.[49]

Moreover, had Bremer been attentive to American policy in

Japan he would have been more anxious to identify individuals from Saddam Hussein's regime who might have seen it to be in their interest to work with the American occupiers. Bremer and his colleagues, however, feared that the United States would fail unless it could clearly demonstrate to the majority of Iraqis, who were Shia Muslims, that the American occupiers had clearly broken with Saddam's Sunni-dominated regime. Had the Americans been more focused on the need for local allies and less convinced of the possibility of regime transformation, they might have chosen differently. Rational choice institutionalism would have provided more effective policy guidance than modernization theory or institutional capacity, the approaches that implicitly informed American policy. The implicit American assumption was that democratization would be relatively easy and that the new Iraqi political elite would want to do the right thing.

Bremer's approach, which was part of a larger American effort to quickly put Iraq on the path to consolidated democracy, quickly failed. In the fall of 2003, when it was already becoming clear that there would be resistance in Iraq, Secretary of Defense Rumsfeld ordered that a new and larger Iraqi army be created more quickly. The resources and planning for this endeavor were never, however, effectively put in place.[50] There was no overlap between the interests of the American occupiers and those of many of the Shia or Sunni leaders of Iraq. Iraqi Shias wanted to govern Iraq on their own terms. Early in the occupation Muqtada al-Sadr, the leader of the Mahdi militia, ordered the assassination of his more moderate rival al-Khoei, and paid no price. The Americans backed Nouri al-Maliki as prime minister in 2005, a choice that proved highly problematic by 2014, when Maliki had driven the country into a sectarian ditch. Maliki might have been the best of a bad set of choices, but his background as a Shia activist and ally of Iran were known in 2005.[51] Betting on the right Iraqi was difficult.[52]

The relationship between the Kurdish region in the North and the rest of the country was not resolved when the United States first occupied Iraq. An explicit commitment to a federal or confederal structure might have served American interests. The Kurds were dependent on external resources, including military support, to ensure their autonomy from the rest of Iraq. They also feared Turkey. With few exceptions, however, such as Senator Joe Biden, who later became Obama's vice-president, American leaders were committed to creating a unified, democratic Iraq that could transform the Middle East. If modernization theory or even institutional capacity approaches adequately explained the fundamental drivers of development and democracy, the American strategy might have made some sense. Rational choice institutionalism, focusing on elite interests, would have suggested much more modest goals in Iraq—good enough governance and a federal structure, goals that might have been achievable.

In Iraq, security deteriorated despite the continued presence of a large number of foreign troops and the American surge in 2007. The surge, which took advantage of the awakening (Sunnis awakening to the danger of Salafists, who threatened the traditional prerogatives of tribal chieftains), did keep the country from collapsing into sectarian strife during President Bush's term in office. Conflict among different groups—Shia, Kurdish, and Sunni—continued even after the increase in American military presence. American civilian officials were more or less trapped in the Green Zone, where the US embassy was located.

In President Obama's second term, long after the initial intervention, ISIS overran Iraqi military positions in many of the Sunni areas of the country. The Iraqi army disintegrated despite the investment of some $25 billion by the United States. This massive investment in Iraq, like more modest investments in Afghanistan, reflected a belief that external actors could build institutional capacity. Training and equipping the army was considered, to some extent, to be a technical problem. The interests of American and Iraqi leaders were, however, far apart. For the sectarian regime of

Nouri al-Maliki, a professional, potentially neutral Iraqi military was a threat. The Maliki regime wanted loyalty from its military. It accepted corruption in the officer corps. Technically competent officers were replaced with sectarian loyalists as US troops left the country. The regime turned a blind eye to death squads. It is hardly surprising that the Iraqi army simply melted away in the face of a much smaller ISIS contingent in 2014.[53]

The Iraqi army, with the help of Kurdish Peshmerga forces and of American troops, intelligence, and air power, was able to retake the country from ISIS in 2017. The Iraqi general who led the equivalent of the Iraqi Special Forces attributed 50 percent of the victory to the United States.[54] The battle for Mosul lasted six months and much of the city was destroyed.

THE BUSH ADMINISTRATION was committed to moving Afghanistan and Iraq along a path that would ultimately lead to consolidated democracy. President Bush and some of his key advisors accepted a utopian vision of what was possible. Consolidated democracy was not an afterthought or a rationalization. It was part of a considered grand strategy that was coherent in its basic design and analysis: the only way that the security of the United States could be ensured was to address the root causes of transnationalism terrorism, and these root causes were understood to be autocratic regimes in many Muslim-majority countries. The administration's policy was not incoherent, but it was based on a flawed understanding of how development takes place. Key figures in the Bush administration implicitly assumed that modernization theory and institutional capacity approaches provided an adequate understanding of how consolidated democracy could be achieved. If per capita incomes could be raised—and some incomes were already relatively high in Iraq, if not in Afghanistan—and if the relevant personnel could be trained and supported, then democracy and economic development would naturally follow. Indigenous officials would want to do the right thing. If the burden of autocracy could be lifted, then countries would naturally move along a democratic path. If the viability of democracy could be demonstrated in Iraq, then it would be irresistible in other Middle Eastern countries, Persian as well as Arab.

This assumption, that consolidated democracy was possible in all countries, framed key elements of the Bush administration's policies. American officials did press forward in both countries to reach markers that would indicate that Afghanistan and Iraq were moving along a democratic path. They used a template that had been derived in part from experiences in the Balkans and that included demobilization; the creation of an interim government; the writing of a constitution; elections within two years; and policy reforms in specific areas, such as training a new military and police, combating corruption, limiting inflation, and providing better access to education.[55] Unlike the Dayton Accords, which ended the Balkan wars of the 1990s, the United States never explicitly endorsed confederal solutions for Afghanistan or Iraq. Even in Iraq, where the Kurdish North had been established as a de facto autonomous region after the Gulf War, the explicitly articulated American goal was a unified country with a strong and effective central government.

In the quest to demonstrate that Afghanistan and Iraq were moving along a democratic path, elections were particularly important. No elections, no democracy. But elections have not necessarily provided stability or security in either country. Without institutions and norms that support inclusivity and accountability, such as a free press, an independent judiciary, and active civic associations, elections can precipitate violence and perpetuate autocratic rule, if the number of votes and the number of guns are misaligned. In a world of winner-take-all politics, those with guns will not passively accept electoral outcomes that exclude them from political power. Karzai in Afghanistan was never interested in creating a consolidated democracy, and al-Maliki in Iraq pursued a sectarian agenda. As secretary of state, John Kerry had to negotiate the outcome of the 2014 election in Afghanistan.

The effort to put Afghanistan and Iraq on a democratic path failed, but it did not fail because the resources committed were too small. American assumptions, based implicitly on modernization or institutional capacity approaches, were flawed. The American leadership, especially at the beginning, had utopian visions for both Afghanistan and Iraq. More than a decade after these interventions the vision of the American leadership was more dystopian: nothing could be done. The United States would have been more successful if it had recognized that for closed access orders like Iraq and Afghanistan, the best that can be hoped for is good enough governance, something that lies between utopian hope and dystopian despair.

If the United States had aimed for good enough governance—better security, possibly achieved through decentralization or even a federal structure; some improvement in service provision; and some economic growth—it might have been more successful. The United States might have been able to identify indigenous leaders with whom it could work effectively, leaders whose own positions would not have been threatened by good enough governance despite being threatened by democratization.

As the years wore on, domestic and international support for both wars eroded. The American rationale for invading Iraq, the presence of weapons of mass destruction, was quickly proved wrong. The mistreatment of prisoners by American forces in Abu Ghraib prison undermined US legitimacy, especially in the Middle East. Corruption was a pervasive problem in both Afghanistan and Iraq. Poor outcomes and doubts about the rationale for war, especially in Iraq, made the American public less tolerant of casualties.[56]

The Obama administration struggled to find a doctrine that would join concerns about US security with some set of broader objectives, which, even if not entirely focused on consolidated democracy, would not be inconsistent with it. In his 2009 speech at West Point, the president announced not only that he would send thirty thousand more troops to Afghanistan but also that "we must make it clear to every man, woman and child around the world who lives under the dark cloud of tyranny that America will speak out on behalf of their human rights, and tend to the light of freedom, and justice, and opportunity, and respect for the dignity of all peoples. That is who we are. That is the moral source of America's authority."[57]

American troops formally left Iraq in 2011 because a status of forces agreement, which would have allowed some residual force to remain in the country, could not be concluded, although thousands of Americans, some of them defense contractors, stayed in the country. Differences between the Kurdish enclave in the North and the national government in Baghdad were not resolved. Suicide bombings swept the country. ISIS took control of large areas of Iraq. The government in Baghdad became more closely allied with Iran, a country whose nuclear ambitions, support for Hamas and Hezbollah, and backing of transnational terrorism threaten US national security. Improvements in corruption, service delivery, and accountability were marginal or nonexistent in both countries.[58]

In 2014 President Obama ordered a small number of American forces to return to the country to help Iraq address the rising threat from ISIS, which had occupied large swaths of the country. President Trump early in his term gave his secretary of defense, James Mattis, authority to determine the number of American troops in Iraq and Syria, but then announced a precipitous withdrawal from both countries in December 2018, prompting Mattis to resign. Trump announced withdrawals from northern Syria in 2019.

While the Bush administration tried to do too much in Iraq and Afghanistan, the Obama and Trump administrations tried to do too little. The key to success for the Obama administration was not democratization, but rather national security forces that could guarantee order and combat terrorism. Better training and resources, it was believed, could achieve this outcome. Implicitly the Obama administration relied on an institutional capacity perspective, which suggested that creating an effective national army was a technical problem that could be addressed through training and the provision of equipment. What is missing from this perspective are the links between civilian officials and the military. Despite the expenditure of billions of dollars in Afghanistan and Iraq, national armies nominally directed from Kabul and Baghdad disintegrated in the face of much smaller and less well-armed Islamist groups.

Success for the United States would have required identifying some alternative end point at which America might aim: if Afghanistan and Iraq could not move in a systematic way toward consolidated democracy, what kind of acceptable political order might be achieved? Many of the policies that were supported to encourage movement along what was conceived of as a democratic path made it more difficult to achieve some alternative outcome that might have created more stability within Afghanistan and Iraq. Combating corruption across the board can make it more difficult to achieve greater control and security, because leaders depend on what would conventionally be understood as corrupt practices to pay their supporters with guns. Advocating full equality for women could create a backlash against more modest changes that might otherwise be acceptable to traditional conservative groups. Insisting on free and fair elections when powerful actors are not willing to risk losing office may lead to elections that are more problematic and violent than they might have been had elections been viewed as mechanisms to ratify agreements that had already been reached among political elites rather than as procedures that could remove those elites from power.

Good enough governance, which would focus on security, some economic growth, and some provision of services, is a realizable objective. It is neither utopian nor dystopian. In Iraq and Afghanistan the United States might have been able to achieve the more modest objectives associated with good enough governance; more ambitious plans to put these countries on the path to consolidated democracy were not achievable.

CHAPTER 10

Colombia, a Model for Good Enough Governance

OF ALL OF THE STATE-BUILDING EFFORTS THAT THE UNITED States has undertaken following the very successful projects in Japan and Germany, many observers have regarded Colombia as the most positive. An op-ed published in the *New York Times* in 2015 by the then vice-president of the United States, Joe Biden, is worth quoting at some length.

In 1999, we initiated Plan Colombia to combat drug trafficking, grinding poverty and institutional corruption—combined with a vicious insurgency—that threatened to turn Colombia into a failed state. Fifteen years later, Colombia is a nation transformed. As one of the architects of Plan Colombia in the United States Senate, I saw that the key ingredient was political will on the ground. Colombia benefited from leaders who had the courage to make significant changes regarding security, governance and human rights. Elites agreed to pay higher taxes. The Colombian government cleaned up its courts, vetted its police force and reformed its rules of commerce to open up its economy. The United States invested $9 billion over the course of Plan Colombia, with $700 million the first year. But our figures show that Colombia outspent us four to one.[1]

Biden was not alone in his praise; it came from sources inside and outside of the government. "A 2007 report from the Center for Strategic and International Studies (CSIS), titled *Colombia: Back from the Brink*, credits Plan Colombia with many accomplishments, including expanding state authority, reducing violence, improving human rights, advancing the peace process, enhancing governance, expanding the economy, and providing social services. . . . 'This critical ally of America has done all of the right things to try to bring stability, democracy, and prosperity to its own citizens,' then Secretary of State Condoleezza Rice said in a 2008 statement supporting further US assistance for Colombia."[2] Winifred Tate, an NGO activist and academic, has written that during her field research in January 2010 at the United States Southern Command, located in Florida, high-level American officers told her that "Colombia has been very good to all of us."[3]

Plan Colombia

Plan Colombia was initially developed under the administrations of Bill Clinton in the United States and Andrés Pastrana in Colombia. Ernesto Samper, who preceded Pastrana and held office from 1994 to 1998, was discredited when it was revealed that his campaign had taken money from drug kingpins.[4] As president, Andrés Pastrana held talks with the Fuerzas Armadas Revolucionarias de Colombia, or Revolutionary Armed Forces of Colombia (FARC) and agreed to give them authority over a large swath of territory, the size of Switzerland. The FARC hid thousands of fighters and weapons in this zone, which the FARC completely controlled. The talks collapsed in 2002. Pastrana's popularity plummeted. His approval rating fell to 22 percent.[5] A previous effort at negotiating with the FARC in the 1980s and creating a left-wing political party had also failed; many members of the party created by the FARC were assassinated. Efforts to reach a negotiated settlement with other left-wing militant movements in the 1980s and the 1990s were successful, but the FARC remained a formidable force. General Barry McCaffrey, who was in charge of the American war on drugs in the late 1990s, described Colombia as "out of control, a flipping nightmare."[6]

Pastrana was interested in social investments. The United States, before 9/11, was focused on counternarcotics activities. The Plan, as it initially emerged from the US Congress, was essentially designed to support counternarcotics programs in Colombia. This was the only rationale that would generate congressional support in the 1990s.[7] The goals of American and Colombian elites were far from perfectly aligned.

Pastrana's failed negotiating strategy helped Álvaro Uribe to win the presidency on a platform that took a hard line against the FARC. Plan Colombia morphed into a broader project, one with ambitions beyond narcotics, under President Uribe. Uribe understood the American political environment and recognized that the surest way to get continued support from the United States was to link Plan Colombia with counterterrorism. Uribe took advantage of the fact that leftist groups had become heavily involved with drug trafficking in Colombia in the 1980s and 1990s. He closely aligned himself with President Bush, who awarded him the Presidential Medal of Freedom. From an American perspective in the post-9/11 era, describing the war against the FARC and narco-trafficking as part of the war against terrorism allowed the Bush administration to cast its policies in nonreligious terms. There could be terrorists that were not Muslims. The United States was not, as President Bush frequently said, engaged in a war against Islam but rather a war against terror, and making Plan Colombia part of the American effort was evidence that the United States was concerned with terror and not with Islam.[8] Uribe obfuscated distinctions among drugs, violence, and terrorism because this allowed him to more effectively appeal to the United States.[9]

During his successful electoral campaign Uribe committed himself to not negotiating with armed groups. Uribe linked Plan Colombia to what he termed his "Democratic Security and Defense Policy." This policy listed five threats and five strategic objectives for Colombia. The threats were terrorism, illegal drugs, criminal finance, trafficking in arms and explosives, and killings. As strategic objectives, the Uribe plan listed effective state control over all of Colombia's territory, providing security to the civilian population, maintaining the effectiveness of the security forces, ending the drug trade, and achieving higher levels of efficiency and transparency in public finances. These were all good-governance objectives, ones that would appeal to the American administration, which saw good governance and democracy as the most effective ways to address the root causes of terrorism.[10]

Uribe's security policy was successful; murder and kidnapping rates plummeted. His popularity increased. He won a second term in 2006.

Under Plan Colombia the United States provided not only financial and material resources, although not nearly as much as Colombia itself, but also logistical and intelligence support that was important, if not critical, for the success of Colombian forces. The United States gave Colombia about two hundred helicopters, allowing mobility in difficult and mountainous terrain that had previously been inaccessible to the Colombian military. American intelligence and surveillance allowed the Colombian government to locate and kill a number of FARC leaders. With American technology, heavily vegetated areas no longer provided a safe haven for guerrillas.

Plan Colombia Outcome

Security in Colombia dramatically improved after 2002. In Bogotá, the nation's capital, housing prices increased at 10 percent a year from 2011 to 2015, tourism boomed, and international chains like Marriott and Four Seasons built new hotels. In 2014 the *New York Times* published a travel story in its 36 Hours travel series about Cartagena, the main Colombian city on the Caribbean Sea. Other areas covered in the series in 2014 included Burgundy in France, Cambridge in Massachusetts, Edinburgh in Scotland, and Richmond in Virginia—hardly war zones. There was no mention of security issues in the story, which focused on must-see tourist attractions. This was not a story that could have been written a decade and a half earlier.[11]

From 2002 to 2008, homicides in Colombia dropped 45 percent. A UN study reported that the murder rate in Bogotá per 100,000 dropped from 24 in 2005 to 16.5 in 2012.[12] Kidnapping dropped 90 percent from 2002 to 2012. The number of kidnappings for ransom, which had been in the thousands, fell to around two hundred.[13] Colombia improved its scores on a number of governance measures, including control of corruption, rule of law, government effectiveness, and government accountability.[14]

The improved security situation in the country reflected a dramatic increase in the capacity of Colombian security forces. Under Uribe, the security budget increased substantially. The size of the Colombian military grew by 45 percent from 2000 to 2007, when it reached four hundred thousand soldiers. Training and equipping efforts by the United States, especially the provision of helicopters, increased the intelligence and mobility of the security forces. The military budget increased from 3.4 to 5.7 percent of GDP. The capacity of the military was enhanced by a number of special units, including mobile brigades, special forces, and high-mountain battalions. Uribe moved to have a police presence throughout the country.[15]

The implementation of these reforms did have a dramatic impact on rebel groups. The FARC was able to operate only with small units, usually of under ten, during Uribe's presidency; in the 1990s they had been able to field as many as one thousand individuals.[16]

The Colombian military was assisted by right-wing paramilitary units that were organized outside of the state's direct control, at least before 2006. Official and nonofficial forces coordinated their activities.[17] The paramilitaries were not constrained in the same way as official forces by human rights norms and other international standards that at least some American politicians would be attentive to.

In the middle of Uribe's term in office, thousands of paramilitaries were demobilized. The government reached an agreement with the Autodefensas Unidas de Colombia (AUC), the largest paramilitary organization. Some members of the AUC were given reduced sentences, which could still reach up to eight years, provided that they confessed to their crimes, agreed to eschew illegal activity in the future, and turned over their assets to provide compensation for their victims.[18] Some AUC members were extradited to the United States, where they stood trial in federal courts and where their trial transcripts were sealed (possibly because they were cooperating with US drug investigators). Many members of the paramilitaries, however, later joined criminal gangs, or *bandas criminales* (BACRIM), that were engaged in drug trafficking.[19]

The official security forces, not just the paramilitaries, were plagued by human rights violations. The most dramatic was the false positives scandal. During Plan Colombia the military sometimes captured and killed young civilians and then placed weapons on their bodies, claiming that they were guerrillas that had been defeated. Security forces were rewarded for higher body counts. When this practice was discovered near the end of Uribe's presidency, it led to the resignation of a number of high-ranking officers. The military also engaged in phone tapping and other activities that were illegal under Colombian law.[20]

The reduction in violence, even if some of it was achieved by methods that were inconsistent with global standards, was accompanied by economic growth. Between 2002 and 2008, average annual economic growth was 4.9 percent for Colombia. This was three times higher than in the previous seven years.[21] In terms of both the reduction in violence and the increase in economic activities, Colombians, at least a significant number of Colombians, were better off near the end of Uribe's term as president than they had been near the beginning. Plan Colombia had contributed to these positive outcomes.

The government did not just rely on economic growth to secure support from the society. Military units protected major roads and the government sponsored private convoys of vehicles, which allowed Colombians to travel between major cities for the first time in years. The number of vehicles that passed through toll stations increased by two and a half times between 2003 and 2009.[22] Plan Colombia did bring greater security and better governance to Colombia.

The narcotics trade, however, continued to thrive. The destruction of the major cartels in Medellín and Cali in the 1990s fragmented illegal drug activities. Drug production and trafficking from Colombia continued. According to US government figures, coca production peaked at 167,000 hectares in 2007, fell to 78,000 hectares in 2012, but then rose to 159,000 in 2015. The increase in production could be the result of the fact that the government of Colombia reduced spraying in certain areas, such as along the border, because of objections from Ecuador, and in other areas because of opposition from peasant groups.[23]

Plan Colombia was not a panacea for Colombia. In many parts of the country the central government's authority remained weak. The port city of Buenaventura, for instance, continued to have poor government services. Sewage was untreated and ran directly into the bay. Gang violence in the city remained high.[24]

With the assistance of the United States, however, the Colombian government was able to reduce violence in many parts of the country, but many other fundamental characteristics of the Colombian polity did not change. In 2014 the Gini index (a measure of income inequality) for Colombia was 53.5, the highest among those countries in Latin America (where Gini indexes are high compared with other parts of the world) for which the World Bank presented data. Although the level of income inequality in Colombia dropped slightly during the first decade of the twenty-first century, the Gini index in 2014 was slightly higher than it had been in 1989, although lower than it had been in 2000. The justice system did not keep pace with improved policing; a culture of impunity remained in Colombia. Throughout the entire period of the Pastrana, Uribe, and Santos presidencies, from 1998 to 2018, the Freedom House score assigned to Colombia hardly changed.[25] During this entire period Colombia remained an electoral rather than a liberal democracy. Elections had been routinely held since the mid-1960s, although in many cases, especially during earlier periods, outcomes were negotiated among competing elites.[26]

Plan Colombia, by degrading the military capacity of the FARC, contributed to a set of agreements between the government and rebel factions during the Santos presidency, which began in 2010. Plan Colombia brought stability and greater security but did not transform the nature of the polity. As a state-building project, Plan Colombia did bring good enough governance, at least some aspects of good enough governance. It did not, however, set Colombia on the path to consolidated democracy.

Accepting Plan Colombia

The Colombian political elite accepted extensive assistance from the United States, including thousands of Americans in the country working on Plan Colombia, not because it was committed to an open access democracy but because the country was threatened with potential collapse and the members of the political elite could not insulate themselves from violence.

In the mid-1990s Colombia was decertified by the United States for not cooperating on counternarcotics measures. This decertification limited American foreign assistance. This was a clear negative signal for the Colombian elite, which had traditionally been pro-American. The Colombian elite feared not only internal enemies but also external abandonment.

In the early 1990s the Medellín and Cali drug cartels were able to field thousands of fighters. The cartels intimidated and sometimes killed public officials to make sure that narco-traffickers were not extradited to the United States.[27] Medellín was the most dangerous city in the world in the early 1990s, with a murder rate of 381 per 100,000. In the late 1990s the FARC took over a military base in Putumayo; attacked a naval base in Antioquia; and took over Mitú, the capital city in the department of Vaupés, killing thirty-seven people and kidnapping sixty-one members of the armed forces. In 2002 there were attacks in 209 municipalities.

Thirty-nine percent of Colombia's municipalities experienced violent events between 1964 and 1984. About a quarter of these events were associated with the FARC. More than eight thousand people died, and 388 towns were captured. Areas that had experienced rebel violence from the 1960s to the 1980s were more likely than other areas to experience rebel violence in the subsequent decades, because such areas had legacies that made it easier to organize violence.[28] The leaders of drug cartels attacked and threatened government officials. Hundreds of judges and police investigators were killed. Three presidential candidates were assassinated.[29]

The FARC, the largest but not the only left-wing group in the country, was estimated to have seventeen thousand to twenty thousand members in 2000. At the turn of the century the FARC controlled large areas of the country, imposed taxes on coca growers, and threatened large landowners. By the end of the 1990s the FARC might have been securing nearly a billion dollars in revenue, a substantial part of that, but not all, from the drug trade. In 1999 a FARC commander, probably operating on his own, killed three American indigenous rights activists.[30] Each was blindfolded and shot multiple times; their bodies were discovered just across the border in Venezuela. Even though the FARC might have eroded some of its support from the population in the 1990s, by becoming the principal in drug operations rather than protecting the population from drug traffickers, the FARC was able to generate enough funds from drug trafficking to recruit new members, strengthen its arsenal, and act more like a state within a state. The ELN, another leftist group, was extorting money from foreign corporations.[31]

This violence, extralegal activity, kidnapping, and mayhem did not affect just the poor. One observer has written that "by far the most important indicator of the crisis for many middle and upper-class Colombians, however, was the fear of escalating attacks by the guerrillas."[32] Kidnappings increased. The elite, including their children, were often targets. For the elite the war had come home.

> One Colombian who had worked in the Foreign Service during this period compared the country to Afghanistan. "The FARC was going to take over the country," while the callous elite fled to Miami. . . . As I heard from other elite Colombians, as well as from US officials in Bogotá, FARC strength was symbolized by its presence in La Calera, a small town about a fifteen-minute drive from the Bogotá city limits over the eastern mountain range, where many wealthy residents had country homes or spent the weekend horse back riding and enjoying leisurely barbeques. "The FARC took over La Calera. La Calera! That is Bogotá!" he exclaimed, concluding, "The state was unraveling. A FARC takeover was likely."[33]

Ernesto Londoño, a writer for the *New York Times* who grew up in Colombia, reports that for a long time the elites were able to keep violence at bay. His wealthy classmates in a private American school in Bogotá arrived, he wrote, in bulletproof cars with bodyguards. When Londoño was nine, a group of armed robbers broke into his house, threatened to kidnap his two-year-old sister, and made off with the family's valuables. The parents of a close high school friend of Londoño's were kidnapped thirty miles from Bogotá, the stepfather held for five months and the mother for an additional six when the FARC reneged on the original ransom deal.[34]

The threat of violence was so palpable that the richest Colombians agreed to a special tax, which was supported by the Uribe administration. The wealth tax, which was imposed on the wealthiest individuals in the country, was earmarked for the security services. In 1999 nearly one million people demonstrated against the FARC. Many people in the middle class left the country in the late 1990s.[35]

By the time that Uribe assumed the presidency in 2002, Plan Colombia, including substantial assistance from the United States, looked like the only good option. Among many in Colombia there was a recognition that the country was near collapse. Pastrana's efforts to negotiate with the FARC had only strengthened the organization. Despite its Marxist roots it had continued to thrive after the Soviet Union collapsed. Violence, bombings, and kidnappings were taking place in the capital city itself.

Latin American elites have always been nervous about the power and intrusiveness of the United States. The United States has frequently shown that it was willing to intervene in the internal affairs of Latin American countries. If anything, the environment after 9/11, in which the United States experienced the first major attack against its home territory since 1941, could only make Latin American elites more nervous. But the leaders of Colombia did not believe that they had any good alternatives to extensive American assistance. The Colombian elite accepted intrusive American assistance not because of a commitment to making the country a consolidated democracy but because the country was near collapse. Without American assistance the elite would not have been able to maintain its position.

Peace Agreement 2016

Even with substantial increases in expenditures, American assistance, and sometimes brutal military tactics, not to speak of the collapse of the Soviet Union and the declining attractiveness of Marxist ideology, the Colombian government was not able to definitively defeat the FARC. Government control over peripheral areas, especially in the South, remained tenuous. President Santos began negotiations for a peace agreement with the FARC in 2012. Santos lost in the first round of elections in 2014 but his opponent did not win the required majority. In the second round of elections Santos prevailed, securing 50.95 percent of the votes.[36] The negotiations were then continued in Havana. Cuba had the only explicitly Marxist regime in the Western Hemisphere, and the Cuban government was sympathetic to the FARC. In March of 2015 Santos stopped bombing FARC encampments and praised the FARC for holding to a partial cease-fire.[37]

An agreement was reached in 2016. Santos, however, had committed to submitting the agreement to a popular plebiscite, and on October 4, 2016, it was defeated by less than 1 percent of the votes cast. The turnout, at 40 percent, was low, perhaps because Colombians expected the agreement to be endorsed, which is what polls had indicated, and perhaps because treacherous weather discouraged voters in some areas. The agreement, which guaranteed to members of the FARC a small number of seats in the legislature and which limited jail time for FARC members who confessed to their crimes, was opposed by former president Uribe, whose father had been killed by the FARC.

In November of 2016 the Santos government took a new agreement to the Colombian legislature, bypassing a popular vote. This new agreement was approved. Santos's party held a majority of seats in both houses of the legislature. The new agreement stipulated that there would be a special tribunal to try FARC members, but those who confessed were still guaranteed limited time in jail. Members of the FARC were guaranteed seats in the Congress but they could not run from districts in former conflict zones. Uribe and other opposition leaders walked out of the Congress and refused to support the new agreement.[38]

In sum, Plan Colombia was successful in bringing Colombia back from the brink. Political authority did not completely disappear, something that had seemed possible in 2000. Levels of violence declined. Parts of the country, most of the major cities, were no longer afflicted with pervasive violence. American assistance had been consequential.

But Colombia was not transformed. External assistance and increased Colombian government commitments returned the country to a degree of stability, but Colombia has not made any jump that would put it securely on the path to an open access or inclusive order. The country is still dominated by a narrow elite. Elections have mattered in Colombia, but power has been swapped among members of the elite. President Uribe, who was the principal architect of the Democratic Security Program, which was linked with Plan Colombia, is a large cattle rancher. Uribe became a senator in Colombia after he left the presidency. President Santos is the son and grandson of former presidents.

Plan Colombia should be understood as helping to provide good enough governance for Colombia. Above all, it did bring greater security to the country. For the Colombian elite the alternative to Plan Colombia could have been the complete disintegration of state authority and the end of any semblance of order and security, even in Bogotá.

Violence in Colombia

That good enough governance, not a path to Denmark, has been the outcome in Colombia is not surprising, given the conditions in the country. Colombia has been a limited access order with a weak central state since it became independent. Since its creation Colombia has been torn by violence. There were eight civil wars in the nineteenth century.[39] Non-state armed groups have been a constant presence. During the period between 1946 and 1964, which Colombians labeled *La Violencia*, power fragmented dramatically.

Violence in Colombia did not end in 1964. After *La Violencia* a number of leftist armed groups emerged in Colombia of which the Revolutionary Armed Forces of Colombia (FARC) became the most important. Right-wing paramilitaries began to form in the early 1980s, at least in part to fight against left-wing guerrillas.[40]

Historically, elections were often contested with weapons.[41] There have never been substantial state-building projects in Colombia. Along with Ecuador and Bolivia, Colombia is a mosaic of regions. Among ten South American countries, excluding Brazil, only two others have less urban concentration than Colombia.[42]

The central government has never been able to effectively assert its authority in all parts of the country. Areas of limited statehood have been the norm. There is not even a system of uniform railway gauges throughout the country. Political elites opposed projects designed to build stronger state institutions. During the nineteenth century the national army never numbered more than six thousand troops.[43]

Drug violence in Colombia was part of a longer history. Colombia has been very violent.[44] Pablo Escobar, the leader of the Medellín cartel who was killed in 1993, was elected as an alternative deputy in the Colombian Chamber of Deputies in 1982. Escobar was responsible for the assassination of at least one presidential candidate in the late 1980s and for many other murders.

In sum, the explosion of violence that occurred in the period when Plan Colombia was formulated and accepted did not emerge from a vacuum. Violence has almost always been present in Colombia. What was different was the inability of the political and economic elites, even those living in Bogotá and its environs, to protect themselves at the turn of the twenty-first century.

————

PLAN COLOMBIA HAS been considered a model for American state-building efforts, the most notable success since Germany and Japan at the end of the Second World War. By providing financial aid, training, military technology (especially helicopters), and intelligence, the United States did contribute to restoring security to large parts of Colombia. The country's political elite, especially President Uribe, was fully on board with this project. Plan Colombia does not, however, vindicate the utopian vision of some American leaders.

Colombia should be understood as an example of how an external actor might contribute to good enough governance, but not good governance. The country was much more peaceful by the end of Uribe's presidency than it had been at the beginning. Colombia did improve its scores on a number of World Bank governance indicators, including control of corruption and government effectiveness, after 2000. Colombia, however, never scored higher than a partial democracy in the Freedom House listing.

With a willing elite, good enough governance can work, but consolidated democracy is much less likely. Despite very substantial US assistance, the basic structure of Colombia's society did not change. The Gini index has not budged. The country is still dominated by a small wealthy elite, but that elite was willing to accept some reforms and intrusive assistance from the United States to avoid personal violence and the possibility of state collapse.

CHAPTER 11

The Rare Occurrence of Consolidated Democracy

THE MOST VISITED DESTINATION IN THE STATE OF GEORGIA IS Stone Mountain Park. Stone Mountain itself is literally a stone mountain, a granite monadnock. On its face is the largest bas-relief sculpture in the world, which depicts three leaders of the Confederacy on horseback, Robert E. Lee, Stonewall Jackson, and Jefferson Davis. The memorial was not completed until 1972, fourteen years after the monadnock and surrounding area was bought by the state of Georgia.

The mountain was the site of the second founding, in 1915, of the Ku Klux Klan, the most successful terrorist organization in American history. In 1915 the mountain was owned by the Venable brothers, one of whom, Sam Venable, was involved with the KKK. Stone Mountain Park was opened by the state of Georgia in 1965, exactly one hundred years after the assassination of Abraham Lincoln. The park and its memorial are testimony to how much of a failure Reconstruction, which took place after the Civil War, actually was. The South remained distinct from the rest of the country and discrimination against former slaves remained in place.

Despite a war that lasted four years, a decisive victory, and a death toll that exceeded any other American war, the Union was not able to create anything like a consolidated democracy in the South or to put the South on a path that would be followed by the rest of the country. Lincoln did succeed in preserving the Union. Several constitutional amendments were passed, which at least formally gave former slaves equal rights, although many of these rights did not become a reality until more than a hundred years after the Civil War ended.

The failure of Reconstruction demonstrates how hard it is for external state-builders to create something resembling a democratic system. The United States had been founded on the notion "that all men are created equal, that they are endowed by their Creator with certain unalienable Rights, that among these are Life, Liberty and the pursuit of Happiness.—That to secure these rights, Governments are instituted among Men, deriving their just powers from the consent of the governed." These inspiring words were written by Thomas Jefferson, who was, if nothing else, a hypocrite and a slave owner, one who fathered illegitimate children with one of his slaves. Nevertheless, when the United States was founded, it was a great experiment. No other country drew its legitimacy from the will of the people. Initially slaves, imported largely from Africa, were not counted as people—well, they were counted as three-fifths of a person in the Constitution, but the term *slave* or *African* is not mentioned in the Declaration of Independence or the original version of the Constitution (the term *slave* is used in the Thirteenth Amendment to the Constitution). Slavery was always at odds with the founding principles of the United States.

Creating a political system in the southern states that was close to a liberal democracy, in which each person had the same rights, was a great challenge. Racism was pervasive in all parts of the country.[1] Only a few northern states allowed blacks to vote in 1860.[2] An 1860 proposal to allow blacks to vote in New York State was defeated by the voters by more than 60 percent.[3] The preservation of the Union, not the abolition of slavery, had been the principal motivation for fighting when the war began, and the Emancipation Proclamation, which was issued by Lincoln in 1863, freed only slaves in those states that had seceded from the Union, not in those states that allowed slavery but had remained in the Union.

The Union army was rapidly demobilized after the war. The army of the Union, which had more than one million men at the end of the war, had only 152,000 by January 1, 1866. The defense budget fell by more than three-quarters after the war.[4]

Lincoln was assassinated shortly after the Civil War ended and replaced by Andrew Johnson from Tennessee, a committed racist. Johnson was consistently at loggerheads with the Radical Republicans who dominated Congress and he was almost convicted by the Senate, which held an impeachment trial. The elections that were held in the South immediately after the war re-created the same ruling structure that had existed before the war, because President Johnson made it easy for the southern states to return to the Union. The vice-president of the Confederate states ended his life as a senator from Georgia.

Leaders in the South quickly moved to reimpose a de facto form of slavery after slavery was outlawed by the Thirteenth Amendment in 1865. The murder of blacks in the South began right after the war ended.[5] There were riots in Memphis in 1866, followed by race riots in New Orleans. Forty-five of the forty-seven killed in Memphis were blacks.[6]

The black codes passed by many southern states limited black employment to certain activities, especially agriculture. Blacks were denied access to guns. Under President Andrew Johnson, slave owners were able to reclaim their land, which had in some cases been given to former slaves. The number of black voters peaked in 1872, then fell. The number of black officials fell dramatically after Union troops were withdrawn from the South in 1877.[7] A Confederate general, Nathan Bedford Forrest, was the first Grand Wizard of the KKK. Segregation was imposed on almost every aspect of life.[8] Blacks were not given the right to vote in the southern states. Even after the war, Maryland law allowed black children to be apprenticed by the courts without the approval of their parents.[9] In the words of W. E. B. Du Bois, "The slave went free; stood a brief moment in the sun; then moved back toward slavery."[10] The South was a white despotism.

The election of 1876 was disputed. The Democratic candidate, Governor Tilden of New York, won the popular vote, but the Republican candidate, Governor Hayes of Ohio, won the Electoral College as a result of the Electoral College votes from four disputed states going to him. To avoid a drawn-out conflict, Republicans agreed to withdraw all Union troops from the last two southern states in which they were stationed in return for Democratic acceptance of Hayes's election. Reconstruction ended with a whimper, not a bang.

The South has continued to remain a distinct region. In 2014 the poorest state in the United States was Mississippi, whose per capita income was a bit more than half that of the richest state, Maryland.[11] In the 2010 census the states with the highest percentage of blacks were all in the Old South, despite massive migrations to the North that took place in the 150 years following the Civil War. In 2015 the five states with the lowest percentages of people with a bachelor's degree were all from the South, although not all from states that had seceded from the Union.[12] The four states in which the highest percentage of people reported that religion was somewhat or very important to them were all in the South.[13] External state-building is hard. Even in the territory of the United States and after a very costly war, the utopian vision of a consolidated democracy for all could not be realized.

Reconstruction and the Civil War did not provide a set of lessons for the United States when it became a global power after the Second World War. In the last sixty years, the United States has been an ambitious state-builder. During the Cold War, the primary concern of American leaders was to put countries, or at least elites in the third world, in the American rather than the Soviet column. Often, however, American leaders have tried to put countries on the path to consolidated, or full, democracy, to replicate American norms, values, and institutions. American national identity has been defined by adherence to a set of Lockean liberal values, enshrined in the Declaration of Independence, even if these values have sometimes been ignored in practice. Despotism was not only wrong but un-American.

In an American political context, these efforts to create something like the United States in other countries even has a proper name, Wilsonianism. Historically, the most important challenger to Wilsonianism has been Jeffersonianism, in which American leaders depicted the United States as a shining city upon a hill that should be emulated by the rest of the world, even if the United States did not actively engage in the promotion of democracy. The two other American perspectives that Walter Russell Mead identified, Jacksonianism and Hamiltonianism, the former fundamentally concerned with American security, the latter with American economic interests, have not had the same salience.[14] As Louis Hartz argued in his *The Liberal Tradition in America*, the United States has vacillated between Wilsonian and Jeffersonian projects, between a utopian view that external actors could help to create liberal democracies and a dystopian view that external actors could do nothing except provide a model that could be emulated by others. When efforts to remake the world in their own image fail, as has frequently occurred, Americans return to more inward-looking policies.[15]

For the first part of American history, Jeffersonianism predominated. The United States did not have the resources to influence other polities. Even in the Western Hemisphere the United States could not, until the end of the nineteenth century, challenge major European powers.

This reticence receded as American power increased. The United States established concessions in China along with other Western powers in the later part of the nineteenth century. With the Spanish-American War, the United States became a colonial power, taking over formerly Spanish colonies not only in the Caribbean but also in the western Pacific. Aside from direct colonization, the United States also engaged in a number of foreign-imposed regime changes (FIRCs) before the Second World War, especially in the Caribbean and Central America, where the target states were geographically close, small, and weak. While these interventions were clothed in the language of democracy, American policies were more focused on protecting well-defined economic interests (Hamiltonianism) than on political transformations.

After the Second World War, the United States eschewed, at least to some extent, the isolationism that was understood to have contributed to the horrific cost of the Second World War. The United States occupied Japan and parts of Germany. In both countries it supported measures that contributed to the creation of consolidated democracies, although only by finding nondemocratic indigenous allies, most notably the emperor of Japan, who could be induced to share the vision of America's political elite. Moreover, both Germany and Japan were relatively developed countries that had experienced some elements of democracy in the past.

Once the fundamental antagonism between the United States and the Soviet Union became apparent—clearly by 1947, probably as early as Churchill's Iron Curtain speech in Fulton, Missouri, in March of 1946—the United States actively intervened in many countries around the world both overtly and covertly. It was involved in hot wars in Korea and Vietnam and in covert interventions in a number of countries, including Iran, Guatemala, and Chile. Although these covert and overt interventions were sometimes rationalized using the language of democracy, the focus of the United States was on preserving regimes that would at the very least rhetorically reject communism and the Soviet Union.

The Soviet Union was a serious challenger for the United States. Ideologically the Soviets rejected American democracy and the market economy. In the two decades immediately after the Second World War, the Soviet economy performed well. In some high-technology sectors, like space travel, the Russians appeared to be ahead of the United States. The American moon landings played an important symbolic role; they showed that the United States was on top, even in space. Once the United States was liberated from external enemies, with the collapse of the Soviet Union, Wilsonianism once again became the default strategy for American leaders.

Most, but not all, of the efforts to create consolidated democracies have failed. In Germany and Japan they succeeded dramatically. In Iraq and Afghanistan the aspirations of the Bush administration failed spectacularly. There have been many explanations for the failure of external state-building and democratization. In some cases, particularly during the Cold War, the United States was interested primarily in its own security and supported autocratic dictators so long as they were willing to back the international position of the United States or at least not support communism and the Soviet Union. In other cases, observers have pointed to inadequate resources or weak coordination among different departments.[16]

There is, however, a more fundamental explanation for the failure to achieve the American utopian vision. Consolidated democracy is not the natural order of things. America is an exceptional country. Its basic constitutional structure has lasted more than two hundred years, during a period when other major powers in the world experienced many dramatic changes in the nature of their political regimes. China, a more than two-thousand-year-old polity, was partly occupied by the Western powers in the nineteenth century, experienced a century of chaos, then became a communist regime under an arbitrary and ruthless dictator, Mao, and then became a more benign regime but one still dominated by the communist party. Germany, since its unification in 1871, has been a monarchy, a democracy, a Nazi regime, defeated in two major wars, divided in 1945, and then united again as a single country in 1990. Since the French Revolution, France has been a republic, a dictatorship, a monarchy, a republic, a dictatorship, and then several different republics. Russia was governed by the autocratic Romanov rulers until the regime collapsed at the end of the First World War, was replaced for a short period by the Mensheviks, then the Bolsheviks, only to have communism collapse in 1990 and the Soviet empire break apart, primarily into political entities whose international legal sovereignty had never before been recognized.

Whether the United States will persist in the future is not clear. It is hard to change the Constitution, and the US Senate, to take the most obvious example, is becoming less and less democratic.

For most Americans, national identity has been associated with one idea, Lockean liberalism. With the exception of the War of 1812, the continental United States has never been invaded by a foreign power. The United States benefited not just from the wisdom of its founding fathers but also from its geographic position, shielded by two oceans from other major powers. The United States initially chose democracy when every other major state was governed by a hereditary regime.

Consolidated democracy is not the natural order of things for the human race. It has existed in a small number of countries in limited parts of the world only in recent history. In the contemporary world, consolidated democracy has become more common, but only in a limited number of countries. Most of the OECD world emerged only after the horrific wars of the twentieth century. The Madisonian sweet spot, in which governments are strong enough to govern effectively but do not abuse their own populations, is unusual.

The conventional story is one of progress beginning with settled agriculture ten thousand years ago. Even this first step almost certainly made most human beings worse off; they lived better and longer lives as hunter-gatherers.[17] Efforts to turn countries into Denmark or to put them on the path to consolidated democracy fly in the face of most human experience. The United States would be more successful in its state-building efforts if it recognized that success is impossible unless the interests of external and internal elites are at least complementary. Good enough governance is the best that can be hoped for in most of the world's polities, which are closed access, extractive orders. In the long run, with luck, good enough governance might provide stability, economic growth, and an intermediate polity, some of whose elites would see their interests furthered by a state that was both effective and constrained. Only in such intermediate states will there be national elites willing to support a more open order.

But even in such intermediate polities, success is not guaranteed. The temptations of corruption remain high. Elections can be manipulated in many ways, most of which are invisible to outside observers.[18] Autocrats will not go quietly into the night.

Consolidated democracy is a very rare occurrence in human history. There is no teleological process inevitably leading to better governance. Things can get better, sometimes with help from external actors, but more frequently they fall back down. The most we can hope for is good enough governance. The dystopian view that nothing can be done must be resisted, but it is also essential that we recognize that the utopian view is unrealistic. Only under specific circumstances and with some luck can external actors create consolidated democracies.

Acknowledgments

IN THE COURSE OF WRITING THIS BOOK I HAVE BEEN HELPED BY many. My friend Josef Joffe, a true bridge between the United States and Germany, helped to clarify my argument. In Berlin Thomas Risse and Tanja Börzel offered many helpful suggestions over the years. They were also instrumental in allowing me to spend several months in Berlin as a Mercator Fellow at the Free University and at the research center on Governance in Areas of Limited Statehood. Eric Stollenwerk was the research director at the center during most of the months that I was there. The Belfer Center at the Kennedy School at Harvard University, then headed by professor Graham Allison, and the Burkle Center at UCLA, directed by professor Kal Raustiala, were generous in allowing me to spend several months at both institutions. My editor, Roby Harrington, has been more than patient and helpful for many years.

My colleagues in the Department of Political Science, the Freeman Spogli Institute for International Affairs, and the Hoover Institution at Stanford University have been of invaluable help in writing this book. There are very few places in the world where not only are people doing important work but every seminar is interesting, mostly because the presenters are great but also because the audience can always be depended on to ask interesting questions. I have learned a great deal from the pre- and postdoctoral fellows at the Center on Democracy, Development and the Rule of Law at the Freeman Spogli Institute. Many of their contributions are recognized in the body of this book.

Notes

Chapter 1: So You Want to Make the World a Better Place

1. United States and Donald Trump, *National Security Strategy of the United States of America* (National Security Strategy Archive, December 2017), p. 41.
2. Lisa Blaydes, *State of Repression: Iraq under Saddam Hussein* (Princeton, NJ: Princeton University Press, 2018).
3. Séverine Autesserre, *Peaceland: Conflict Resolution and the Everyday Politics of International Intervention* (Cambridge: Cambridge University Press, 2014).
4. James Scott, *Seeing Like a State* (New Haven, CT: Yale University Press, 1998).
5. M. A. Thomas, *Govern Like Us: U.S. Expectations of Poor Countries* (New York, Columbia University Press, 2015), p. 10.
6. Scott, *Seeing Like a State*, pp. 89–90.
7. John Helliwell, Richard Layard, and Jeffrey Sachs, eds., *World Happiness Report 2016*, vol. 1 (New York: Sustainable Development Solutions Network, 2016), p. 20.
8. For human mortality improvement in evolutionary context, see Oskar Burger, Annette Baudisch, and James W. Vaupel, "Human Mortality Improvement in Evolutionary Context," *PNAS* 109, no. 44 (October 30, 2012).
9. Jared Diamond, *Guns, Germs, and Steel* (New York: W. W. Norton, 1997).
10. Steven Pinker, *The Better Angels of Our Nature* (New York: Penguin Books, 2012), chap. 3.

11. Manuel Eisner, "Long-Term Historical Trends in Violent Crime," *Crime and Justice* 30 (2003): pp. 85, 96, 97.

12. Angus Maddison, "Poor until 1820," *Wall Street Journal*, January 11, 1999.

13. Josiah Ober, *The Rise and Fall of Classical Greece* (Princeton, NJ: Princeton University Press, 2015), pp. xiv–xv.

14. Douglass North, John Wallis, and Barry Weingast, *Violence and Social Orders* (Cambridge: Cambridge University Press, 2009); Daron Acemoglu and James A. Robinson, *Why Nations Fail* (New York: Crown, 2012). North, Wallis, and Weingast use the term *open access order*; Acemoglu and Robinson use the term *inclusive society.*

15. Ober, *Rise and Fall*, p. xiii. (Italics in original.)

16. North, Wallis, and Weingast, *Violence and Social Orders.*

17. North, Wallis, and Weingast, *Violence and Social Orders*, p. 6.

18. North, Wallis, and Weingast, *Violence and Social Orders*, p. 5.

19. North, Wallis, and Weingast, *Violence and Social Orders*, chaps. 1–2; Daron Acemoglu and James A. Robinson, *Why Nations Fail* (New York: Crown, 2012), chap. 3.

20. Francis Fukuyama, *Political Order and Political Decay* (New York: Farrar, Straus, Giroux, 2014); William G. Howell and Terry Moe, *Relic: How Our Constitution Undermines Effective Government* (New York: Basic Books, 2016).

21. North, Wallis, and Weingast, *Violence and Social Orders*; Acemoglu and Robinson, *Why Nations Fail.*

22. John M. Owen IV, *The Clash of Ideas in World Politics* (Princeton, NJ: Princeton University Press, 2010), p. 2.

23. Frank Schimmelfennig, "The Community Trap: Liberal Norms, Rhetorical Action, and the Eastern Enlargement of the European Union," *International Organization* 55, no. 1 (Winter 2001).

24. OECD, "OECD Trends from 1960 to 2012: Interactive Charts," October 16, 2013.

25. Condoleezza Rice, "Rethinking the National Interest," *Foreign Affairs* 87, no. 4 (July/August 2008).

26. Rice, "Rethinking the National Interest," p. 14.

27. For a discussion of the relationship between ideology and power, see Stephen D. Krasner, *Defending the National Interest* (Princeton, NJ: Princeton University Press, 1978).

28. Stephen D. Krasner, "An Orienting Principle for Foreign Policy," *Policy Review* (Stanford University, Hoover Institution, October 1, 2010).

29. Krasner, "An Orienting Principle."

30. Paul H. Wise and Michele Barry, "Civil War and the Global Threat of Pandemics," *Daedalus* 146, no. 4 (Fall 2017).

31. "HIV/AIDS," World Health Organization, July 19, 2018.

32. Krasner, "An Orienting Principle."

33. Merilee Grindle, "Good Enough Governance: Poverty Reduction and Reform in Developing Countries," *Governance: An International Journal of Policy, Administration, and Institutions* 17, no. 4 (2004); John Rawls, *The Law of Peoples* (Cambridge, MA: Harvard University Press, 1999). The term, although not the specifics elaborated here, originated with Grindle; the term *benevolent absolutism* is elaborated by Rawls.

34. On the importance of distinguishing between corruption that removes wealth from a country and corruption that keeps resources within a polity, see Sarah Chayes, *Thieves of State: Why Corruption Threatens Global Security* (New York: W. W. Norton, 2015); see also Michael Johnston, *Syndromes of Corruption* (Cambridge: Cambridge University Press, 2005).

35. Stephen D. Krasner, "Seeking Good-Enough-Governance—Not Democracy," *The Great Debate* (blog), Reuters, September 23, 2013.

36. Stephen D. Krasner and Thomas Risse, "External Actors, State-Building, and Service Provision in Areas of Limited Statehood: Introduction," *Governance* 27, no. 4 (2014); Marco Schäferhoff, "External Actors and the Provision of Public Health Services in Somalia," *Governance* 27, no. 4 (2014).

37. For an illuminating discussion of infrastructure corruption in contemporary Russia, see Joshua Yaffa, "Oligarchy 2.0," *The New Yorker*, May 29, 2017.

38. Krasner, "Seeking Good-Enough-Goverance."

Chapter 2: **The Nature of Threats in the Modern Era**

1. Vanda Felbab-Brown, "Organized Crime, Illicit Economies, Civil Violence and International Order: More Complex Than You Think," *Daedalus* 146, no. 4 (Fall 2017).

2. Stewart Patrick, *The Sovereignty Wars* (Washington, DC: The Brookings Institution Press, 2017).

3. Paul H. Wise and Michele Barry, "Civil War and the Global Threat of Pandemics," *Daedalus* 146, no. 4 (Fall 2017).

4. Wise and Barry, "Civil War," pp. 1–5.

5. Wise and Barry, "Civil War," pp. 6–9.

6. Wise and Barry, "Civil War," pp. 9–11.

7. Wise and Barry, "Civil War," pp. 12–13.

8. Joel Achenbach and Lena H. Sun, "Trump Budget Seeks Huge Cuts to Science and Medical Research, Disease Prevention," *Washington Post*, May 23, 2017.

9. Ohio Center of Excellence for Bioterrorism Preparedness and Response, "Anthrax," Ohio State University Wexner Medical Center Department of Family Medicine (website).

10. Heidi Ledford, "CRISPR, the Disruptor," *Nature* 522, no. 7554 (June 4, 2015).

11. For an example of this debate see Tim Trevan, "Do Not Censor Science in the Name of Biosecurity," *Nature* 486, no. 7403 (June 21, 2012); and "Sunday Dialogue: Bird Flu Experiments," *New York Times*, Sunday Review: Letters, January 28, 2012.

12. Stockholm International Peace Research Institute, "Global Nuclear Weapons: Downsizing but Modernizing," June 13, 2016.

13. Steve Coll, *Directorate S: The C.I.A. and America's Secret Wars in Afghanistan and Pakistan* (New York: Penguin Books, 2018), pp. 45, 366, 402, 437, 454.

14. "Estonia and Russia: A Cyber-Riot," *The Economist*, May 10, 2007.

15. Matt Zapotosky, "FBI Has Accessed San Bernardino Shooter's Phone without Apple's Help," *Washington Post*, March 28, 2016.

16. United Nations High Commissioner for Refugees (UNHCR), *Global Trends: Forced Displacement in 2017* (United Nations publication), p. 16.

17. UNHCR, *Forced Displacement in 2017*, p. 6, fig. 1.

18. United States Holocaust Memorial Museum, "Voyage of the St. Louis," Holocaust Encyclopedia (website), last edited June 16, 2016.

19. Laura Barnett, "Global Governance and the Evolution of the International Refugee Regime," *International Journal of Refugee Law* 14, no. 2/3 (2002); and Nicole Triola, "The International Refugee Regime: A Failing System," *Ramapo Journal of Law and Society* 1, no. 2 (Fall 2014).

20. "Asylum and the Rights of Refugees," International Justice Resource Center (website), n.d.

21. United Nations High Commissioner for Refugees, *Global Trends: Forced Displacement in 2015* (United Nations publication, June 20, 2016), p. 18, fig. 6.

22. Sarah Kenyon Lischer, "The Global Refugee Crisis," *Daedalus* 146, no. 4 (Fall 2017).

23. Dan Bilefsky, "Sweden Toughens Rules for Refugees Seeking Asylum," *New York Times*, June 21, 2016.

24. Benjamin Wittes and Gabriella Blum, *The Future of Violence: Robots and Germs, Hackers and Drones* (New York: Basic Books, 2015), chap. 1.

25. Abraham Lowenthal, *The Dominican Intervention* (Cambridge, MA: Harvard University Press, 1972).

Chapter 3: **Accounting for History and Human Nature**

1. Daniel Kurtz-Phelan, *The China Mission: George Marshall's Unfinished War 1945–47* (New York: W. W. Norton, 2018).

2. See, for instance, Henry Rowen, "When Will the Chinese People Be Free?" *Journal of Democracy* 18, no. 3 (July 2007).

3. Francis Fukuyama, *Political Order and Political Decay* (New York: Farrar, Straus, Giroux, 2014).

4. For one of the original statements of the modernization thesis, see Seymour M. Lipset, "Some Social Requisites of Democracy: Economic Development and Political Legitimacy," *American Political Science Review* 53, no. 1 (March 1959). For more recent statements, see Ronald Inglehart and Christian Welzel, *Modernization, Cultural Change, and Democracy* (Cambridge: Cambridge University Press, 2005) and "How Development Leads to Democracy: What We Know about Modernization," *Foreign Affairs* 88, no. 2 (2009).

5. W. W. Rostow, *The Stages of Economic Growth: A Non-Communist Manifesto* (Cambridge: Cambridge University Press, 1960). Rostow became a special assistant to President Lyndon Johnson after leaving MIT.

6. Michael Clemens and Todd Moss, "Ghost of 0.7%: Origins and Relevance of the International Aid Target" (working paper, Center for Global Development, September 6, 2005).

7. Adam Przeworski et al., *Democracy and Development: Political Institutions and Well-Being in the World, 1950–1990* (New York: Cambridge University Press, 2000), pp. 78–79.

8. Przeworski et al., *Democracy and Development*, pp. 19–22.

9. Przeworski et al., *Democracy and Development*, p. 98.

10. Carles Boix, "Democracy, Development, and the International System," *American Political Science Review* 105, no. 4 (November 2011): p. 809.

11. Carles Boix, "Democracy, Development"; Przeworski et al., *Democ-*

racy and Development, p. 98. Carles Boix and Susan Stokes, "Endogenous Democratization," *World Politics* 55, no. 4 (July 2003), found a weak positive relationship between per capita income and transitions to democracy; transitions were more likely at higher levels of income, but other empirical studies have found no relationship.

12. Carles Boix, "Democracy, Development," pp. 812, 813.

13. Samuel P. Huntington, *The Third Wave* (Norman: University of Oklahoma Press, 1993); Seva Gunitsky, *Aftershocks: Great Powers and Domestic Reforms in the Twentieth Century* (Princeton, NJ: Princeton University Press, 2017).

14. Acemoglu and Robinson put the case against modernization theory with particular vigor and clarity: "Modernization theory is both incorrect and unhelpful for thinking about how to confront the major problems of extractive institutions in failing nations. The strongest piece of evidence in favor of modernization theory is that rich nations are the ones that have democratic regimes, respect civil and human rights, and enjoy functioning markets and generally inclusive economic institutions. Yet interpreting this association as supporting modernization theory ignores the major effect of inclusive economic political institutions on economic growth. As we have argued throughout this book, it is the societies with inclusive institutions that have grown over the past three hundred years and have become relatively rich today." Daron Acemoglu and James Robinson, *Why Nations Fail* (New York: Crown, 2012), p. 454.

15. For an exhibition of Greek bronzes, see Jens Daehner and Kenneth Lapatin, *Power and Pathos: Bronze Sculpture of the Hellenistic World* (Los Angeles: Getty Museum, 2015, exhibition catalog).

16. Peer Vries, "Europe in the World, 1500–2000," in *Global Economic History*, ed. Tirthankar Roy and Giorgio Riello (London: Bloomsbury, 2018). Original data in S. Broadberry and K. O'Rourke, introduction to *The Cambridge Economic History of Modern Europe*, vol. 1, *1700–1870*, ed. S. Broadberry and K. O'Rourke (Cambridge: Cambridge University Press, 2010), p. 2.

17. Carles Boix and Scott Abramson, "The Roots of the Industrial Revolution or Socially Embedded Know-How?" (paper presented at the Annual Meeting of the American Political Science Association, 2013), p. 48.

18. M. H. Robb et al., *Teotihuacan: City of Water, City of Fire* (Berkeley: University of California Press, 2017, exhibition catalog).

19. Karl Marx, *The Eighteenth Brumaire of Louis Bonaparte*, trans. Terrell Carver, in *Marx's Eighteenth Brumaire: (Post)Modern Interpretations*, ed. Mark Cowling and James Martin (London: Pluto Press, 2002), p. 19.

20. Two of the most prominent rebuttals of modernization theory are by Samuel P. Huntington. In 1965 he published "Political Order and Political Decay" in the journal *World Politics*, followed in 1968 by his book *Political Order in Changing Societies*.

21. Samuel P. Huntington, *Political Order in Changing Societies* (New Haven, CT: Yale University Press, 1968), p. 47.

22. Huntington, *Political Order*, pp. 81–82.

23. Huntington, *Political Order*, p. 1.

24. "Case Study: Congo," in *The Story of Africa*, BBC World Service (website).

25. Francis Fukuyama, *State-Building: Governance and World Order in the 21st Century* (Ithaca, NY: Cornell University Press, 2004), pp. 8–12.

26. World Bank, *World Development Report 1997: The State in a Changing World* (New York: Oxford University Press, 1997), p. 27, table 1.1.

27. Martha Finnemore, "International Organizations as Teachers of Norms: The United Nations Educational, Scientific, and Cultural Organization and Science Policy," *International Organization*, 47 (1993).

28. Finnemore, "International Organizations."

29. For discussions of the problem of decoupling, see Meyer et al., "World Society and the Nation-State," *American Journal of Sociology* 103, no. 1 (July 1997); Lant Pritchett, Michael Woolcock, and Matt Andrews, "Looking Like a State: Techniques of Persistent Failure in State Capability for Implementation" (CID Working Paper No. 239, Kennedy School, Harvard University, June 2012); and especially Martha Finnemore, "Norms, Culture, and World Politics: Insights from Sociology's Institutionalism," *International Organization* 50, no. 2 (Spring 1996).

30. Hendrik Spruyt, *The Sovereign State and Its Competitors* (Princeton, NJ: Princeton University Press, 1994).

31. Charles Tilly, *Coercion, Capital, and European States, AD 990–1992* (New York: Wiley-Blackwell, 1992), pp. 45, 65, 77–78; Spruyt, *The Sovereign State*.

32. Jan Glete, *War and the State in Early Modern Europe: Spain, the Dutch Republic and Sweden as Fiscal-Military States 1500–1660* (London: Routledge, 2002).

33. Janice Thomson, *Mercenaries, Pirates, and Sovereigns* (Princeton, NJ: Princeton University Press, 1994).

34. Tilly, *Coercion*, p. 53.

35. Tilly, *Coercion*, p. 53.

36. Tilly, *Coercion*, p. 20.

37. Nicholas Sambanis, Stergios Skaperdas, and William C. Wohlforth, "Nation-Building through War," *American Political Science Review* 109, no. 2 (May 2015).

38. Timothy Besley and Torsten Persson, *Pillars of Prosperity: The Political Economics of Development Clusters* (Princeton, NJ: Princeton University Press, 2011), fig. 1.8, p. 17.

39. Victoria Tin-bor Hui, *War and State Formation in Ancient China and Early Modern Europe* (Cambridge: Cambridge University Press, 2005), pp. 7–8; Francis Fukuyama, *The Origins of Political Order* (New York: Farrar, Straus, Giroux, 2011), chap. 7.

40. Acemoglu and Robinson, *Why Nations Fail*, p. 310; W. G. Beasley, *The Meiji Restoration* (Stanford: Stanford University Press, 1972).

41. Tanisha M. Fazal, *State Death: The Politics and Geography of Conquest, Occupation, and Annexation* (Princeton, NJ: Princeton University Press, 2011), chap. 2, fig. 2.2.

42. Tong Vu, "Studying the State through State Formation," *World Politics* 62, no. 1 (2010); Spruyt, *The Sovereign State*.

43. Marco Schäferhoff, "External Actors and the Provision of Public Health Services in Somalia," *Governance* 27, no. 4 (2014).

44. Francis Fukuyama, *Political Order*, chap. 10.

45. For other societal arguments about state strengthening, especially in Latin America, that emphasize dominant social coalitions at the time of independence or during the Great Depression, see Marcus Kurtz, *Latin American State Building in Comparative Perspective: Social Foundations of Institutional Order* (Cambridge: Cambridge University Press, 2013), pp. 6–10, 36–48; and Marcus Kurtz, "The Social Foundations of Institutional Order: Reconsidering War and the 'Resource Curse' in Third World State Building," *Politics and Society* 37, no. 4 (2009).

46. Matthew Lange, *Lineages of Despotism and Development: British Colonialism and State Power* (Chicago: University of Chicago Press, 2009), chaps. 1–2; David Laitin, *Hegemony and Culture* (Chicago: University of Chicago Press, 1986). British law protected property rights and promoted growth more effectively than French, and French law more effectively than Spanish or Portuguese; see David Landes, *The Wealth and Poverty of Nations* (New York: W. W. Norton, 1999), chaps. 19, 20.

47. Reo Matsuzaki, *Statebuilding by Imposition: Resistance and Control in Colonial Taiwan and the Philippines* (Ithaca, NY: Cornell University Press, 2019), p. 165.

48. Atul Kohli, "Where Do High Growth Political Economies Come From? The Japanese Lineage of Korea's 'Developmental State,'" *World Development* 22, no. 9 (1994); for a counterargument view, see Stephan Haggard, David Kang, and Chung-in Moon, "Japanese Colonialism and Korean Development: A Critique," *World Development* 25, no. 6 (1997).

49. Francis Fukuyama, *Political Order*, chap. 1.

50. Philip S. Gorski, *The Disciplinary Revolution: Calvinism and the Rise of the State in Early Modern Europe* (Chicago: University of Chicago Press, 2003), pp. 17, 158–59.

51. Gorski, *The Disciplinary Revolution*, chaps. 2 and 3.

52. Steven Rosefielde and Stefan Hedlund, *Russia Since 1980* (Cambridge: Cambridge University Press, 2008), p. 87, table 5.7.

53. Landes, *Wealth and Poverty*; Jonathan Spence, *Treason by the Book* (New York: Penguin Books, 2002).

54. See Tilly, *Coercion*; Spruyt, *The Sovereign State*; Rostow, *Stages of Economic Growth*, pp. 5–7, 15–16; Timothy Besley and Torsten Persson, "The Origins of State Capacity: Property Rights, Taxation, and Politics," *American Economic Review* 99, no. 4 (September 2009); Hui, *War and State Formation*, pp. 1–37, 137–42; Fukuyama, *Origins*, chaps. 7, 8, 9.

55. Amelia Peck, *Interwoven Globe: The Worldwide Textile Trade, 1500–1800* (New York: Metropolitan Museum of Art, 2013, exhibition catalog).

56. James Scott, *The Art of Not Being Governed* (New Haven, CT: Yale University Press, 2009), p. 85.

57. James Scott, *Seeing Like a State* (New Haven, CT: Yale University Press, 1998).

Chapter 4: **The Difficulty in Replicating Success**

1. Daron Acemoglu and James A. Robinson, *Why Nations Fail* (New York: Crown, 2012).

2. Daron Acemoglu and James A. Robinson, *Economic Origins of Dictatorship and Democracy* (New York: Cambridge University Press, 2006), pp. xii, 15–23; Gary W. Cox, Douglass C. North, and Barry R. Weingast, "The Violence Trap: A Political-Economic Approach to the Problems of Development," SSRN (February 13, 2015); Raghuram G. Rajan, "Rent Preservation and the Persistence of Underdevelopment," *American Economic Journal: Macroeconomics* 1, no. 1 (2009); Dou-

glass North, John Wallis, and Barry Weingast, *Violence and Social Orders* (Cambridge: Cambridge University Press, 2009); Acemoglu and Robinson, *Why Nations Fail.*

3. Colin Martin and Geoffrey Parker, *The Spanish Armada* (New York: W. W. Norton, 1988), pp. 15–16.

4. Robert Hutchinson, *The Spanish Armada* (London: Weidenfeld and Nicolson, 2013), pp. xi, 121.

5. Hutchinson, *The Spanish Armada*, p. 175.

6. Joseph A. Schumpeter, *Capitalism, Socialism and Democracy* (London: Routledge, 2003, first published 1942), p. 83; Cox, North, and Weingast, "The Violence Trap," p. 3.

7. Ricardo Hausmann, Lant Pritchett, and Dani Rodrik, "Growth Accelerations" (NBER Working Paper 10566, 2004).

8. North, Wallis, and Weingast, *Violence and Social Orders*, p. 4.

9. Cox, North, and Weingast, "The Violence Trap," p. 2.

10. Cox, North, and Weingast, "The Violence Trap," pp. 5–6.

11. Timothy Besley and Torsten Persson, *Pillars of Prosperity: The Political Economics of Development Clusters* (Princeton, NJ: Princeton University Press, 2011), chap. 1.

12. North, Wallis, and Weingast, *Violence and Social Orders*, pp. 18–19.

13. North, Wallis, and Weingast, *Violence and Social Orders*, pp. 24, 157–59.

14. In a similar vein, Besley and Persson, *Pillars of Prosperity*, pp. 56–63, argue that there are three kinds of states: common interest states, in which revenue is used for the collective; redistributive states, in which leaders can collect some taxes and make some investments in collective goods but, because the leaders want to stay in power, the distribution of benefits favors some groups over others; and weak states with incoherent institutions, where leaders make no investments in collective goods.

15. Paul David, "Clio and the Economics of QWERTY," *American Economic Review* 75, no. 2 (1985); and W. Brian Arthur, "Competing Technologies, Increasing Returns, and Lock-In by Historical Events," *The Economic Journal* 99, no. 394 (March 1989).

16. Saumitra Jha, "Financial Asset Holdings and Political Attitudes: Evidence from Revolutionary England," *Quarterly Journal of Economics* 130, no. 3 (2015).

17. Douglass North and Barry Weingast, "Constitutions and Commitment: The Evolution of Institutions Governing Public Choice in Seventeenth-Century England," *Journal of Economic History* 49, no. 4 (December 1989).

18. North, Wallis, and Weingast, *Violence and Social Orders*, p. 78.
19. Daron Acemoglu and James A. Robinson, *Economic Origins of Dictatorship and Democracy* (New York: Cambridge University Press, 2006), pp. 16–28.
20. Acemoglu and Robinson, *Economic Origins*, pp. 31–40.
21. University of Uppsala Department of Peace and Conflict Research, "Uppsala Conflict Data Program" (website).
22. "Botswana," *The World Factbook* (Washington, DC: Central Intelligence Agency, n.d.).
23. "Botswana."
24. Acemoglu and Robinson, *Why Nations Fail*, p. 127; Willie Henderson, "Seretse Khama: A Personal Appreciation," *African Affairs* 89 (January 1990); Anne Pitcher, Mary H. Moran, and Michael Johnston, "Rethinking Patrimonialism and Neopatrimonialism in Africa," *African Studies Review* 52, no. 1 (April 2009); Nicolas van de Walle, "Presidentialism and Clientelism in Africa's Emerging Party Systems," *Journal of Modern African Studies* 41, no. 2 (June 2003).
25. Acemoglu and Robinson, *Economic Origins*, pp. 4–14.
26. Derived from figures in José Jurado Sánchez, "Military Expenditure, Spending Capacity and Budget Constraint in Eighteenth-Century Spain and Britain," *Revista de Historia Económica/Journal of Iberian and Latin American Economic History* (Second Series) 27, no. 1 (Spring 2008), p. 148, table 1.
27. Jurado Sánchez, "Military Expenditure," pp. 146–47.
28. Jurado Sánchez, "Military Expenditure," p. 155, table 2.
29. Gary W. Cox, *Marketing Sovereign Promises* (New York: Cambridge University Press, 2016), p. 136.
30. Cox, *Marketing Sovereign Promises*, p. 133.
31. John Brewer, *The Sinews of Power* (Cambridge, MA: Harvard University Press, 1988); North and Weingast, "Constitutions and Commitment"; Cox, *Marketing Sovereign Promises*.
32. Gary W. Cox, "Development Traps of Britain," unpublished manuscript, Stanford University, 2016.
33. Roger Knight and Martin Wilcox, *Sustaining the Fleet, 1793–1815* (Woodbridge, UK: Boydell Press, 2010), p. 9.
34. Knight and Wilcox, *Sustaining the Fleet*, p. 20.
35. Cox, "Development Traps of Britain," p. 1; Cox, *Marketing Sovereign Promises*, p. 150. North, Wallis, and Weingast have emphasized that the Victualling Board was one of the important mechanisms that allowed Britain to have an effective military, because the board created a credible commitment that the state would not have arbitrary

control over the centralized instruments of violence. The Victualling Board, which was first created in 1683, was, however, something more: it was a structure that demonstrated to the commercial class that there could be an efficient and nonarbitrary state, that a rule-of-law budget could work in the civilian as well as the military sector.

36. Isabela Mares, *From Open Secrets to Secret Voting: Democratic Electoral Reforms and Voter Autonomy* (Cambridge: Cambridge University Press, 2015), p. 1.

37. Mares, *From Open Secrets*, chap. 1.

38. A first step in identifying polities that might be in the middle is to look at the distribution of per capita income. The following table is derived from World Bank data.

Gross National Income Per Capita Atlas Method, 2015	Number of Countries: excluding mini-states, e.g., Andorra; dependencies, e.g., Hong Kong; and oil rich states, e.g., Brunei
Above $20,000	41
$10,000–19,999	24
$5,000–$9,999	31
$2,500–$4,999	33
$0–$2,499	59

Source: World Bank, "Gross National Income Per Capita 2017, Atlas Method and PPP," World Development Indicators Database, April 25, 2019.

There is clustering at the top and bottom of the per capita income scales. All of the countries with incomes above $20,000 per capita (excluding mini-states and oil-exporting states) are classified by Freedom House as free, with one exception, Singapore, which is classified as partly free. Of the twenty-six countries with per capita incomes above $20,000 for which scores are available from Polity IV (Polity does not provide data for countries with populations under 500,000), twenty-one received a 10, the highest possible rating on the democracy scale; four others received scores between 6 and 9, which would place them within the Polity IV democracy category; only one, Singapore, was not classified as a democracy.

Of the twenty-four countries with incomes between $10,000 and $19,999 (again excluding mini-states and oil-exporting states), nineteen were classified by Freedom House as free, two as partly free, and three as not free. Of the sixteen countries for which Polity IV scores are available for this same income category, eight received the top score of 10, and of the eight others, only Russia and Malaysia received scores of less than 6.

Of the countries with incomes between $5,000 and $9,999, twenty-seven received scores from the Polity IV data set. Of these twenty-seven, only one received a score of 10, Mauritius; nineteen received scores between 6 and 9; seven received scores of less than 6. Freedom House scores thirty-three countries in this same income bracket. Of these thirty-three, sixteen received a score of free; eight, a score of partly free; and nine, a score of not free.

Of the countries with incomes between $2,500 and $4,999, Polity IV provides scores for twenty-five countries. Two received a score of 10 (Mongolia and Cape Verde); thirteen received scores between 6 and 9; the rest were below 6. Freedom House provides scores for thirty-three countries in this same income bracket: twelve received a score of free; fifteen, a score of partly free; the rest, not free.

Of the fifty-nine countries with per capita incomes below $2,500, only six were classified by Freedom House as free (São Tomé and Príncipe, India, Ghana, Lesotho, Senegal, and Benin); twenty-seven as partly free; and the remaining as not free. Polity IV scores fifty-three countries with per capita incomes below $2,500. Not one of these countries receives a 10; twenty-three receive scores between 6 and 9; the rest, below 6.

The Freedom House scores and Polity scores are highly correlated but not perfectly so. See J. Högström, "Does the Choice of Democracy Measure Matter? Comparisons between the Two Leading Democracy Indices, Freedom House and Polity IV," *Government and Opposition* 48, no. 2 (April 2013). Freedom House scores from *Freedom in the World 2015*; Polity scores from Wikipedia, s.v. "Polity Data Series"; per capita income scores from World Bank, "Gross National Income Per Capita 2017."

39. Polity scores from Wikipedia, "Polity Data Series"; per capita income scores from World Bank, "Gross National Income Per Capita 2017."
40. "GDP Per Capita," World Bank (website).
41. Polity scores from Wikipedia, "Polity Data Series"; per capita income scores from World Bank, "Gross National Income Per Capita 2017."
42. Per capita incomes and Polity scores are obviously not the only factors that could be used to describe states that have a mixed or intermediate polity, that are neither open nor closed access. Another data set, which assesses state fragility, suggests similar conclusions, if a Polity score of 10 is the right score to focus on for open access orders. The Center for Systemic Peace, the same people that bring you the Polity data set, have also constructed an index of state fragility. The following table shows the relationship between the state fragility index for 2014 (divided into

three groups, where 0 is the most stable and 24 is the highest fragility score), Polity scores of 10 for 2015, and scores of 6–9 for 2015.

State Fragility and Polity IV Scores

Polity Scores	High Fragility, 12–24 scores on fragility index	Medium Fragility, 4–11 scores on fragility index	Low Fragility, scores of 0–3 on fragility index
Not a democracy, scores of 5 to -10	31	28	2
Non-consolidated democracy, scores of 6–9	13	34	16
Consolidated democracy, score of 10	0	3	32

Sources: State Fragility Scores from Monty G. Marshall and Benjamin R. Cole, "State Fragility Index and Matrix," Center for Systemic Peace; Polity scores from Wikipedia, s.v. "Polity Data Series."

Again, there is nirvana at the top. There are thirty-two countries with low state fragility scores and Polity scores of 10. There are also thirty-one countries at the bottom that are not democracies and where fragility is high. Nevertheless, there are a few countries that might be in the middle, that might be transitioning from closed to open access orders or where open access attributes might apply to some aspects of the political order. There are fifty countries with Polity IV scores of 6–9 that have a medium or low fragility index. One key analytic claim made by rational choice institutionalism, however, is that there is no guarantee that this transition to an open access or consolidated democracy will take place.

43. Bradley Christopher Parks, "Brokering Development Policy Change: The Parallel Pursuit of Millennium Challenge Account Resources and Reform" (PhD diss., London School of Economics, 2013); Barbara Geddes, *Politician's Dilemma: Building State Capacity in Latin America* (Berkeley: University of California Press, 1994).

44. Albert O. Hirschman, *Exit, Voice, and Loyalty* (Cambridge, MA: Harvard University Press, 1970).

45. "Faculty Spotlight: Onyinye Iweala, MD," Duke University School of Medicine, July 6, 2015.

46. Stephen D. Krasner and Jeremy Weinstein, "Improving Governance from the Outside In," *Annual Review of Political Science* 17 (2014): pp. 131–34.

Chapter 5: **Good Enough Governance**

1. See Naazneen Barma, *The Peacebuilding Puzzle: Political Order in Post-Conflict States* (Cambridge: Cambridge University Press, 2017), for an analysis that emphasizes the need for interest complementarity between external and internal elites.
2. Séverine Autesserre, *Peaceland: Conflict Resolution and the Everyday Politics of International Intervention* (Cambridge: Cambridge University Press, 2014), especially pp. 9–13.
3. Sarah Bush, *The Taming of Democracy Assistance: Why Democracy Promotion Does Not Confront Dictators* (Cambridge: Cambridge University Press, 2015), p. x.
4. Bush, *Taming*, p. 14.
5. Bush, *Taming*, pp. 4, 25, 53.
6. Stephen D. Krasner and Jeremy Weinstein, "Improving Governance from the Outside In," *Annual Review of Political Science* 17 (2014): p. 128.
7. Polity IV Project. "Polity IV Individual Country Regime Trends, 1946–2013," Center for Systemic Peace (website).
8. Monty Marshall and Benjamin Cole, *Global Report 2014: Conflict, Governance, and State Fragility* (Vienna, VA: Center for Systemic Peace, 2014), p. 23. For Tunisia's 2015 rating, see Polity IV Project, "Regime Trends, 1946–2013."
9. "Inclusive enough" from the World Bank, *World Development Report 2011: Conflict, Security, and Development* (Washington, DC: World Bank, May 26, 2011), pp. xvii, 104, 112, 120.
10. Lisa Blaydes, *State of Repression: Iraq under Saddam Hussein* (Princeton, NJ: Princeton University Press, 2018).
11. For a discussion of growth spurts, see Ricardo Hausmann, Lant Pritchett, and Dani Rodrik, "Growth Accelerations" (NBER Working Paper 10566, 2004).
12. Benjamin J. Kaplan, *Divided by Faith: Religious Conflict and the Practice of Toleration in Early Modern Europe* (Cambridge, MA: Harvard University Press, 2007), chap. 8.
13. Merilee Grindle, "Good Enough Governance: Poverty Reduction and Reform in Developing Countries," *Governance: An International Journal of Policy, Administration, and Institutions* 17, no. 4 (2004); and Merilee Grindle, "Good Enough Governance Revisited," *Development Policy Review* 25, no. 5 (2007): pp. 553–74.
14. For a list of the SDGs and associated targets, see Liz Ford, "Sustainable Development Goals: All You Need to Know," *The Guardian*,

January 19, 2015; and "Sustainable Development Goals," United Nations (website).

15. Stephen Biddle, "Building Security Forces and Stabilizing Nations: The Problem of Agency," *Daedalus* 146, no. 4 (Fall 2017).

16. Gordon Adams and Richard Sokolsky, "Governance and Security Sector Assistance: The Missing Link—Part II," Lawfare (blog), July 19, 2015.

17. Adams and Sokolsky, "Governance and Security Sector."

18. Steve Coll, *Directorate S: The C.I.A. and America's Secret Wars in Afghanistan and Pakistan* (New York: Penguin Books, 2018), p. 110.

19. Mark Mazzetti, "The Devastating Paradox of Pakistan," *The Atlantic*, March 2018.

20. Biddle, "Building Security Forces."

21. Dexter Filkins, "What We Left Behind: An Increasingly Authoritarian Leader, a Return of Sectarian Violence, and a Nation Worried for Its Future," *New Yorker*, April 28, 2014.

22. David Lake, *The Statebuilder's Dilemma* (Ithaca, NY: Cornell University Press, 2016).

23. Sullivan and Koch have collected data on all military interventions by major powers (the five permanent members of the UN Security Council) between 1946 and 2003. There were 126 military interventions (defined as a military action involving more than five hundred troops) during this time period. Their findings are summarized in table IV of Patricia L. Sullivan and Michael T. Koch, "Military Intervention by Powerful States, 1945–2003," *Journal of Peace Research* 46, no. 5 (September 2009), p. 715.

In 100 percent of interventions with state targets, external actors were able to maintain state authority, although the number of cases, at five, is small, and the selection may be endogenous, that is, external actors might intervene in favor of existing authorities only if they believe they can be successful. In 50 percent of interventions with state targets, they were successful in achieving protection and order.

24. "Egypt: Mohammed Morsi Death Sentence Overturned," BBC News, November 15, 2016.

25. Roberta Rampton and Arshad Mohammed, "Obama Ends Freeze on U.S. Military Aid to Egypt," Reuters, March 31, 2015.

26. Matthew Lee, "US to Release $1.2 Billion in Military Aid to Egypt," Fox News, September 7, 2018.

27. Angus Deaton, *The Great Escape: Health, Wealth, and the Origins of Inequality* (Princeton, NJ: Princeton University Press, 2013), chaps. 1 and 2.

28. "Life Expectancy at Birth, Female (Years)," World Bank, n.d.

29. "PEPFAR Now Reaches Over 14 Million People Globally with Life-saving HIV Treatment," United States President's Emergency Plan for AIDS Relief, May 16, 2018.

30. "Poliomyelitis," World Health Organization, March 1, 2019.

31. Joseph L. Dieleman et al., "Sources and Focus of Health Development Assistance, 1990–2014," *JAMA* 313, no. 23 (2015): p. 2361.

32. "Official Bilateral Commitments by Sector" and "Aid to Developing Countries," OECD iLibrary..

33. Dieleman et al., "Sources and Focus," p. 2361.

34. Dieleman et al., "Sources and Focus," p. 2366.

35. World Health Organization, *The World Health Report 2000: Health Systems; Improving Performance*, June 2000, pp. vii–viii.

36. Pan American Health Organization, *Public Health in the Americas: Conceptual Renewal, Performance Assessment, and Bases for Action* (Washington, DC: Pan American Health Organization, 2002).

37. Sameen Siddiqi et al., "Framework for Assessing Governance of the Health System in Developing Countries: Gateway to Good Governance," *Health Policy* 90 (2009): p. 17, table 1.

38. Stephen D. Krasner and Thomas Risse, "External Actors, State-Building, and Service Provision in Areas of Limited Statehood: Introduction," *Governance* 27, no. 4 (2014).

39. Transparency International, Corruption Perceptions Index 2017.

40. Conversation with Dr. Stephen Luby.

41. Hristos Doucouliagos and Martin Paldam, "The Aid Effectiveness Literature: The Sad Results of 40 Years of Research," *Journal of Economic Surveys* 23, no. 3 (2009), p. 433; see also Raghuram Rajan and Arvind Subramanian, "What Undermines Aid's Impact on Growth?" (Working Paper No. 05/126, Research Department, IMF, June 2005), who conclude that neither cross-national nor panel results suggest that aid enhances growth.

42. Raghuram Rajan and Arvind Subramanian, "Does Aid Affect Governance?" *American Economic Review* 97, no. 2 (May 2007): p. 322.

43. Nathan Nunn and Nancy Qian, "US Food Aid and Civil Conflict," *American Economic Review* 104, no. 6 (2014): pp. 1630–31.

44. Rajan and Subramanian, "What Undermines Aid's Impact."

45. Bruce Bueno de Mesquita and Hilton L. Root, "The Political Roots of Poverty: The Economic Logic of Autocracy," *The National Interest* 68 (Summer 2002).

46. William Easterly, *The White Man's Burden* (Oxford: Oxford University Press, 2006).

47. Derek Headey, "Geopolitics and the Effect of Foreign Aid on Economic Growth: 1970–2001," *Journal of International Development* 20, no. 2 (March 2008), especially pp. 161–64; Camelia Minoiu and Sanjay G. Reddy, "Development Aid and Economic Growth: A Positive Long-Run Relation," *Quarterly Review of Economics and Finance* 50, no. 1 (February 2010), pp. 30, 34; Craig Burnside and David Dollar, "Aid Spurs Growth—in a Sound Policy Environment," *Finance and Development* 34, no. 4 (1997); Desha Girod, *Explaining Post-Conflict Reconstruction* (New York: Oxford University Press, 2015).

48. Rajan and Subramanian, "Does Aid Affect Governance," pp. 654, 657.

49. Rajan and Subramanian, "Does Aid Affect Governance," p. 655.

50. Rajan and Subramanian, "What Undermines Aid's Impact," p. 23.

51. Tim Buthe and Helen Milner, "Bilateral Investment Treaties and Foreign Direct Investment: A Political Analysis," in *The Effect of Treaties on Foreign Direct Investment: Bilateral Investment Treaties, Double Taxation Treaties, and Investment Flows*, ed. Karl P. Sauvant and Lisa E. Sachs (New York: Oxford University Press, 2009).

52. Srividya Jandhyala, Witold J. Henisz, and Edward D. Mansfield, "Three Waves of BITs: The Global Diffusion of Foreign Investment Policy," *Journal of Conflict Resolution* 55, no. 6 (2011): p. 1047.

53. John Rawls, *The Law of Peoples* (Cambridge, MA: Harvard University Press, 1999).

54. Rod Nordland, "Afghan Women, Eager to Play, Are Relegated to the Sidelines," *New York Times*, April 26, 2016; Alex Horton, "Pentagon Tried to Block Independent Report on Child Sex among Afghan Forces, Senate Office Says," *Washington Post*, November 26, 2017; Zahra Nader and Mujib Mashal, "Despite Ban, Invasive Virginity Tests Remain Prevalent in Afghanistan," *New York Times*, January 6, 2017.

Chapter 6: **Corruption Is Unavoidable**

1. Brian M. Rosenthal, "The Most Expensive Mile of Subway Track on Earth," *New York Times*, December 28, 2017.

2. Rosenthal, "The Most Expensive Mile"; Emma G. Fitzsimmons and Michael LaForgia, "How Cuts in Basic Subway Upkeep Can Make Your Commute Miserable," *New York Times*, December 20, 2017.

3. Between 1976 and 2013, the rate of federal corruption convictions in

Illinois was 1.40 per 100,000 of population, the largest of any state with a population more than 5,000,000.

4. Thomas J. Gradel and Dick Simpson, *Corrupt Illinois: Patronage, Cronyism, and Criminality* (Urbana: University of Illinois Press, 2015).

5. See Jack Paine, "Rethinking the Conflict 'Resource Curse': How Oil Wealth Prevents Center-Seeking Civil Wars," *International Organization* 70, no. 4 (2017), and Stephen Haber and Victor Menaldo, "Do Natural Resources Fuel Authoritarianism? A Reappraisal of the Resource Curse," *American Political Science Review* 105, no. 1 (2011) on why resources might be beneficial. For an exposition of why natural resources are often a curse, see Michael L. Ross, *The Oil Curse: How Petroleum Wealth Shapes the Development of Nations* (Princeton, NJ: Princeton University Press, 2012).

6. Crude oil export values for 2015 from Daniel Workman, "Crude Oil Exports by Country," World's Top Exports (website), March 9, 2017; population figures from the World Bank.

7. David Blair, "Embarrassment as Nigerian Navy 'Loses' Impounded Tanker," *The Telegraph*, September 21, 2004.

8. Christina Katsouris and Aaron Sayne, "Nigeria's Criminal Crude: International Options to Combat the Export of Stolen Oil," Chatham House, September 1, 2013.

9. Institute for Economics and Peace, *Global Terrorism Index 2015* (IEP Report 36, November 2015), p. 4; *Global Terrorism Index 2016* (IEP Report 43, November 2016), p. 4.

10. Drew Hinshaw, "Nigeria President Orders Probe into Army Corruption," *Wall Street Journal*, January 15, 2016; Nick Schifrin, "Did Corruption in Nigeria Hamper Its Fight against Boko Haram?" NPR, December 27, 2015.

11. Transparency International, Corruption Perceptions Index 2018.

12. Hugh Naylor, "Fall of Ramadi Reflects Failure of Iraq's Strategy against ISIS, Analysts Say," *Washington Post*, May 19, 2015; Austin Ramzy, "Malaysia's New Leader Agrees to a Pardon for an Old Foe, Anwar Ibrahim," *New York Times*, May 11, 2018.

13. Bo Rothstein and Aiysha Varraich, *Making Sense of Corruption* (Cambridge: Cambridge University Press, 2017), chap. 3, especially p. 57.

14. Susan Rose-Ackerman, *Corruption and Government: Causes, Consequences, and Reform* (New York: Cambridge University Press, 1999), pp. 1, 5, 226–28.

15. Bob Rijkers, Leila Baghdadi, and Gael Raballand, *Political Connections*

and Tariff Evasion: Evidence from Tunisia (World Bank, Policy Research Working Paper 7336, 2015).

16. Michael Ross, *The Oil Curse: How Petroleum Wealth Shapes the Development of Nations* (Princeton, NJ: Princeton University Press, 2012), chap. 3.

17. Data from the World Bank.

18. United Nations Development Program, "Human Development Index Trends, 1990–2017," *Human Development Reports*, table 2.

19. David Cameron, "PM Speech at Open Government Partnership 2013," Gov.UK, October 31, 2013.

20. Reuters, "Equatorial Guinea: Heir Buys $35 Million U.S. House," *New York Times*, November 9, 2006; Reuters, "Equatorial Guinea: A Vice President Is Ordered to Forfeit Assets in the U.S.," *New York Times*, October 10, 2014; Angelique Chrisafis, "Son of Equatorial Guinea's President Is Convicted of Corruption in France," *The Guardian*, October 27, 2017.

21. David Barstow, "Longtime Critic of Modi Is Now a Target," *New York Times*, August 19, 2015.

22. Austin Ramzy, "Now Free, Malaysia's Anwar Ibrahim Attacks System That Jailed Him Twice," *New York Times*, May 15, 2018.

23. Thomas Fuller, "Malaysian Court Upholds Opposition Leader's Sodomy Conviction," *New York Times*, February 9, 2015.

24. Melanie Kirkpatrick, "Lee Kuan Yew vs. the News," *Wall Street Journal*, March 22, 2015; "International Commission of Jurists," *Singapore Window*, August 22, 1997.

25. Data from the World Bank.

26. David Segal, "Petrobras Oil Scandal Leaves Brazilians Lamenting a Lost Dream," *New York Times*, August 7, 2015; Richard House, "Petrobras Scandal Runs Rolls-Royce through 'Car Wash,'" *Financial Times*, October 29, 2015.

27. Ajit Mishra, "Persistence of Corruption: Some Theoretical Perspectives," *World Development* 34, no. 2 (February 2006): pp. 349–58; Pranab Bardhan, "The Economist's Approach to the Problem of Corruption," *World Development* 34, no. 2 (2006): pp. 341–48; Raymond Fisman and Miriam Golden, *Corruption: What Everyone Needs to Know* (New York: Oxford University Press, 2017), especially introduction.

28. For research on the weak relationship between formal institutions and corruption, see Nan Zhang, "Corruption and Social Norms: Explaining Corruption's Persistence in the Face of Moral Condemnation" (PhD diss., Stanford University, May 2014), fig. 1.3. In the

upper right-hand corner of the table, all of the polities listed are open access or inclusive orders; formal organizations conform with actual practice. In the upper left-hand quadrant, populated mostly by closed access orders, there is no relationship between formal institutions and actual practice.

29. At least according to Transparency International's 2017 ranking.

30. Njoya Tikum, "Guest Post: Time to Go Beyond Anti-Corruption Agencies in Sub-Saharan Africa," *The Global Anticorruption Blog*, January 21, 2016; Rosa Ehrenreich Brooks, "The New Imperialism: Violence, Norms, and the 'Rule of Law,'" *Michigan Law Review* 101, no. 7 (June 2003): pp. 2284–85.

31. Michael Johnston, *Syndromes of Corruption* (Cambridge: Cambridge University Press, 2005).

32. Johnston, *Syndromes of Corruption*, chaps. 1–8.

33. Nicholas Confessore, Sarah Cohen, and Karen Yourish, "Small Pool of Rich Donors Dominates Election Giving," *New York Times*, August 1, 2015.

34. World Bank, World Development Indicators, various years.

35. Paula Hancocks, Yoonjung Seo, and James Griffiths, "Former South Korean President Park Sentenced to 24 Years in Prison," CNN, April 6, 2018.

36. Joyce Lee, and Yuna Park, "Samsung Leader Jay Y. Lee Given Five-Year Jail Sentence for Bribery," Reuters, August 24, 2017.

37. GDP growth rate figures for Kenya from World Bank, World Development Indicators.

38. "How a Cancer of Corruption Steals Nigerian Oil, Weapons and Lives," PBS, December 2, 2015.

39. Sarah Chayes, *Thieves of State: Why Corruption Threatens Global Security* (New York: W. W. Norton, 2015).

40. Chayes, *Thieves of State*, p. 41.

41. Mark Rosenberg, "Trail of Fraud and Vengeance Leads to Kabul Bank Convictions," *New York Times*, March 15, 2013.

42. Bardhan, "The Economist's Approach"; Mary Beth Goodman and Trevor Sutton, "Tackling Corruption in Afghanistan: It's Now or Never," Center for American Progress, March 17, 2015; Rose-Ackerman, *Corruption and Government*, chaps. 4–5.

43. Kempe Ronald Hope, "Liberia's Governance and Economic Management Assistance Program (GEMAP): An Impact Review and Analytical Assessment of a Donor Policy Intervention for Democratic State-Building in a Post-Conflict State," *South African Journal of International Affairs* 17, no. 2 (2010).

44. Transparency International, Corruption Perceptions Index 2017.
45. Transparency International, Corruption Perceptions Index 2004; United States Agency for International Development, *Electoral Security Framework: Technical Guidance Handbook for Democracy and Governance Officers* (Washington, DC: USAID, July 2010); Hope, "Liberia's Governance," p. 250.
46. Desha Girod, *Explaining Post-Conflict Reconstruction* (New York: Oxford University Press, 2015).
47. Matthew Taylor, *Lessons from Guatemala's Commission against Impunity: What Other Countries Can Learn from CICIG's First Decade* (New York: Council on Foreign Relations, 2017); Elisabeth Malkin, "Guatemala Expels U.N.-Backed Anti-Corruption Panel, Claiming Overreach," *New York Times*, January 7, 2019; Aila M. Matanock and Natalia Garbiras-Díaz, "Invited Intervention: A Mechanism to Restore the Rule of Law in Weak States?" Unpublished paper, University of California, Berkeley, August 24, 2016.
48. Michael Lohmuller, "Mandate Renewed, but CICIG Will Not Save Guatemala," InSight Crime, April 23, 2015.
49. "Head of OAS Anti-Corruption Mission in Honduras Resigns," Reuters, February 15, 2018.
50. *Criterio* (@criteriohn), "La MACCIH decepciona porque no da resultados contundentes contra la corrupción," Twitter, March 21, 2019, 11:57 a.m.
51. Mo Ibrahim, "Celtel's Founder on Building a Business on the World's Poorest Continent," *Harvard Business Review*, October 2012; World Bank, *World Development Report 2011* (Washington, DC: World Bank, May 26, 2011), p. 158.
52. Percentile ranks for corruption can be found in World Bank, World Development Indicators.
53. Bruce Bueno de Mesquita et al., *The Logic of Political Survival* (Cambridge: MIT Press, 2003).

Chapter 7: **Elections Sometimes Lead to Bad Outcomes**

1. Francis Fukuyama, "The End of History?" *The National Interest*, 16 (Summer 1989); Francis Fukuyama, *The End of History and the Last Man* (New York: Free Press, 1992).
2. Samuel P. Huntington, *The Third Wave* (Norman: University of Oklahoma Press, 1993); to quote: "A political system is democratic to the extent that its most powerful collective decision makers are selected

through fair, honest, and periodic elections in which candidates freely compete for votes and in which virtually all the adult population is eligible to vote." This definition incorporates the two central elements of democracy: contestation and participation.

3. Adam Przeworski et al., *Democracy and Development: Political Institutions and Well-Being in the World, 1950–1990* (New York: Cambridge University Press, 2000), in one of the most widely used definitions of democracy, require not just free and fair elections but also regular changes of government. Botswana, for instance, is classified as free by Freedom House and as a democracy but not a full democracy by its Polity score, but would not be classified as a democracy according to the Przeworski criteria because the Botswana Democratic Party has never lost an election.

4. Nicholas Cheeseman and Brian Klaas, *How to Rig an Election* (New Haven, CT: Yale University Press, 2018), introduction and chaps. 1 and 2.

5. For an example, see Farishte Jalalzai, "Purple Ink: For Many Women, a Sign of Responsible Citizenship," Radio Free Europe Radio Liberty, April 8, 2014.

6. Pippa Norris, "What Works? Evaluating Electoral Assistance" (paper presented at the Annual Meeting of the American Political Science Association, 2015).

7. Fareed Zakaria, "The Rise of Illiberal Democracy," *Foreign Affairs* 76, no. 6 (1997).

8. Zakaria, "Rise of Illiberal Democracy," p. 26; Arch Puddington, *Breaking Down Democracy: Goals, Strategies, and Methods of Modern Authoritarians* (Washington, DC: Freedom House, June 2017).

9. Carles Boix, "Democracy, Development, and the International System," *American Political Science Review* 105, no. 4 (November 2011); Thomas Carothers, *Aiding Democracy Abroad* (Washington, DC: Carnegie Endowment for International Peace, 1999), chap. 1.

10. Carothers, *Aiding Democracy Abroad*, chap. 6.

11. United States Agency for International Development, *Electoral Security Framework: Technical Guidance Handbook for Democracy and Governance Officers* (Washington, DC: USAID, July 2010), pp. 41–47.

12. Norris, "What Works?"

13. David McFadden, "President: Haiti Runoff Vote Will Take Place as Scheduled," *Washington Post*, January 21, 2016; David McFadden, "Haiti Delays Presidential Runoff Again in Electoral Dispute," *Washington Post*, January 22, 2016.

14. David McFadden, "For 2nd Day in Row, Protest Turns Violent in Haiti Capital," *Washington Post*, January 19, 2016.
15. Susan Hyde, *The Pseudo-Democrat's Dilemma: Why Election Observation Became an International Norm* (Ithaca, NY: Cornell University Press, 2011).
16. Judith Kelley, *Monitoring Democracy: When International Election Observation Works and Why It Often Fails* (Princeton, NJ: Princeton University Press, 2012); James Fearon, "Self-Enforcing Democracy," *Quarterly Journal of Economics* 126, no. 4 (2011); Hyde, *The Pseudo-Democrat's Dilemma*.
17. Kelley, *Monitoring Democracy*.
18. Hyde, *The Pseudo-Democrat's Dilemma*, pp. 159–60.
19. European Stability Initiative, *Disgraced: Azerbaijan and the End of Election Monitoring as We Know It* (November 5, 2013).
20. Emily Beaulieu and Susan D. Hyde, "In the Shadow of Democracy Promotion: Strategic Manipulation, International Observers, and Election Boycotts," *Comparative Political Studies* 42, no. 3 (March 2009).
21. Joseph Asunka et al., "Electoral Fraud or Violence: The Effect of Observers on Party Manipulation Strategies," *British Journal of Political Science* (2017), p. 3.
22. Palko Karasz, "Five Takeaways from Turkey's Election," *New York Times*, June 25, 2018.
23. Hyde, *The Pseudo-Democrat's Dilemma*, p. 168.
24. Bo Rothstein and Jan Torrell, "Defining and Measuring Quality of Government," in *Good Governance: The Relevance of Political Science*, ed. Sören Holmberg and Bo Rothstein (Cheltenham, UK: Edward Elgar, 2012), p. 14.
25. Brett L. Carter, "Repression and Foreign Aid in Autocracies: Exploiting Day-Level Shocks in Post-Cold War Africa" (unpublished manuscript, June 25, 2015), p. 15.
26. Nicolas van de Walle, "Presidentialism and Clientelism in Africa's Emerging Party Systems," *Journal of Modern African Studies* 41, no. 2 (June 2003).
27. "Congo's Presidential Election Result Looks to Be an Enormous Fraud," editorial, *Washington Post*, January 17, 2019.
28. Quoted in Saleh Mwanamilongo and Krista Larson, "Congo President to Leave After 2017 Vote under New Deal," *Washington Post*, December 31, 2016.
29. Carter, "Repression and Foreign Aid," pp. 6–7.
30. Emilie Hafner-Burton, Susan D. Hyde, and Ryan S. Jablonski, "When

Do Governments Resort to Election Violence?" *British Journal of Political Science* 44 (January 2014): pp. 151, 153; Yusuf Ahmad et al., *Reducing Violence and Improving the Rule of Law, Organized Crime, Marginalized Communities, and the Political Machine* (World Justice Project, Washington, DC: Carnegie Endowment for International Peace, 2015).

31. Thomas Edward Flores and Irfan Nooruddin, "The Effect of Elections on Postconflict Peace and Reconstruction," *The Journal of Politics* 74, no. 2 (March 2012).

32. Paul Collier, *War, Guns, and Votes: Democracy in Dangerous Places* (New York: HarperCollins, 2009), p. 11.

33. Jack A. Goldstone and Jay Ulfelder, "How to Construct Stable Democracies," *Washington Quarterly* 28, no. 1 (2004).

34. Goldstone and Ulfelder, "How to Construct."

35. Carter, "Repression and Foreign Aid."

36. Abbey Steele, "Unsettling: Displacement During Civil Wars" (PhD diss., Yale University, 2010), chap. 2.

37. Gardiner Harris, "Campaign for Prime Minister in India Gets Off to Violent Start," *New York Times*, September 17, 2013.

38. Herbert Kitschelt and Steven Wilkinson, "Citizen Politician Linkages," in *Patrons, Clients, and Policies: Patterns of Democratic Accountability and Political Competition*, ed. Herbert Kitschelt and Steven Wilkinson (Cambridge: Cambridge University Press, 2006).

39. Isabela Mares, *From Open Secrets to Secret Voting: Democratic Electoral Reforms and Voter Autonomy* (Cambridge: Cambridge University Press, 2015), chap. 1.

40. Anoop Sadanandan, "Patronage and Decentralization: The Politics of Poverty in India," *Comparative Politics* 44, no. 2 (2012).

41. Teacher absentee rates from Transparency International, *Global Corruption Report: Education* (New York: Routledge, 2013), p. 71; Polity IV scores for 2007 from country pages, Polity IV Project, "Political Regime Characteristics and Transitions, 1800–2013," Center for Systemic Peace.

42. Kitschelt and Wilkinson, "Citizen Politician Linkages"; Susan Stokes and Luis Fernando Medina, "Monopoly and Monitoring: An Approach to Political Clientelism," in *Patrons, Clients, and Policies: Patterns of Democratic Accountability and Political Competition*, ed. Herbert Kitschelt and Steven Wilkinson (New York: Cambridge University Press, 2006).

43. Kitschelt and Wilkinson, "Citizen Politician Linkages"; Stokes and Medina, "Monopoly and Monitoring."

44. Steven Wilkinson, "Explaining Changing Patterns of Party-Voter Linkages in India," in *Patrons, Clients, and Policies: Patterns of Democratic Accountability and Political Competition*, ed. Herbert Kitschelt and Steven Wilkinson, chap. 5 (New York: Cambridge University Press, 2006).

45. Colin Poulton, *Democratisation and the Political Economy of Agricultural Policy in Africa* (FAC Working Paper 43, London: Future Agricultures Consortium, 2012).

46. Van de Walle, "Presidentialism and Clientelism."

47. Andrew Higgins, "Ukraine Palace Is Still Emblem of Dysfunction," *New York Times*, September 8, 2014.

48. David Lake and Matthew Baum, "The Political Economy of Growth: Democracy and Human Capital," *American Journal of Political Science* 47, no. 2 (April 2003).

49. Michael L. Ross, "Is Democracy Good for the Poor?" *American Journal of Political Science* 50, no. 4 (October 2006).

50. Alberto Diaz-Cayeros, Federico Estévez, and Beatriz Magaloni, *The Political Logic of Poverty Relief: Electoral Strategies and Social Policy in Mexico* (New York: Cambridge University Press, 2015), chap. 1.

51. Banik, Dan (2011), p. 103; see also Poulton, *Democratisation*, p 18.

52. Diaz-Cayeros et al., *Political Logic of Poverty*.

53. Diaz-Cayeros et al., *Political Logic of Poverty*, conclusion.

54. Elliott Green, "Patronage, District Creation and Reform in Uganda," *Studies in Comparative International Development* 45 (2010).

55. "The Rwandan Patriotic Front's Business Empire," *The Economist*, March 2, 2017.

56. Gary W. Cox, *Marketing Sovereign Promises* (New York: Cambridge University Press, 2016), pp. 136–38.

57. Cox, *Marketing Sovereign Promises*, chaps. 10, 11.

58. Communication with Gary Cox.

59. Cox, *Marketing Sovereign Promises*, chap. 11, conclusion.

60. Scott Seward Smith, "Elections and Democratization in Afghanistan," in *State Strengthening in Afghanistan: Lessons Learned, 2001–14*, ed. Scott Smith and Colin Cookman (Washington, DC: United States Institute of Peace, 2015), p. 37.

61. Smith, "Elections and Democratization in Afghanistan," pp. 36–37.

62. William Reno, "Fictional States and Atomized Public Spheres," *Daedalus* 146, no. 4 (Fall 2017); United States Agency for International Development, *USAID Support for Kenya's 2013 Elections: Rapid Assessment Review* (Washington, DC: USAID, February 2014), p. 3.

Chapter 8: **Historical Examples of Forcing Your Neighbor's Hand**

1. For a favorable portrait of Genghis Khan, see Jack Weatherford, *Genghis Khan and the Making of the Modern World* (New York: Crown Publishers, 2004).

2. David Laitin, *Hegemony and Culture* (Chicago: University of Chicago Press, 1986).

3. Reo Matsuzaki, *Statebuilding by Imposition: Resistance and Control in Colonial Taiwan and the Philippines* (Ithaca, NY: Cornell University Press, 2019).

4. Nigel Lo, Barry Hashimoto, and Dan Reiter, "Ensuring Peace: Foreign-Imposed Regime Change and Postwar Peace Duration, 1914–2001," *International Organization* 62, no. 4 (Fall 2008); Jeffrey Pickering and Mark Peceny, "Forging Democracy at Gunpoint," *International Studies Quarterly* 50 (2006); John M. Owen IV, *The Clash of Ideas in World Politics* (Princeton, NJ: Princeton University Press, 2010); Jonathan Monten and Alexander B. Downes, "Forced to Be Free? Why Foreign-Imposed Regime Change Rarely Leads to Democratization," *International Security* 37, no. 4 (Spring 2013). Lo, Hashimoto, and Reiter find thirty-three or thirty-seven FIRCs (depending on the underlying database) for the period 1914 to 2001, but they are examining only FIRCs that are associated with the termination of wars. Some scholars have focused only on great power interventions. For the period 1946–1996, Pickering and Peceny identify seventy-nine hostile interventions by the United States, UK, United Nations, and France, where an intervention involved the deployment of troops.

5. Bruce Bueno de Mesquita and George Downs, "Intervention and Democracy," *International Organization* 60, no. 3 (July 2006).

6. Stephen Walt, "Why Is America So Bad at Promoting Democracy in Other Countries?" *Foreign Policy*, April 25, 2016; Walt finds that the United States is rarely successful in promoting democracy. Pickering and Peceny, in "Forging Democracy at Gunpoint," examine all military interventions by major powers and the UN from 1946 to 1996; of the seventy-nine hostile interventions, those that could be construed as FIRCs, few resulted in a positive movement toward democratization.

7. David Lake and Christopher Fariss, "Why International Trusteeship Fails: The Politics of External Authority in Areas of Limited Statehood," *Governance* 27, no. 4 (October 2014).

8. David Lake, *The Statebuilder's Dilemma* (Ithaca, NY: Cornell University Press, 2016).

9. Fritz Scharpf, *Governing in Europe* (New York: Oxford University Press, 1999); and Cord Schmelzle and Eric Stollenwerk, "Causes and Consequences of Legitimacy in Areas of Limited Statehood" (paper presented at the Annual Meeting of the American Political Science Association, 2017).

10. Jonathan Haslam, *Russia's Cold War* (New Haven, CT: Yale University Press, 2011), p. ix.

11. Haslam, *Russia's Cold War*, p. 295.

12. Haslam, *Russia's Cold War*, pp. 75–80.

13. Dimitri Pronin, "Land Reform in Poland: 1920–1945," *Land Economics* 25, no. 2 (May 1949).

14. Grzegorz Ekiert, *The State against Society: Political Crises and Their Aftermath in East Central Europe* (Princeton, NJ: Princeton University Press, 1996), pp. 9–10.

15. Ekiert, *The State against Society*, pp. 42–43.

16. Ekiert, *The State against Society*, pp. 45–49.

17. Haslam, *Russia's Cold War*, pp. 168–72.

18. Ekiert, *The State against Society*, chap. 1 and pp. 58, 59.

19. Ekiert, *The State against Society*, p. 70.

20. Ekiert, *The State against Society*, p. 67.

21. Ekiert, *The State against Society*, p. 83.

22. Ekiert, *The State against Society*, p. 157.

23. Jiri Valenta, "The Bureaucratic Politics Paradigm and the Soviet Invasion of Czechoslovakia," *Political Science Quarterly* 94, no. 1 (Spring 1979), pp. 114–15.

24. Ekiert, *The State against Society*, pp. 162, 163.

25. Ekiert, *The State against Society*, pp. 148–51; Condoleezza Rice, *The Soviet Union and the Czechoslovak Army, 1948–1983* (Princeton, NJ: Princeton University Press, 1984), chap. 6.

26. Ekiert, *The State against Society*, pp. 165–72.

27. Diego Cordovez and Selig S. Harrison, *Out of Afghanistan: The Inside Story of the Soviet Withdrawal* (New York: Oxford University Press, 1995), chap. 1.

28. For data, see James D. Fearon and David D. Laitin, "Does Contemporary Armed Conflict Have 'Deep Historical Roots'"? (paper prepared for delivery at the Annual Meeting of the American Political Science Association, 2014).

29. "Hungary," Countries, Clio Infra (website).

30. World Bank, World Development Indicators.

31. Carles Boix, "Democracy, Development, and the International System," *American Political Science Review* 105, no. 4 (November 2011).

32. *Oxford Handbooks Online* (Oxford University Press, 2015); Cornelius Torp, "The Great Transformation: German Economy and Society, 1850–1914," in *The Oxford Handbook of Modern German History*, ed. Helmut Walser Smith (New York: Oxford University Press, 2015).

33. Alexander Gerschenkron, *Economic Backwardness in Historical Perspective* (Cambridge, MA: Harvard University Press, 1962).

34. Sheri Berman, "Modernization in Historical Perspective: The Case of Imperial Germany," *World Politics* 53, no. 3 (April 2001); Eva Bellin, "The Iraqi Intervention and Democracy in Comparative Historical Perspective," *Political Science Quarterly* 119, no. 4 (2004).

35. James Dobbins et al., *America's Role in Nation-Building: From Germany to Iraq* (Santa Monica, CA: RAND, 2003).

36. John Dower, *Embracing Defeat* (New York: W. W. Norton, 1999), chap. 1.

37. Dower, *Embracing Defeat*, p. 214.

38. Dower, *Embracing Defeat*, pp. 278–79.

39. Dower, *Embracing Defeat*, pp. 330–49.

40. Dower, *Embracing Defeat*, pp. 293–95.

41. Chalmers Johnson, *MITI and the Japanese Miracle: The Growth of Industrial Policy 1925–1975* (Stanford: Stanford University Press, 1982); Daniel Okimoto, *Between MITI and the Market: Japanese Industrial Policy for High Technology* (Stanford, CA: Stanford University Press, 1989).

42. Dower, *Embracing Defeat*, chap. 13.

43. Dower, *Embracing Defeat*, pp. 80–85.

44. Dower, *Embracing Defeat*, chap. 13.

45. Dobbins et al., *America's Role*, pp. 14–15.

46. Richard L. Merritt, *Democracy Imposed: U.S. Occupation Policy and the German Public, 1945–1949* (New Haven, CT: Yale University Press, 1995), p. xiv.

47. Alison Smale, "A Front-Row Seat to Germany's Long Reckoning with Its Past," *New York Times*, June 17, 2016.

48. Norbert Frei, *Adenauer's Germany and the Nazi Past: The Politics of Amnesty and Integration* (New York: Columbia University Press, 2003), p. 6.

49. Peter Katzenstein, "United Germany in an Integrating Europe," in *Tamed Power: Germany in Europe*, ed. Peter Katzenstein, pp. 1–48 (Ithaca, NY: Cornell University Press, 1997).

Chapter 9: **What Happened in Afghanistan and Iraq?**

1. Data from the World Bank.
2. United States and George W. Bush, *National Security Strategy of the United States of America* (National Security Strategy Archive, September 2002).
3. Bruce L. Benson and Zafar R. Siddiqui, "Pashtunwali—Law for the Lawless, Defense for the Stateless," *International Review of Law and Economics* 37 (2014).
4. "Agreement on Provisional Arrangements in Afghanistan Pending the Re-establishment of Permanent Government Institutions," United Nations, December 2001.
5. Kimberley Marten, "Warlordism in Comparative Perspective," *International Security* 31, no. 3 (Winter 2006/07); M. A. Thomas, *Govern Like Us: U.S. Expectations of Poor Countries* (New York, Columbia University Press, 2015), pp. 1–6; Sudarsan Raghavan, "Afghanistan's Defining Fight: Technocrats vs. Strongmen," *Washington Post* (April 12, 2015).
6. Seth G. Jones, "The Rise of Afghanistan's Insurgency: State Failure and Jihad," *International Security* 32, no. 4 (Spring 2008).
7. United States Agency for International Development, *US Mission Afghanistan, U.S. Foreign Assistance for Afghanistan: Post Performance Management Plan—2011–2015* (Washington, DC: USAID, n.d.).
8. Anthony H. Cordesman, "The Afghan Narcotics Industry: A Summary," Center for Strategic and International Studies, November 12, 2009.
9. Liana Rosen and Kenneth Katzman, "Afghanistan: Drug Trafficking and the 2014 Transition," Congressional Research Service, May 9, 2014, p. 21; United Nations Office on Drugs and Crime, *Afghanistan Opium Survey 2016: Cultivation and Production* (United Nations publication, December 2016).
10. Joseph Goldstein, "Bribery Frees a Drug Kingpin in Afghanistan, Where Cash Often Overrules Justice," *New York Times*, December 31, 2014.
11. Rod Nordland and Azam Ahmed, "Afghan Opium Cultivation and Production Seen Rising," *New York Times*, November 13, 2013.
12. Vanda Felbab-Brown, "Organized Crime, Illicit Economies, Civil Violence and International Order: More Complex Than You Think," *Daedalus* 146, no. 4 (Fall 2017).
13. Matthew Rosenberg, "Political Meddling Hampers Inquiry into Kabul Bank Debacle," *New York Times*, November 28, 2012; Mat-

thew Rosenberg, "Trail of Fraud and Vengeance Leads to Kabul Bank Convictions," *New York Times*, March 5, 2013.

14. Mujib Mashal, "Greed, Corruption and Danger: A Tarnished Afghan Gem Trade," *New York Times*, June 5, 2016.

15. "Afghanistan," Transparency International.

16. Mary Beth Goodman and Trevor Sutton, "Tackling Corruption in Afghanistan: It's Now or Never," Center for American Progress, March 17, 2015; United States Special Inspector General for Afghanistan Reconstruction, Office of Special Projects, *Afghanistan's High Office of Oversight: Personal Asset Declarations of High Ranking Afghan Government Officials Are Not Consistently Registered and Verified*, SIGAR-16-60-SP (Arlington, VA: SIGAR, September 2016).

17. Matthew Rosenberg, "Breaking with the West, Afghan Leader Supports Russia's Annexation of Crimea," *New York Times*, March 23, 2014.

18. Jennifer Cafarella, ISIS Plotting Attacks from Afghanistan (Washington, DC: Institute for the Study of War, 2017); Kate Clark, "Record Numbers of Civilian Casualties Overall, from Suicide Attacks and Air Strikes: UNAMA Reports on the Conflict in 2018," Afghan Analysts Network, February 24, 2019; Rod Nordland, "Death Toll in Kabul Bombing Has Hit 150, Afghan President Says," *New York Times*, June 6, 2017.

19. United States Department of the Army, *Counterinsurgency*, Field Manual No. 3-24 (Washington, DC: Department of the Army, December 2006).

20. United States Department of the Army, *Counterinsurgency*, pp. 1–21.

21. United States Department of the Army, *Counterinsurgency*, pp. 1–21.

22. United States Department of the Army, *Counterinsurgency*, pp. 5–15.

23. Karl W. Eikenberry, "The Limits of Counterinsurgency Doctrine in Afghanistan," *Foreign Affairs* 92, no. 5 (September–October 2013).

24. Barack H. Obama, "Remarks by the President in Address to the Nation on the Way Forward in Afghanistan and Pakistan" (speech, United States Military Academy, West Point, NY, December 2009).

25. United States Agency for International Development, *US Mission Afghanistan*.

26. International Security Assistance Force (ISAF), COMISAF/CDR USFOR-A, *Command Brief*, updated December 1, 2014.

27. Rod Nordland, "Taliban End Takeover of Kunduz After 15 Days," *New York Times*, October 13, 2015.

28. Jeffrey Goldberg, "The Obama Doctrine," *The Atlantic*, April 2016.

29. Karl Eikenberry, Cables on U.S. Strategy in Afghanistan, United

States Department of State (*New York Times* documents, November 2009).

30. Data from the World Bank.
31. Rod Nordland, "Top Afghans Tied to '90s Carnage, Researchers Say," *New York Times*, July 22, 2012; Rod Nordland and Jawad Sukhanyar, "Afghanistan Police Surround Vice President's House," *New York Times*, February 21, 2017.
32. Mujib Mashal, "Calling Successor a 'Traitor,' Afghan Ex-Leader Denounces U.S. Bombing," *New York Times*, April 15, 2017; Mujib Mashal, "Afghanistan Is in Chaos. Is That What Hamid Karzai Wants?" *New York Times*, August 5, 2016.
33. Data from World Bank Governance Indicators.
34. World Bank Governance Indicators; Transparency International, Corruption Perceptions Index 2017.
35. "Immunization, Measles (% of Children Ages 12–23 Months)," World Bank; "Afghanistan GDP Per Capita," Trading Economics.
36. World Bank, *World Development Report 2011* (Washington, DC: World Bank, May 26, 2011), p. 267.
37. Prisca Benelli, Antonio Donini, and Norah Niland, *Afghanistan: Humanitarianism in Uncertain Times* (Somerville, MA: Feinstein International Center, Tufts University, 2012), pp. 6–7.
38. World Bank, *World Development Report 2011*, p. 133.
39. World Bank, *National Solidarity Program III*, Report No. P117103 (Washington, DC: World Bank, 2016).
40. Rushda Majeed, *Building Trust in Government: Afghanistan's National Solidarity Program, 2002–2013* (Princeton, NJ: Innovations for Successful Societies, Princeton University, May 2014), especially pp. 6, 9, 12, 16.
41. Nematullah Bizhan, "Budget Transparency in Afghanistan: A Pathway to Building Public Trust in the State," International Budget Partnership, 2012, p. 11; "The Open Budget Survey," International Budget Partnership.
42. Bizhan, "Budget Transparency in Afghanistan," p. 4.
43. Robert Jervis, *American Foreign Policy in a New Era* (New York: Routledge, 2005), chap. 5.
44. "Top Secret Polo Step," National Security Archive, February 14, 2007; Michael O'Hanlon, "Iraq without a Plan," *Policy Review*, 128 (December 2004/January 2005); Nora Bensahel et al., *After Saddam: Prewar Planning and the Occupation of Iraq* (Santa Monica, CA: RAND, 2008).
45. Data from the World Bank; "Iraq: Life Expectancy," World Health Rankings, World Life Expectancy, 2018.

46. Transparency International, Corruption Perceptions Index 2017.

47. James Dobbins et al., *Occupying Iraq: A History of the Coalition Provisional Authority* (Santa Monica, CA: RAND, 2009), pp. 59–60.

48. Quoted in Dobbins et al., *Occupying Iraq*, p. 54.

49. Dobbins et al., *Occupying Iraq*, pp. 102–104.

50. Dobbins et al., *Occupying Iraq*, pp. 68–70.

51. Dexter Filkins, "What We Left Behind: An Increasingly Authoritarian Leader, a Return of Sectarian Violence, and a Nation Worried for Its Future," *New Yorker*, April 28, 2014.

52. Conversation with congressional staff member in 2016.

53. Stephen Biddle, "Building Security Forces and Stabilizing Nations: The Problem of Agency," *Daedalus* 146, no. 4 (Fall 2017).

54. Peter Bergen, "It Wasn't Trump but This General's Elite Soldiers Who Defeated ISIS," CNN, December 16, 2017.

55. Marina Ottaway, "Promoting Democracy after Conflict: The Difficult Choices," *International Studies Perspectives* 4, no. 3 (August 2003).

56. Christopher Gelpi, Peter D. Feaver, and Jason Reifler, "Success Matters: Casualty Sensitivity and the War in Iraq," *International Security* 30, 3 (Winter 2005/2006).

57. Barack Obama, "Full President Obama Speech Text on Afghanistan," Top of the Ticket (blog), *Los Angeles Times*, December 1, 2009.

58. Data from World Bank Governance Indicators.

Chapter 10: **Colombia, a Model for Good Enough Governance**

1. Joseph R. Biden, "A Plan for Central America," *New York Times*, January 29, 2015.

2. Winifred Tate, *Drugs, Thugs, and Diplomats: U.S. Policymaking in Colombia* (Stanford, CA: Stanford University Press, 2015), p. 221.

3. Tate, *Drugs, Thugs, and Diplomats*, p. 221.

4. Tate, *Drugs, Thugs, and Diplomats*, p. 91.

5. Jonathan D. Rosen, *Plan Colombia: The Losing War* (Albany, NY: SUNY Press, 2014), p. 26.

6. Quoted in Rosen, *Plan Colombia*, p. 22.

7. Michael Shifter, "Plan Colombia: A Retrospective," *Americas Quarterly* 6, no. 3 (2012).

8. Rosen, *Plan Colombia*, pp. 75–76.

9. Rosen, *Plan Colombia*, pp. 50–55.

10. Raúl Benítez Manaut, "U.S. Assistance and the Fight against

Organized Crime," in *One Goal, Two Struggles: Confronting Crime and Violence in Mexico and Colombia*, ed. Cynthia J. Arnson, Eric L. Olson, and Christine Zaino (Washington, DC: Wilson Center, 2014); see also United States and George W. Bush, *National Security Strategy of the United States of America* (National Security Strategy Archive, September 2002).

11. Freda Moon, "36 Hours in Cartagena, Colombia," *New York Times*, September 10, 2014.

12. United Nations Office on Drugs and Crime, *Global Study on Homicide 2013: Trends, Contexts, Data* (United Nations publication, sales no. 14.IV.1).

13. María Llorente and Jeremy McDermott, "Colombia's Lessons for Mexico," in *One Goal, Two Struggles: Confronting Crime and Violence in Mexico and Colombia*, ed. Cynthia J. Arnson, Eric L. Olson, and Christine Zaino (Washington, DC: Wilson Center, 2014), p. 12.

14. World Bank, *World Development Report 2011*, p. 113.

15. Tate, *Drugs, Thugs, and Diplomats*, p. 230.

16. Llorente and McDermott, "Colombia's Lessons for Mexico," pp. 10–13.

17. Tate, *Drugs, Thugs, and Diplomats*, pp. 10–11.

18. Llorente and McDermott, "Colombia's Lessons for Mexico," p. 5.

19. Zill de Granados Oriana and Chisun Lee, "Colombian Paramilitaries Extradited to the U.S., Where Cases Are Sealed," *Washington Post*, September 11, 2010; Llorente and McDermott, "Colombia's Lessons for Mexico," pp. 11–13.

20. William Neuman, "Colombia Military Accused of Deception on Civilian Deaths," *New York Times*, June 24, 2015; Llorente and McDermott, "Colombia's Lessons for Mexico," pp. 17–18.

21. World Bank, *World Development Report 2011*, pp. 145–50.

22. World Bank, *World Development Report 2011*, pp. 145–50.

23. Office of National Drug Control Policy, "Coca in the Andes," Obama White House Archives; William Neuman, "More Land in Colombia Used to Grow Coca, U.S. Says," *New York Times*, May 6, 2015.

24. William Neuman, "Colombian City's New Face and Violent Underbelly Collide," *New York Times*, July 13, 2015.

25. "GINI Index (World Bank Estimate)," World Bank; "Colombia," Freedom House Rankings; World Bank, *World Development Report 2011*, p. 150.

26. Aila Matanock and Miguel García-Sánchez, "The Colombian Paradox: Peace Processes, Elite Divisions and Popular Plebiscites," *Daedalus* 146, no. 4 (Fall 2017).

27. Rosen, *Plan Colombia*, pp. 10–11; Tate, *Drugs, Thugs, and Diplomats*, p. 89.

28. Sarah Zukerman Daly, "Organizational Legacies of Violence: Conditions Favoring Insurgency Onset in Colombia, 1964–1984," *Journal of Peace Research* 49, no. 3 (2012), p. 479

29. Tate, *Drugs, Thugs, and Diplomats*, p. 89.

30. Shifter, "Plan Colombia"; Tate, *Drugs, Thugs, and Diplomats*, p. 146.

31. Vanda Felbab-Brown, "Organized Crime, Illicit Economies, Civil Violence and International Order: More Complex Than You Think," *Daedalus* 146, no. 4 (Fall 2017), p. 4; Rosen, *Plan Colombia*, pp. 15–30.

32. Tate, *Drugs, Thugs, and Diplomats*, p. 92.

33. Quoted in Tate, *Drugs, Thugs, and Diplomats*, p. 92.

34. Londoño, Ernesto, "The Men Who Haunted Me as a Child in Colombia," *New York Times*, January 17, 2015.

35. Shifter, "Plan Colombia."

36. Matanock and García-Sánchez, "The Colombian Paradox," pp. 155–57; "Elección de Presidente y Vicepresidente," *Registraduría Nacional del Estado Civil*, República de Colombia.

37. "Colombia President Halts Bombing of Rebel Camps," *New York Times*, March 10, 2015.

38. Nicholas Casey, "Colombia's Congress Approves Peace Accord with FARC," *New York Times*, November 30, 2016; "Colombia's Peace Deal Has Taken Effect, but the Country Remains Divided," *The Economist*, December 10, 2016.

39. Harvey F. Kline, *Showing Teeth to the Dragons: State Building by Colombian President Alvaro Uribe Velez, 2002–2006* (Tuscaloosa: University of Alabama Press, 2009), p. 8.

40. Matanock and García-Sánchez, "The Colombian Paradox," pp. 158–60.

41. Kline, *Showing Teeth*, pp. 9–10.

42. Hillel David Soifer, *State Building in Latin America* (Cambridge University Press, 2015), p. 236.

43. Soifer, *State Building*, pp. 1–20, 211–239.

44. Timothy Besley and Torsten Persson, *Pillars of Prosperity: The Political Economics of Development Clusters* (Princeton, NJ: Princeton University Press, 2011), fig. 8.1.

Chapter 11: **The Rare Occurrence of Consolidated Democracy**

1. C. Vann Woodward, *The Strange Career of Jim Crow* (New York: Oxford University Press, 1955), p. 6.
2. Eric Foner, *Reconstruction: America's Unfinished Revolution, 1863–1877* (New York: Harper and Row, 1988), chap. 1.
3. Bennett Liebman, "The Quest for Black Voting Rights," *Albany Government Law Review* 11, no. 2 (2018), p. 412.
4. William R. Nester, *The Age of Lincoln and the Art of American Power, 1848–1876* (Lincoln: University of Nebraska Press, 2013), p. 120.
5. Nester, *The Age of Lincoln*, p.129; Foner, *Reconstruction*, chap. 5.
6. Foner, *Reconstruction*, p. 262.
7. Nester, *The Age of Lincoln*, p. 125.
8. Woodward, *Strange Career*, pp. 6–10.
9. Foner, *Reconstruction*, pp. 39–42.
10. "Reconstruction vs. Redemption," National Endowment for the Humanities, February 11, 2014.
11. Data from "American FactFinder," United States Census Bureau.
12. Data from "American FactFinder," United States Census Bureau.
13. Pew Research Center, *America's Changing Religious Landscape* (Pew Research Center, May 12, 2015), pp. 143–146.
14. Walter Russell Mead, *Special Providence: American Foreign Policy and How It Changed the World* (New York: Knopf, 2001).
15. Louis Hartz, *The Liberal Tradition in America* (New York: Harvest Books, 1955).
16. William J. Burns, Michèle Flournoy, and Nancy Lindborg, *U.S. Leadership and the Challenge of State Fragility*, Fragility Study Group report (Washington, DC: 2016).
17. James Scott, *Against the Grain: A Deep History of the Earliest States* (New Haven, CT: Yale University Press, 2017).
18. Nicholas Cheeseman and Brian Klaas, *How to Rig an Election* (New Haven, CT: Yale University Press, 2018).

References

Acemoglu, Daron, and James A. Robinson. *Economic Origins of Dictatorship and Democracy*. New York: Cambridge University Press, 2006.
———. *Why Nations Fail*. New York: Crown, 2012.

Ahmad, Yusuf, Alyssa Dougherty, Rachel Kleinfeld, and Alejandro Ponce. *Reducing Violence and Improving the Rule of Law, Organized Crime, Marginalized Communities, and the Political Machine*. World Justice Project, Washington, DC: Carnegie Endowment for International Peace, 2015.

Arnson, Cynthia J., Eric L. Olson, and Christine Zaino. "Introduction" in *One Goal, Two Struggles: Confronting Crime and Violence in Mexico and Colombia*, edited by Cynthia J. Arnson, Eric L. Olson, and Christine Zaino. Washington, DC: Wilson Center, 2014.

Arthur, W. Brian. "Competing Technologies, Increasing Returns, and Lock-In by Historical Events." *The Economic Journal* 99, no. 394 (March 1989): pp. 116–31.

Asunka, Joseph, Sarah Brierley, Miriam Golden, Eric Kramon, and George Ofosu. "Electoral Fraud or Violence: The Effect of Observers on Party Manipulation Strategies." *British Journal of Political Science* (2017): pp. 1–23.

Autesserre, Séverine. *Peaceland: Conflict Resolution and the Everyday Politics of International Intervention*. Cambridge: Cambridge University Press, 2014.

Banik, Dan. "Growth and Hunger in India." *Journal of Democracy* 22, no. 3 (July 2011): pp. 90–104.

Bardhan, Pranab. "The Economist's Approach to the Problem of Corruption." *World Development* 34, no. 2 (2006): pp. 341–8.

Barma, Naazneen. *The Peacebuilding Puzzle: Political Order in Post-Conflict States*. Cambridge: Cambridge University Press, 2017.

Barnett, Laura. "Global Governance and the Evolution of the International Refugee Regime." *International Journal of Refugee Law* 14, no. 2/3 (2002): pp. 38–45.

Beasley, W. G. *The Meiji Restoration*. Stanford: Stanford University Press, 1972.

Beaulieu, Emily, and Susan D. Hyde. "In the Shadow of Democracy Promotion: Strategic Manipulation, International Observers, and Election Boycotts." *Comparative Political Studies* 42, no. 3 (March 2009): pp. 392–415.

Bellin, Eva. "The Iraqi Intervention and Democracy in Comparative Historical Perspective." *Political Science Quarterly* 119, no. 4 (2004): pp. 595–608.

Benelli, Prisca, Antonio Donini, and Norah Niland. *Afghanistan: Humanitarianism in Uncertain Times*. Somerville, MA: Feinstein International Center, Tufts University, 2012.

Bensahel, Nora, Olga Oliker, Keith Crane, Richard R. Brennan Jr., Heather S. Gregg, Thomas Sullivan, and Andrew Rathmell. *After Saddam: Prewar Planning and the Occupation of Iraq*. Santa Monica, CA: RAND, 2008.

Benson, Bruce L., and Zafar R. Siddiqui. "Pashtunwali—Law for the Lawless, Defense for the Stateless." *International Review of Law and Economics* 37 (2014): pp. 108–20.

Berman, Sheri. "Modernization in Historical Perspective: The Case of Imperial Germany." *World Politics* 53, no. 3 (April 2001): pp. 431–62.

Besley, Timothy, and Torsten Persson. "The Origins of State Capacity: Property Rights, Taxation, and Politics." *American Economic Review* 99, no. 4 (September 2009): pp. 1218–44.

———. *Pillars of Prosperity: The Political Economics of Development Clusters*. Princeton, NJ: Princeton University Press, 2011.

Biddle, Stephen. "Building Security Forces and Stabilizing Nations: The Problem of Agency." *Daedalus* 146, no. 4 (Fall 2017): pp. 126–38.

Bizhan, Nematullah. "Budget Transparency in Afghanistan: A Pathway to Building Public Trust in the State." International Budget Partnership, 2012.

Blaydes, Lisa. *State of Repression: Iraq under Saddam Hussein*. Princeton, NJ: Princeton University Press, 2018.

Boix, Carles. "Democracy, Development, and the International System." *American Political Science Review* 105, no. 4 (November 2011): pp. 809–28.

Boix, Carles, and Scott Abramson. "The Roots of the Industrial Revolution or Socially Embedded Know-How?" Paper presented at the Annual Meeting of the American Political Science Association, 2013.

Boix, Carles, and Susan Stokes. "Endogenous Democratization." *World Politics* 55, no. 4 (July 2003): pp. 517–49.

Brewer, John. *The Sinews of Power.* Cambridge, MA: Harvard University Press, 1988.

Broadberry, S., and K. O'Rourke. Introduction to *The Cambridge Economic History of Modern Europe*, vol. 1, *1700–1870*, edited by S. Broadberry and K. O'Rourke. Cambridge: Cambridge University Press, 2010.

Brooks, Rosa Ehrenreich. "The New Imperialism: Violence, Norms, and the 'Rule of Law.'" *Michigan Law Review* 101, no. 7 (June 2003): pp. 2275–340.

Bueno de Mesquita, Bruce, and George Downs. "Intervention and Democracy." *International Organization* 60, no. 3 (July 2006): pp. 627–49.

Bueno de Mesquita, Bruce, and Hilton L. Root. "The Political Roots of Poverty: The Economic Logic of Autocracy." *The National Interest* 68 (Summer 2002): pp. 27–37.

Bueno de Mesquita, Bruce, Alastair Smith, Randolph Siverson, and James Morrow. *The Logic of Political Survival.* Cambridge: MIT Press, 2003.

Burger, Oskar, Annette Baudisch, and James W. Vaupel. "Human Mortality Improvement in Evolutionary Context." *PNAS* 109, no. 44 (October 30, 2012): pp. 18210–14.

Burns, William J., Michèle Flournoy, and Nancy Lindborg. *U.S. Leadership and the Challenge of State Fragility.* Fragility Study Group report. Washington, DC: 2016.

Burnside, Craig, and David Dollar. "Aid Spurs Growth—in a Sound Policy Environment." *Finance and Development* 34, no. 4 (1997): pp. 4–7.

Bush, Sarah. *The Taming of Democracy Assistance: Why Democracy Promotion Does Not Confront Dictators.* Cambridge: Cambridge University Press, 2015.

Buthe, Tim, and Helen Milner. "Bilateral Investment Treaties and Foreign Direct Investment: A Political Analysis." In *The Effect of Treaties on Foreign Direct Investment: Bilateral Investment Treaties, Double Taxation Treaties, and Investment Flows*, edited by Karl P. Sauvant and Lisa E. Sachs. New York: Oxford University Press, 2009.

Cafarella, Jennifer. *ISIS Plotting Attacks from Afghanistan.* Washington, DC: Institute for the Study of War, 2017.

Carothers, Thomas. *Aiding Democracy Abroad.* Washington, DC: Carnegie Endowment for International Peace, 1999.

Carter, Brett L. "Repression and Foreign Aid in Autocracies: Exploiting Day-Level Shocks in Post-Cold War Africa." Unpublished manuscript, June 25, 2015.

Case, Ann, and Angus Deaton. "Rising Morbidity and Mortality in Mid-life among White Non-Hispanic Americans in the 21st Century." *Proceedings of the National Academy of Sciences* 112, no. 49 (2015): pp. 15078–83.

Chayes, Sarah. *Thieves of State: Why Corruption Threatens Global Security*. New York: W. W. Norton, 2015.

Cheeseman, Nicholas, and Brian Klaas. *How to Rig an Election*. New Haven, CT: Yale University Press, 2018.

Clark, Kate. "Record Numbers of Civilian Casualties Overall, from Suicide Attacks and Air Strikes: UNAMA Reports on the Conflict in 2018." Afghan Analysts Network, February 24, 2019.

Clemens, Michael, and Todd Moss. "Ghost of 0.7%: Origins and Relevance of the International Aid Target." Working paper, Center for Global Development, September 6, 2005.

Coll, Steve. *Directorate S: The C.I.A. and America's Secret Wars in Afghanistan and Pakistan*. New York: Penguin Books, 2018.

Collier, Paul. *War, Guns, and Votes: Democracy in Dangerous Places*. New York: HarperCollins, 2009.

Cordovez, Diego, and Selig S. Harrison. *Out of Afghanistan: The Inside Story of the Soviet Withdrawal*. New York: Oxford University Press, 1995.

Cox, Gary W. "Development Traps of Britain." Unpublished manuscript, Stanford University, 2016.

———. *Marketing Sovereign Promises*. New York: Cambridge University Press, 2016.

———, Douglass C. North, and Barry R. Weingast. "The Violence Trap: A Political-Economic Approach to the Problems of Development." SSRN, February 13, 2015.

Daehner, Jens, and Kenneth Lapatin. *Power and Pathos: Bronze Sculpture of the Hellenistic World*. Los Angeles: Getty Museum, 2015.

Daly, Sarah Zukerman. "Organizational Legacies of Violence: Conditions Favoring Insurgency Onset in Colombia, 1964–1984." *Journal of Peace Research* 49, no. 3 (2012): pp. 473–91.

David, Paul. "Clio and the Economics of QWERTY." *American Economic Review* 75, no. 2 (1985): pp. 332–37.

Deaton, Angus. *The Great Escape: Health, Wealth, and the Origins of Inequality*. Princeton, NJ: Princeton University Press, 2013.

Diamond, Jared. *Guns, Germs, and Steel*. New York: W. W. Norton, 1997.

Diaz-Cayeros, Alberto, Federico Estévez, and Beatriz Magaloni. *The Political Logic of Poverty Relief: Electoral Strategies and Social Policy in Mexico*. New York: Cambridge University Press, 2015.

Dieleman, Joseph L., Casey Graves, Elizabeth Johnson, Tara Templin, Maxwell Birger, Hannah Hamavid, Michael Freeman, Katherine Leach-Kemon, Lavanya Singh, Annie Haakenstad, and Christopher J. L. Murray. "Sources and Focus of Health Development Assistance, 1990–2014." *JAMA* 313, no. 23 (2015): pp. 2359–68.

Dobbins, James, Seth G. Jones, Benjamin Runkle, and Siddharth Mohandas. *Occupying Iraq: A History of the Coalition Provisional Authority.* Santa Monica, CA: RAND, 2009.

Dobbins, James, John G. McGinn, Keith Crane, Seth G. Jones, Rollie Lal, Andrew Rathmell, Rachel M. Swanger, and Anga R. Timilsina. *America's Role in Nation-Building: From Germany to Iraq.* Santa Monica, CA: RAND, 2003.

Doucouliagos, Hristos, and Martin Paldam. "The Aid Effectiveness Literature: The Sad Results of 40 Years of Research." *Journal of Economic Surveys* 23, no. 3 (2009): pp. 433–61.

Dower, John. *Embracing Defeat.* New York: W. W. Norton, 1999.

Easterly, William. *The White Man's Burden.* Oxford: Oxford University Press, 2006.

Eikenberry, Karl W. "The Limits of Counterinsurgency Doctrine in Afghanistan." *Foreign Affairs* 92, no. 5 (September–October 2013): pp. 59–74.

Eisner, Manuel. "Long-Term Historical Trends in Violent Crime." *Crime and Justice* 30 (2003): pp. 83–142.

Ekiert, Grzegorz. *The State against Society: Political Crises and Their Aftermath in East Central Europe.* Princeton, NJ: Princeton University Press, 1996.

European Stability Initiative. *Disgraced: Azerbaijan and the End of Election Monitoring as We Know It.* November 5, 2013.

Fazal, Tanisha M. *State Death: The Politics and Geography of Conquest, Occupation, and Annexation.* Princeton, NJ: Princeton University Press, 2011.

Fearon, James. "Self-Enforcing Democracy." *Quarterly Journal of Economics* 126, no. 4 (2011): pp. 1661–708.

Felbab-Brown, Vanda. "Organized Crime, Illicit Economies, Civil Violence and International Order: More Complex Than You Think." *Daedalus* 146, no. 4 (Fall 2017): pp. 98–111.

Filkins, Dexter. "What We Left Behind: An Increasingly Authoritarian Leader, a Return of Sectarian Violence, and a Nation Worried for Its Future." *New Yorker*, April 28, 2014.

Finnemore, Martha. "International Organizations as Teachers of Norms: The United Nations Educational, Scientific, and Cultural Organization and Science Policy." *International Organization*, 47 (1993): pp. 565–97.

———. "Norms, Culture, and World Politics: Insights from Sociology's Institutionalism." *International Organization* 50, no. 2 (Spring 1996): pp. 325–47.

Fisman, Raymond, and Miriam Golden. *Corruption: What Everyone Needs to Know*. New York: Oxford University Press, 2017.

Flores, Thomas Edward, and Irfan Nooruddin. "The Effect of Elections on Postconflict Peace and Reconstruction." *The Journal of Politics* 74, no. 2 (March 2012): pp. 558–70.

Foner, Eric. *Reconstruction: America's Unfinished Revolution, 1863–1877*. New York: Harper and Row, 1988.

Frei, Norbert. *Adenauer's Germany and the Nazi Past: The Politics of Amnesty and Integration*. New York: Columbia University Press, 2003.

Fukuyama, Francis. "The End of History?" *The National Interest*, 16 (Summer 1989): pp. 3–18.

———. *The End of History and the Last Man*. New York: Free Press, 1992.

———. *The Origins of Political Order*. New York: Farrar, Straus, Giroux, 2011.

———. *Political Order and Political Decay*. New York: Farrar, Straus, Giroux, 2014.

———. *State-Building: Governance and World Order in the 21st Century*. Ithaca, NY: Cornell University Press, 2004.

Geddes, Barbara. *Politician's Dilemma: Building State Capacity in Latin America*. Berkeley: University of California Press, 1994.

Gelpi, Christopher, Peter D. Feaver, and Jason Reifler. "Success Matters: Casualty Sensitivity and the War in Iraq." *International Security* 30, 3 (Winter 2005/2006): pp. 7–46.

Gerschenkron, Alexander. *Economic Backwardness in Historical Perspective*. Cambridge, MA: Harvard University Press, 1962.

Girod, Desha. *Explaining Post-Conflict Reconstruction*. New York: Oxford University Press, 2015.

Glete, Jan. *War and the State in Early Modern Europe: Spain, the Dutch Republic and Sweden as Fiscal-Military States 1500–1660*. London: Routledge, 2002.

Goldstone, Jack A., and Jay Ulfelder. "How to Construct Stable Democracies." *Washington Quarterly* 28, no. 1 (2004): pp. 9–20.

Goodman, Mary Beth, and Trevor Sutton. "Tackling Corruption in Afghanistan: It's Now or Never." Washington, DC: Center for American Progress, 2015.

Gorski, Philip S. *The Disciplinary Revolution: Calvinism and the Rise of the State in Early Modern Europe*. Chicago: University of Chicago Press, 2003.

Gradel, Thomas J., and Dick Simpson. *Corrupt Illinois: Patronage, Cronyism, and Criminality.* Urbana: University of Illinois Press, 2015.

Green, Elliott. "Patronage, District Creation and Reform in Uganda." *Studies in Comparative International Development* 45 (2010): pp. 83–103.

Grindle, Merilee. "Good Enough Governance: Poverty Reduction and Reform in Developing Countries." *Governance: An International Journal of Policy, Administration, and Institutions* 17, no. 4 (2004): pp. 525–48.

———. "Good Enough Governance Revisited." *Development Policy Review* 25, no. 5 (2007): pp. 553–74.

Gunitsky, Seva. *Aftershocks: Great Powers and Domestic Reforms in the Twentieth Century.* Princeton, NJ: Princeton University Press, 2017.

Haber, Stephen, and Victor Menaldo. "Do Natural Resources Fuel Authoritarianism? A Reappraisal of the Resource Curse." *American Political Science Review* 105, no. 1 (2011): pp. 1–26.

Hafner-Burton, Emilie, Susan D. Hyde, and Ryan S. Jablonski. "When Do Governments Resort to Election Violence?" *British Journal of Political Science* 44 (January 2014): pp. 149–79.

Haggard, Stephan, David Kang, and Chung-in Moon. "Japanese Colonialism and Korean Development: A Critique." *World Development* 25, no. 6 (1997): pp. 867–81.

Hamilton, Alexander, James Madison, and John Jay. *The Federalist Papers.* Mineola, NY: Dover Thrift Edition, 2016.

Hartz, Louis. *The Liberal Tradition in America.* New York: Harvest Books, 1955.

Haslam, Jonathan. *Russia's Cold War.* New Haven, CT: Yale University Press, 2011.

Hausmann, Ricardo, Lant Pritchett, and Dani Rodrik. "Growth Accelerations." NBER Working Paper 10566, 2004.

Headey, Derek. "Geopolitics and the Effect of Foreign Aid on Economic Growth: 1970–2001." *Journal of International Development* 20, no. 2 (March 2008): pp. 161–80.

Henderson, Willie. "Seretse Khama: A Personal Appreciation." *African Affairs* 89 (January 1990): pp. 27–56.

Hirschman, Albert O. *Exit, Voice, and Loyalty.* Cambridge, MA: Harvard University Press, 1970.

Hope, Kempe Ronald. "Liberia's Governance and Economic Management Assistance Program (GEMAP): An Impact Review and Analytical Assessment of a Donor Policy Intervention for Democratic State-Building in a Post-Conflict State." *South African Journal of International Affairs* 17, no. 2 (2010): pp. 243–63.

Högström, J. "Does the Choice of Democracy Measure Matter? Comparisons between the Two Leading Democracy Indices, Freedom House and Polity IV." *Government and Opposition* 48, no. 2 (April 2013): pp. 201–21.

Howell, William G., and Terry Moe. *Relic: How Our Constitution Undermines Effective Government.* New York: Basic Books, 2016.

Hui, Victoria Tin-bor. *War and State Formation in Ancient China and Early Modern Europe.* Cambridge: Cambridge University Press, 2005.

Huntington, Samuel P. *Political Order in Changing Societies.* New Haven, CT: Yale University Press, 1968.

———. *The Third Wave.* Norman: University of Oklahoma Press, 1993.

Hutchinson, Robert. *The Spanish Armada.* London: Weidenfeld and Nicolson, 2013.

Hyde, Susan. *The Pseudo-Democrat's Dilemma: Why Election Observation Became an International Norm.* Ithaca, NY: Cornell University Press, 2011.

Inglehart, Ronald, and Christian Welzel. "How Development Leads to Democracy: What We Know about Modernization." *Foreign Affairs* 88, no. 2 (2009): pp. 33–48.

———. *Modernization, Cultural Change, and Democracy.* Cambridge: Cambridge University Press, 2005.

International Security Assistance Force (ISAF), COMISAF/CDR USFOR-A. *Command Brief.* Updated December 1, 2014.

Jandhyala, Srividya, Witold J. Henisz, and Edward D. Mansfield. "Three Waves of BITs: The Global Diffusion of Foreign Investment Policy." *Journal of Conflict Resolution* 55, no. 6 (2011): pp. 1047–73.

Jervis, Robert. *American Foreign Policy in a New Era.* New York: Routledge, 2005.

Jha, Saumitra. "Financial Asset Holdings and Political Attitudes: Evidence from Revolutionary England." *Quarterly Journal of Economics* 130, no. 3 (2015): pp. 1485–545.

Johnson, Chalmers. *MITI and the Japanese Miracle: The Growth of Industrial Policy 1925–1975.* Stanford: Stanford University Press, 1982.

Johnston, Michael. *Syndromes of Corruption.* Cambridge: Cambridge University Press, 2005.

Jones, Seth G. "The Rise of Afghanistan's Insurgency: State Failure and Jihad." *International Security* 32, no. 4 (Spring 2008): pp. 7–40.

Jurado Sánchez, José. "Military Expenditure, Spending Capacity and Budget Constraint in Eighteenth-Century Spain and Britain." *Revista de Historia Económica/Journal of Iberian and Latin American Economic History* (Second Series) 27, no. 1 (Spring 2008): pp. 141–74.

Kaplan, Benjamin J. *Divided by Faith: Religious Conflict and the Practice of Toleration in Early Modern Europe*. Cambridge, MA: Harvard University Press, 2007.

Katzenstein, Peter. "United Germany in an Integrating Europe." In *Tamed Power: Germany in Europe*, edited by Peter Katzenstein, 1–48. Ithaca, NY: Cornell University Press, 1997.

Kelley, Judith. *Monitoring Democracy: When International Election Observation Works and Why It Often Fails*. Princeton, NJ: Princeton University Press, 2012.

Kitschelt, Herbert, and Steven Wilkinson. "Citizen Politician Linkages." In *Patrons, Clients, and Policies: Patterns of Democratic Accountability and Political Competition*, edited by Herbert Kitschelt and Steven Wilkinson. Cambridge: Cambridge University Press, 2006.

Kline, Harvey F. *Showing Teeth to the Dragons: State Building by Colombian President Alvaro Uribe Velez, 2002–2006*. Tuscaloosa: University of Alabama Press, 2009.

Knight, Roger, and Martin Wilcox. *Sustaining the Fleet, 1793–1815*. Woodbridge, UK: Boydell Press, 2010.

Kohli, Atul. "Where Do High Growth Political Economies Come From? The Japanese Lineage of Korea's 'Developmental State.'" *World Development* 22, no. 9 (1994): pp. 1269–93.

Krasner, Stephen D. *Defending the National Interest*. Princeton, NJ: Princeton University Press, 1978.

———. "An Orienting Principle for Foreign Policy." *Policy Review* (Stanford University, Hoover Institution, October 1, 2010).

Krasner, Stephen D., and Thomas Risse. "External Actors, State-Building, and Service Provision in Areas of Limited Statehood: Introduction." *Governance* 27, no. 4 (2014): pp. 545–67.

Krasner, Stephen D., and Jeremy Weinstein. "Improving Governance from the Outside In." *Annual Review of Political Science* 17 (2014): pp. 123–45.

Kurtz, Marcus J. *Latin American State Building in Comparative Perspective: Social Foundations of Institutional Order*. Cambridge: Cambridge University Press, 2013.

———. "The Social Foundations of Institutional Order: Reconsidering War and the 'Resource Curse' in Third World State Building." *Politics and Society* 37, no. 4 (2009): pp. 479–520.

Kurtz-Phelan, Daniel. *The China Mission: George Marshall's Unfinished War 1945–47*. New York: W. W. Norton, 2018.

Laitin, David. *Hegemony and Culture*. Chicago: University of Chicago Press, 1986.

Lake, David. *The Statebuilder's Dilemma*. Ithaca, NY: Cornell University Press, 2016.

Lake, David, and Matthew Baum. "The Political Economy of Growth: Democracy and Human Capital." *American Journal of Political Science* 47, no. 2 (April 2003): pp. 333–47.

Lake, David, and Christopher Fariss. "Why International Trusteeship Fails: The Politics of External Authority in Areas of Limited Statehood." *Governance* 27, no. 4 (October 2014): pp. 569–87.

Landes, David. *The Wealth and Poverty of Nations.* New York: W. W. Norton, 1999.

Lange, Matthew. *Lineages of Despotism and Development: British Colonialism and State Power.* Chicago: University of Chicago Press, 2009.

Ledford, Heidi. "CRISPR, the Disruptor." *Nature* 522, no. 7554 (June 4, 2015): pp. 20–24.

Lipset, Seymour Martin. "Some Social Requisites of Democracy: Economic Development and Political Legitimacy." *American Political Science Review* 53, no. 1 (March 1959): pp. 69–105.

Lischer, Sarah Kenyon. "The Global Refugee Crisis." *Daedalus* 146, no. 4 (Fall 2017): pp. 85–97.

Llorente, María, and Jeremy McDermott. "Colombia's Lessons for Mexico." In *One Goal, Two Struggles: Confronting Crime and Violence in Mexico and Colombia*, edited by Cynthia J. Arnson, Eric L. Olson, and Christine Zaino. Washington, DC: Wilson Center, 2014.

Lo, Nigel, Barry Hashimoto, and Dan Reiter. "Ensuring Peace: Foreign-Imposed Regime Change and Postwar Peace Duration, 1914–2001." *International Organization* 62, no. 4 (Fall 2008): pp. 717–36.

Lowenthal, Abraham. *The Dominican Intervention.* Cambridge, MA: Harvard University Press, 1972.

Majeed, Rushda. *Building Trust in Government: Afghanistan's National Solidarity Program, 2002–2013.* Princeton, NJ: Innovations for Successful Societies, Princeton University, May 2014.

Manaut, Raúl Benítez. "U.S. Assistance and the Fight against Organized Crime." In *One Goal, Two Struggles: Confronting Crime and Violence in Mexico and Colombia*, edited by Cynthia J. Arnson, Eric L. Olson, and Christine Zaino. Washington, DC: Wilson Center, 2014.

Martin, Colin, and Geoffrey Parker. *The Spanish Armada.* New York: W. W. Norton, 1988.

Mares, Isabela. *From Open Secrets to Secret Voting: Democratic Electoral Reforms and Voter Autonomy.* Cambridge: Cambridge University Press, 2015.

Marshall, Monty, and Benjamin Cole. *Global Report 2014.* Vienna, VA: Center for Systemic Peace, 2014.

Marten, Kimberley. "Warlordism in Comparative Perspective." *International Security* 31, no. 3 (Winter 2006/07): pp. 41–73.

Marx, Karl. *The Eighteenth Brumaire of Louis Bonaparte*. Translated by Terrell Carver. In *Marx's Eighteenth Brumaire: (Post)Modern Interpretations*, edited by Mark Cowling and James Martin. London: Pluto Press, 2002. First published 1852 in *Die Revolution*, New York.

Matanock, Aila, and Natalia Garbiras-Díaz. "Invited Intervention: A Mechanism to Restore the Rule of Law in Weak States?" Unpublished paper, University of California, Berkeley, August 24, 2016.

Matanock, Aila, and Miguel García-Sánchez. "The Colombian Paradox: Peace Processes, Elite Divisions and Popular Plebiscites." *Daedalus* 146, no. 4 (Fall 2017): pp. 152–66.

Matsuzaki, Reo. *Statebuilding by Imposition: Resistance and Control in Colonial Taiwan and the Philippines*. Ithaca, NY: Cornell University Press, 2019.

Mazzetti, Mark. "The Devastating Paradox of Pakistan." *The Atlantic*, March 2018.

Mead, Walter Russell. *Special Providence: American Foreign Policy and How It Changed the World*. New York: Knopf, 2001.

Merritt, Richard L. *Democracy Imposed: U.S. Occupation Policy and the German Public, 1945–1949*. New Haven, CT: Yale University Press, 1995.

Meyer, John W., John Boli, George M. Thomas, and Francisco O. Ramirez. "World Society and the Nation-State." *American Journal of Sociology* 103, no. 1 (July 1997): pp. 144–81.

Minoiu, Camelia, and Sanjay G. Reddy. "Development Aid and Economic Growth: A Positive Long-Run Relation." *Quarterly Review of Economics and Finance* 50, no. 1 (February 2010): pp. 27–39.

Mishra, Ajit. "Persistence of Corruption: Some Theoretical Perspectives." *World Development* 34, no. 2 (February 2006): pp. 349–58.

Monten, Jonathan, and Alexander B. Downes. "Forced to Be Free? Why Foreign-Imposed Regime Change Rarely Leads to Democratization." *International Security* 37, no. 4 (Spring 2013): pp. 90–131.

Nester, William R. *The Age of Lincoln and the Art of American Power, 1848–1876*. Lincoln: University of Nebraska Press, 2013.

Norris, Pippa. "What Works? Evaluating Electoral Assistance." Paper presented at the Annual Meeting of the American Political Science Association, 2015.

North, Douglass, John Wallis, and Barry Weingast. *Violence and Social Orders*. Cambridge: Cambridge University Press, 2009.

North, Douglass, and Barry Weingast. "Constitutions and Commitment: The Evolution of Institutions Governing Public Choice in Seventeenth-Century England." *Journal of Economic History* 49, no. 4 (December 1989): pp. 803–32.

Nunn, Nathan, and Nancy Qian. "US Food Aid and Civil Conflict." *American Economic Review* 104, no. 6 (2014): pp. 1630–66.

Ober, Josiah. *The Rise and Fall of Classical Greece.* Princeton, NJ: Princeton University Press, 2015.

O'Hanlon, Michael. "Iraq without a Plan." *Policy Review*, 128 (December 2004/January 2005): pp. 33–46.

Okimoto, Daniel. *Between MITI and the Market: Japanese Industrial Policy for High Technology.* Stanford, CA: Stanford University Press, 1989.

Ottaway, Marina. "Promoting Democracy after Conflict: The Difficult Choices." *International Studies Perspectives* 4, no. 3 (August 2003): pp. 314–22.

Owen, John M., IV. *The Clash of Ideas in World Politics.* Princeton, NJ: Princeton University Press, 2010.

Paine, Jack. "Rethinking the Conflict 'Resource Curse': How Oil Wealth Prevents Center-Seeking Civil Wars." *International Organization* 70, no. 4 (2017): pp. 726–61.

Pan American Health Organization. *Public Health in the Americas: Conceptual Renewal, Performance Assessment, and Bases for Action.* Washington, DC: Pan American Health Organization, 2002.

Parks, Bradley Christopher. "Brokering Development Policy Change: The Parallel Pursuit of Millennium Challenge Account Resources and Reform." PhD diss., London School of Economics, 2013.

Patrick, Stewart. *The Sovereignty Wars.* Washington, DC: The Brookings Institution Press, 2017.

Peck, Amelia. *Interwoven Globe: The Worldwide Textile Trade, 1500–1800.* New York: Metropolitan Museum of Art, 2013. Exhibition catalog.

Pei, Minxin. "The Paradoxes of American Nationalism." *Foreign Policy* (May/June 2003): pp. 31–37.Pickering, Jeffrey, and Mark Peceny. "Forging Democracy at Gunpoint." *International Studies Quarterly* 50 (2006): pp. 539–59.

Pinker, Steven. *The Better Angels of Our Nature.* New York: Penguin Books, 2012.

Pitcher, Anne, Mary H. Moran, and Michael Johnston. "Rethinking Patrimonialism and Neopatrimonialism in Africa." *African Studies Review* 52, no. 1 (April 2009): pp. 125–56.

Poulton, Colin. *Democratisation and the Political Economy of Agricul-*

tural Policy in Africa. FAC Working Paper 43. London: Future Agricultures Consortium, 2012.

Pronin, Dimitri. "Land Reform in Poland: 1920–1945." *Land Economics* 25, no. 2 (May 1949): pp. 133–45.

Pritchett, Lant, Michael Woolcock, and Matt Andrews. "Looking like a State: Techniques of Persistent Failure in State Capability for Implementation." CID Working Paper No. 239. Kennedy School, Harvard University, June 2012.

Przeworski, Adam, Michael E. Alvarez, Jose Antonio Cheibub, and Fernando Limongi. *Democracy and Development: Political Institutions and Well-Being in the World, 1950–1990.* New York: Cambridge University Press, 2000.

Rajan, Raghuram G. "Rent Preservation and the Persistence of Underdevelopment." *American Economic Journal: Macroeconomics* 1, no. 1 (2009): pp. 178–218.

Rajan, Raghuram, and Arvind Subramanian. "Does Aid Affect Governance?" *American Economic Review* 97, no. 2 (May 2007): pp. 322–7.

———. "What Undermines Aid's Impact on Growth?" Working Paper No. 05/126. Research Department, IMF, June 2005.

Rawls, John. *The Law of Peoples.* Cambridge, MA: Harvard University Press, 1999.

Reno, William. "Fictional States and Atomized Public Spheres." *Daedalus* 146, no. 4 (Fall 2017): pp. 139–51.

Rice, Condoleezza. "Rethinking the National Interest." *Foreign Affairs* 87, no. 4 (July/August 2008): pp. 2–16.

———. *The Soviet Union and the Czechoslovak Army, 1948–1983.* Princeton, NJ: Princeton University Press, 1984.

Rijkers, Bob, Leila Baghdadi, and Gael Raballand. *Political Connections and Tariff Evasion: Evidence from Tunisia.* World Bank, Policy Research Working Paper 7336, 2015.

Robb, Matthew H., Rubén Cabrera Castro, David M. Carballo, Erika Carrillo, George L. Cowgill, Laura Filloy Nadal, Julie Gazzola, Sergio Gómez Chávez, Nikolai Grube, Christophe Helmke, Leonardo López Luján, Diana Magaloni, Linda R. Manzanilla, Jesper Nielsen, Nelly Zoé Núñez Rendon, Hillary Olcott, Megan E. O'Neil, Jorge Pérez de Lara Elías, Alejandro Sarabia González, Nawa Sugiyama, and Saburo Sugiyama. *Teotihuacan: City of Water, City of Fire.* Berkeley: University of California Press, 2017. Exhibition catalog.

Rose-Ackerman, Susan. *Corruption and Government: Causes, Consequences, and Reform.* New York: Cambridge University Press, 1999.

Rosefielde, Steven, and Stefan Hedlund. *Russia Since 1980*. Cambridge: Cambridge University Press, 2008.

Rosen, Jonathan D. *Plan Colombia: The Losing War*. Albany, NY: SUNY Press, 2014.

Ross, Michael L. "Is Democracy Good for the Poor?" *American Journal of Political Science* 50, no. 4 (October 2006): pp. 860–74.

———. *The Oil Curse: How Petroleum Wealth Shapes the Development of Nations*. Princeton, NJ: Princeton University Press, 2012.

Rostow, W. W. *The Stages of Economic Growth: A Non-Communist Manifesto*. Cambridge: Cambridge University Press, 1960.

Rothstein, Bo, and Jan Torrell. "Defining and Measuring Quality of Government." In *Good Governance: The Relevance of Political Science*, edited by Sören Holmberg and Bo Rothstein. Cheltenham, UK: Edward Elgar, 2012.

Rothstein, Bo, and Aiysha Varraich. *Making Sense of Corruption*. Cambridge: Cambridge University Press, 2017.

Rowen, Henry. "When Will the Chinese People Be Free?" *Journal of Democracy* 18, no. 3 (July 2007): pp. 38–52.

Sadanandan, Anoop. "Patronage and Decentralization: The Politics of Poverty in India." *Comparative Politics* 44, no. 2 (2012): pp. 211–28.

Sambanis, Nicholas, Stergios Skaperdas, and William C. Wohlforth. "Nation-Building through War." *American Political Science Review* 109, no. 2 (May 2015): pp. 276–96.

Schäferhoff, Marco. "External Actors and the Provision of Public Health Services in Somalia." *Governance* 27, no. 4 (2014): pp. 675–95.

Scharpf, Fritz. *Governing in Europe*. New York: Oxford University Press 1999.

Schimmelfennig, Frank. "The Community Trap: Liberal Norms, Rhetorical Action, and the Eastern Enlargement of the European Union." *International Organization* 55, no. 1 (Winter 2001): pp. 47–80.

Schmelzle, Cord, and Eric Stollenwerk. "Causes and Consequences of Legitimacy in Areas of Limited Statehood." Paper presented at the Annual Meeting of the American Political Science Association, 2017.

Schumpeter, Joseph A. *Capitalism, Socialism and Democracy*. London: Routledge, 2003. First published 1942.

Scott, James. *Against the Grain: A Deep History of the Earliest States*. New Haven, CT: Yale University Press, 2017.

———. *The Art of Not Being Governed*. New Haven, CT: Yale University Press, 2009.

———. *Seeing Like a State*. New Haven, CT: Yale University Press, 1998.

Shifter, Michael. "Plan Colombia: A Retrospective." *Americas Quarterly* 6, no. 3 (2012): pp. 36–42.

Siddiqi, Sameen, Tayyeb I. Masud, Sania Nishtar, David H. Peters, Belgacem Sabri, Khalif M. Bile, and Mohamed A. Jama. "Framework for Assessing Governance of the Health System in Developing Countries: Gateway to Good Governance." *Health Policy* 90 (2009): pp. 13–25.

Smith, Scott Seward. "Elections and Democratization in Afghanistan." In *State Strengthening in Afghanistan: Lessons Learned, 2001–14*, edited by Scott Smith and Colin Cookman. Washington, DC: United States Institute of Peace, 2015.

Soifer, Hillel David. *State Building in Latin America*. Cambridge University Press, 2015.

Spence, Jonathan. *Treason by the Book*. New York: Penguin Books, 2002.

Spruyt, Hendrik. *The Sovereign State and Its Competitors*. Princeton, NJ: Princeton University Press, 1994.

Steele, Abbey. "Unsettling: Displacement During Civil Wars." PhD diss., Yale University, 2010.

Stokes, Susan, and Luis Fernando Medina. "Monopoly and Monitoring: An Approach to Political Clientelism." In *Patrons, Clients, and Policies: Patterns of Democratic Accountability and Political Competition*, edited by Herbert Kitschelt and Steven Wilkinson. New York: Cambridge University Press, 2006.

Sullivan, Patricia, and Michael T. Koch. "Military Intervention by Powerful States, 1945–2003." *Journal of Peace Research* 46, no. 5 (September 2009): pp. 707–18.

Tate, Winifred. *Drugs, Thugs, and Diplomats: U.S. Policymaking in Colombia*. Stanford, CA: Stanford University Press, 2015.

Taylor, Matthew. *Lessons from Guatemala's Commission against Impunity: What Other Countries Can Learn from CICIG's First Decade*. New York: Council on Foreign Relations, 2017.

Thomas, M. A. *Govern Like Us: U.S. Expectations of Poor Countries*. New York, Columbia University Press, 2015.

Thomson, Janice. *Mercenaries, Pirates, and Sovereigns*. Princeton, NJ: Princeton University Press, 1994.

Tilly, Charles. *Coercion, Capital, and European States, AD 990–1992*. New York: Wiley-Blackwell, 1992.

Torp, Cornelius. "The Great Transformation: German Economy and Society, 1850–1914." In *The Oxford Handbook of Modern German History*, edited by Helmut Walser Smith. New York: Oxford University Press, 2015.

Transparency International. *Global Corruption Report: Education.* New York: Routledge, 2013.

Trevan, Tim. "Do Not Censor Science in the Name of Biosecurity." *Nature* 486, no. 7403 (June 21, 2012).

Triola, Nicole. "The International Refugee Regime: A Failing System." *Ramapo Journal of Law and Society* 1, no. 2 (Fall 2014): pp. 1–20.

United Nations High Commissioner for Refugees. *Global Trends: Forced Displacement in 2017.* United Nations publication, June 25, 2018.

United Nations Office on Drugs and Crime. *Afghanistan Opium Survey 2016: Cultivation and Production.* United Nations publication, December 2016.

———. *Global Study on Homicide 2013: Trends, Contexts, Data.* United Nations publication, sales no. 14.IV.1.

United States Agency for International Development. *Electoral Security Framework: Technical Guidance Handbook for Democracy and Governance Officers.* Washington, DC: USAID, July 2010.

———. *Final Evaluation of USAID GEMAP Activities.* Washington, DC: USAID, June 2010.

———. *USAID Support for Kenya's 2013 Elections: Rapid Assessment Review.* Washington, DC: USAID, February 2014.

———. *US Mission Afghanistan. U.S. Foreign Assistance for Afghanistan: Post Performance Management Plan—2011–2015.* Washington, DC: USAID. (n.d.).

United States, and Donald Trump. *National Security Strategy of the United States of America.* National Security Strategy Archive, December 2017.

United States Department of the Army. *Counterinsurgency.* Field Manual No. 3-24. Washington, DC: Department of the Army, December 2006.

United States Special Inspector General for Afghanistan Reconstruction, Office of Special Projects. *Afghanistan's High Office of Oversight: Personal Asset Declarations of High Ranking Afghan Government Officials Are Not Consistently Registered and Verified.* SIGAR-16-60-SP. Arlington, VA: SIGAR, September 2016.

Valenta, Jiri. "The Bureaucratic Politics Paradigm and the Soviet Invasion of Czechoslovakia." *Political Science Quarterly* 94, no. 1 (Spring 1979): pp. 55–76.

Van de Walle, Nicolas. "Presidentialism and Clientelism in Africa's Emerging Party Systems." *Journal of Modern African Studies* 41, no. 2 (June 2003): pp. 297–321.

Vries, Peer. "Europe in the World, 1500–2000." In *Global Economic His-*

tory, edited by Tirthankar Roy and Giorgio Riello. London: Bloomsbury, 2018.

Vu, Tong. "Studying the State through State Formation." *World Politics* 62, no. 1 (2010): pp. 148–75.

Walt, Stephen. "Why Is America So Bad at Promoting Democracy in Other Countries?" *Foreign Policy*, April 25, 2016.

Weatherford, Jack. *Genghis Khan and the Making of the Modern World.* New York: Crown Publishers, 2004.

Wilkinson, Steven. "Explaining Changing Patterns of Party-Voter Linkages in India." In *Patterns of Democratic Accountability and Political Competition*, edited by Herbert Kitschelt and Steven Wilkinson, chap. 5. Cambridge: Cambridge University Press, 2006.

Wise, Paul H., and Michele Barry. "Civil War and the Global Threat of Pandemics." *Daedalus* 146, no. 4 (Fall 2017): pp. 71–84.

Wittes, Benjamin, and Gabriella Blum. *The Future of Violence: Robots and Germs, Hackers and Drones.* New York: Basic Books, 2015.

Woodward, C. Vann. *The Strange Career of Jim Crow.* New York: Oxford University Press, 1955.

Woodward, Susan. *The Ideology of Failed States: Why Intervention Fails.* Cambridge: Cambridge University Press, 2017.

World Bank. *National Solidarity Program III.* Report No. P117103. Washington, DC: World Bank, 2016.

Yaffa, Joshua. "Oligarchy 2.0." *The New Yorker*, May 29, 2017.

Zakaria, Fareed. "The Rise of Illiberal Democracy." *Foreign Affairs* 76, no. 6 (1997): pp. 22–43.

Index